COMPUTER SOFTWARE ENGINEERING RESEARCH

Computer Software Engineering Research

Ari D. Klein
Editor

Nova Science Publishers, Inc.
New York

For permission to use material from this book please contact us:
Telephone 631-231-7269; Fax 631-231-8175
Web Site: http://www.novapublishers.com

LIBRARY OF CONGRESS CATALOGING-IN-PUBLICATION DATA

Computer software engineering research / Ari D. Klein, Editor.
p. cm.
Includes index.
ISBN-13: 978-1-60021-774-6 (hardcover)
ISBN-10: 1-60021-774-5 (hardcover)
1. Software engineering--Congresses. 2. Computer software--Development--Congresses. I. Klein, Ari D.
QA76.758.C674 2007
005.1--dc22 2007019182

Published by Nova Science Publishers, Inc. ✢ New York

CONTENTS

PREFACE

Computer hardware continues to get smaller and computer software continues to get more complicated. Computer programming (often shortened to programming or coding) is the process of writing, testing, and maintaining the source code of computer programs. The source code is written in a programming language. This code may be a modification of existing source or something completely new. The process of writing source code requires expertise in many different subjects, including knowledge of the application domain and algorithms to implement the desired behavior. Within software engineering, programming (the implementation) is regarded as one phase in a software development process. This book presents new leading-edge international research in the field.

Readable code is the key to correct and maintainable programs. Pure class-oriented programming does not scale and tends to lead to code that is hard to read. Extensive subclassing is an effective obfuscator and should often be replaced with delegation. A strategy of divide and conquer can be achieved with suitably structured components. This opens a path to readable, object-oriented programs. Pair programming and, even better, peer review are work processes that help in getting it right the first time.

Chapter 1 deals with implementing agile software development methods in software projects. It focuses on aspects that expose the problems of the software engineering field that mainly concern customer requirements, software defects, management of software projects, and characteristics of the actual development work. Action Research is the research paradigm that we used. Using this paradigm, researchers perform a rigorous, systematic, and criticized process on their own work in the research field. The research is iterative when each research cycle is composed of planning – action – collection of data available as a result of the action – data analysis – reflection – refinement of the results.

The authors present a conceptual model that has emerged as part of a comprehensive qualitative research that deals with the implementation of the agile approach in software teamwork. The model is composed of a three-dimensional analogy of the following concepts: action research, agile software development method, and teaching the agile approach. Using the analogy, the authors analyze findings from our research settings in both industry and academia. For clarity of what such a research setting means, they focus in this chapter on the academic research setting.

The main contribution of this chapter is the 3D analogy that is suggested as a tool to analyze software processes. Illustrating its usage provides a better understanding of the implementation of the agile approach in software processes.

The goal of the BabyUML project is to increase my confidence in my programs. The keywords are simplicity and leverage. Simplicity helps me to think clearly and a reader to understand and audit my code. Leverage lets me say more with less. The end result shall be a new interactive development environment with appropriate languages and tools for supporting high level abstractions.

The essence of object orientation is that objects interact to produce some desired result. Yet current programming languages are focused on individual objects as they are specified by their classes; there are no explicit language constructs for describing communities of interacting objects. In BabyUML, I will zoom back from the classes and let my code specify the roles that objects play in collaborations and interactions.

The BabyUML project is experimental; its ideas and concepts are explored and their feasibility demonstrated with actual code and running programs. One experiment is completed, it explores an old and a new paradigm for organizing objects in clear and explicit structures. The old is MVC, the Model-View-Controller paradigm that describes the objects bridging the gap between a human mental model and the corresponding data stored in the computer. The new is DCA, the Data-Collaboration-Algorithm paradigm where the collaborating objects are explicitly identified by the role they play in an interaction, and where the interaction pattern is explicitly defined in terms of these roles.

Another experiment shall lead to BabyIDE, an integrated development environment that exhibits a balance between classes and roles. BabyIDE will be part of a new discipline of programming where programmers can work consistently at a high conceptual level throughout coding, debugging, testing, and maintenance. It will be implemented in a corner of Smalltalk that I have called the BabyIDE Laboratory. The last part of Chapter 2 describes the laboratory and how it will support new programming paradigms and tools. The author finally indicates the future direction towards a workable BabyIDE.

Requirements Engineering (RE) is a very active and decisive field of Software Engineering (SE). In Chapter 3 the research aims to define a components selection method whose development is fast, agile and requirements driven. The authors try to ensure that an exact correspondence exists between the requirements and the architecture (components) and to raise the abstraction level in the development. In order to do so, it is necessary to study the state-of-the-art of the main approaches of components selection that pay special attention to the system requirements. In addition, the authors present the preliminary ideas for a possible proposal for this aim within the framework of the RE SIREN method. The final aim of proposal is to achieve a RE method that guides the selection, the development and the composition of a set of independent software components, and whose application is the simplest possible. This approach can be used in any Information System (IS) in general, and some simple examples related to the domain of the electronic mail applications are provided.

Systems modularisation is one of the requirements for software development today due to applications complexity. One cannot build systems as a single piece of software. Moreover, reuse is one of the development principles highly required. Object-oriented programming, for example, is an initiative of programs modularisation and reuse in the sense that classes are abstraction units, from which objects inherit behaviour, and a set of objects work together to build a system. Component-based systems have also become popular because systems are built from a set of object-components and the reuse principle is mainly applied, making systems costly effective and in the time to market.

Despite highly required, reusing components and making them work together to accomplish the desired system behaviour is still a challenging task. This requires finding the appropriate components to generate the required behaviour and assembling instances of components (object-components) to result in the whole system. Chapter 4 presents a study on the use of planning techniques to assembling software components to build systems. In this study, a tool, based on goal-driven planning techniques, has been developed together with a software components library and an analysis on the effectiveness of building systems using such techniques is conducted.

Software inspection is a manual software quality technique for ensuring that software defects are identified early in the software development lifecycle, and therefore prevents these defects from propagating to the later stages of development where rework would be a lot more expensive. There is abundant evidence in the literature that if properly applied, it improves the overall productivity of developers by reducing unnecessary effort and time [10]. Most empirical investigations test relative effectiveness of different defect detection methods. Given the complexity of software, and the lack of proper training of software engineers in institutions, more empirical investigations is warranted to understand how to better train inspectors. Constraints in the real-world (limited time and effort resources) and the size/complexity of software also mean that not all software artefacts can be inspected; and any time consuming activity such as inspector training should be as optimal as possible. Defects left undetected in artefacts are deemed as risks to the final quality of the software product.

In recent years, a series of experiments compare methods of training software inspectors [7, 8]. Chapter 5 builds on these experiments, by proposing that a value-based approach is consistent with existing support for the overall discipline of value-based software engineering [5], and therefore should be built in as a strategy for training software inspectors. We report on a laboratory experiment testing the impact of a value-based approach to training software inspectors, and compared the performance of these inspectors to a control group with no specific defect detection training. The authors derived the value-based training approach by modifying the taxonomy of software development risk proposed by SEI to suit the inspection task [5]. This taxonomy ensures that the breadth of all software development risks is dealt with in a systematic way. For comparisons with previous results, these were also compared with a treatment group where inspectors were trained using work examples. An initial pilot was conducted to validate the instruments and experimental procedure, and a main experiment was conducted following the pilot. The results showed significant improvement in the number of defects identified using the value-based approach, over the other treatment groups. This study has implications for how inspectors should be trained for both students and practitioners.

Chapter 6 gives an overview and a comparison of the existing coupling approaches of B and UML for circumventing the shortcomings of these two specification languages with respect to their practical applicability. The authors also deal with our contribution to documenting B specifications with graphical UML notations more intuitive and readable.

Building various program comprehension tools for various object-oriented (OO) languages has been viewed as a necessity to help maintainers to understand legacy OO systems. Due to the difficulty of building such a tool, several generator-based approaches have been proposed. In Chapter 7, the authors view building program comprehension tools for OO languages as a domain engineering problem and propose a domain engineering based approach. The basis of our approach is an XML-based intermediate representation for OO source code. Thus, source code in various OO languages can be easily transformed into this common representation and the target program comprehension tool can be built on the intermediate representation with little consideration of the difference in original languages. It should also be emphasized that our approach is a high-level one, and it does not exclude the co-using of previous generator-based language manipulation methods.

User profiles play an important role on information retrieval. Chapter 8 proposes a method, OAUP, of the construction of ontology-based adaptive user profiles. The OAUP method employs collaborative filtering combined with data mining and soft computing to build ontology-based user profiles. One key feature of OAUP is that collaborative filtering, association rules, simulated annealing and fuzzy genetic algorithms are combined to build user profiles. Another key feature of OAUP is that it employs the hybrid algorithm of exploiting the desirable properties of both complete-link clustering algorithms and inference mechanism to build user ontologies. The method can make user profiles strong expressive, more self-adaptive and less manually interfered.

EXPERT COMMENTARY

In: Computer Software Engineering Research
Editor: Ari D. Klein, pp. 3-8

ISBN: 1-60021-774-5

THE CASE FOR READABLE CODE

Trygve Reenskaug
Dept. of Informatics, University of Oslo

Abstract

Readable code is the key to correct and maintainable programs. Pure class-oriented programming does not scale and tends to lead to code that is hard to read. Extensive subclassing is an effective obfuscator and should often be replaced with delegation. A strategy of divide and conquer can be achieved with suitably structured components. This opens a path to readable, object-oriented programs. Pair programming and, even better, peer review are work processes that help in getting it right the first time.

Introduction

There is no end to the number of different programs that can be executed in a computer. A program may crash or it may go into an infinite loop. It is all the same; the machine executes the instructions given to it.

There is almost no end to the number of programs that will satisfy a given specification and pass the acceptance tests. But tests only cover a minuscule number of the potential executions. Untold glitches and errors may lurk within the untested parts of the code only to be found by undisciplined users who run the program in ways not anticipated by the testers.

There are relatively few programs that will satisfy a given specification, pass the acceptance tests with flying colors, and have been read, understood and accepted by a human reader. These are the "no surprises" programs that blend in with the users' work and that can be adapted to the inevitable changes in the users' needs.

The remainder of this comment is about how to create one of these very desirable programs. This gives me an opportunity to ride a dear hobbyhorse of mine: *The key to quality programs is that the code must be readable, and in addition, that it must actually be read.*

I will first discuss why class-oriented programming makes it difficult to write readable code and look at ways to overcome these problems. I end this commentary by discussing some work processes that facilitate the writing of readable code.

Subclassing is Evil

The *procedure* in procedure-oriented programming is an ideal unit for independent reading. There is one entry point, one exit point, and well-defined calls upon required services. Compare with the code defining a class with its methods. There are a potentially large number of entry points, each having its own exit point. Required services are invoked indirectly through expressions that give the links to the service providers. This can get very complex, and we will have to restrict ourselves to the subset of all possible classes where the code is readable and checkable.

Subclassing is a very powerful feature of object-oriented programming. Common code can be factored out into a superclass; common changes can be done in the superclass and apply equally to all its subclasses. In theory, this practice should be straight forward, but there is a serious snag. Subclassing adds another dimension to the already complex class. It is often necessary to read the superclass code to understand the behavior specification. The services provided by the superclass can be less than obvious and they may have changed since a previous reading. A reviewer can only trust the superclasses if they are part of a trusted and well-known library.

One or more levels of superclasses may be evolving as parts of the current project. Any previous check of a class is invalidated when one of its superclasses is changed. Do we recheck all the subclasses? I hear the word "refactoring", but semiautomatic refactoring cannot replace code reading in a world of careful code review.

My conclusion is that subclassing should be severely restricted because the inevitable superclass evolution will make us lose control. I suggest that subclassing can often be replaced by *delegation*, thus keeping the number of inheritance levels within reasonable bounds.

I work at finding a discipline of object-oriented programming that ameliorates the obfuscation associated with class-oriented programming. I believe we need to

- replace most of the subclassing with delegation,
- enforce an object structure that gives us readable code through a strategy of *divide and conquer*.

Delegation with the Andersen Representation Objects

In his cand.scient. Thesis, Jørn Andersen discussed how the query operations from relational algebra can be translated into an object-oriented context [1]. His premise was that there was a set of encapsulated, black box objects and that the results of the queries should likewise be sets of encapsulated, black box objects. In relational terms, a *relation* became a set of objects, a *tuple* became an object, and an *attribute* became a message.

The SELECT operation is simple; it just returns a subset of the original objects. A JOIN is harder, the result should appear as instances of a new class with attributes from both the argument classes. Andersen's solution was to introduce a *Representation* class. An instance of this class associates the message names with the objects that shall handle them. His solution is similar to the *Facade* pattern [2], but he utilized the stored program facility of Smalltalk to make all facade objects instances of the same, *Representation* class. The result was a very powerful delegation mechanism. A Representation object will dynamically and automatically extend its interface when a new handling object is added. A Representation object will dynamically and automatically shrink its interface when an object is removed.

The Andersen Representation object appears to give dynamic, multiple inheritance in a simple way. It should be explored as a readable replacement of uncontrolled subclassing.

Divide and Conquer with Components

The Facade pattern and the Andersen Representation objects are both open constructs; their handling objects may simultaneously participate in other constructs. This may lead to unduly complex structures that make the code hard to read. I close the constructs by defining a *component* as an object that encapsulates a number of *member objects*. Being encapsulated, a component is characterized by its *provided and required interfaces*. Components are ideal building blocks in a strategy of divide and conquer since they divide the object space into manageable parts. A reader can check the code for each provided operation in turn. The code is local to the component; any required services are captured in the required interfaces. The implementations of the required interfaces are in other components that can be checked separately.

An Andersen Representation can serve as the port into a component. The member objects can be structured according to a suitable paradigm in order to make the code more readable (and thus reliable). An example is the DCA (Data-Collaboration-Algorithm) paradigm discussed in [3].

Testing Cannot Inject Quality into an Inferior Product

Testing has never been in the forefront of my attention because no industry has ever been able to test quality into an inferior product. In programming, this means that it is too late to save an inferior program when it gets to the testing stage. The best thing to do is to focus on getting it right the first time and use testing to check that we have made no serious blunders.

A minimum requirement for a reasonable test is that all statements shall have been executed at least once. Otherwise, a program may pass the tests while glaring deficiencies remain unnoticed. This requirement is hard to satisfy in procedural programming, and I have never been able to satisfy it with objects. I still work at finding a discipline of object oriented programming that facilitates this reasonable level of testing.

Literate Programming

Donald Knuth had proposed the notion of *literate programming*. The main idea was to treat a program as a piece of literature in the form of a textbook. The text could be formatted and printed like a book, and a filter could extract the code and compile it. This idea fitted very well with our idea that a program should primarily be written for a human reader, and it looked like a good idea to develop code and textbook together. So we extended our multimedia authoring tool with two new media: Smalltalk class definitions and Smalltalk method definitions. Our experience with literate programming was reported at OOPSLA-89 [4]

A colleague and I worked together on a major project where we wrote the code directly into a literate programming document. This combination of authoring and coding was very inspiring and great fun. We were highly motivated to write about a good idea whenever we hit upon it. We once saw an obvious way to optimize a certain method. We worked on it for some time before discovering a catch; the optimization could not work. There and then we were very motivated to write a warning to future maintainers directly below the relevant code in the document. The next day would have been too late; we were on to other problems and other solutions.

Literate programming worked beautifully until we got to a stage where we wanted to refactor the program. The program structure was easy to change, but it implied a radical change to the structure of the book. There was no way we could spend a great deal of time on restructuring the book so we ended up with writing appendices and appendices to appendices that explained what we had done. The final book became unreadable and only fit for the dustbin.

The lesson was that the textbook metaphor is not applicable to program development. A textbook is written on a stable and well known subject while a program is under constant evolution. We abandoned literate programming as being too rigid for practical programming. Even if we got it right the first time, it would have failed in the subsequent maintenance phases of the program's life cycle.

Pair Programming

Dijkstra is the source of many pregnant maxims such as *program testing can be used to show the presence of bugs, but never show their absence* and *nothing is cheaper than not introducing the bugs in the first place.* [5] This is all well and good, but easier said than done.

One of the keys to success is to admit the fallibility of humans and make sure that at least two people are involved in the creation of a program. One solution is to let two programmers work together in front of a common computer. I have one very successful experience with this mode of working when a colleague and I developed the base architecture and core program of a family of software products. We spent almost a year on the architecture before getting down to the concrete programming. We were a very good team; one being creative and jumping to conclusions, the other insisting on stopping to think whenever the code was less than obvious. (This effort was also an exercise in literate programming as described previously). Other attempts at pair programming have failed because conflicting personalities made the effort more competitive than cooperative.

I believe that pair programming can be very effective under the right conditions. If a fairly stable team is working on a common body of programs, the pairing can be varied. All team members get to know the programs intimately well and any of them can confidently work on the inevitable changes and extensions.

Pair programming is still not the ideal solution because two programmers working closely together can easily fall into the same trap. Further, they get intimately acquainted with the intricacies of the programs so that the code may not be readable for a future, uninitiated maintainer.

Peer Review

I believe it was an article in the *Datamation* magazine some time in the sixties that first brought peer review to my notice. It sounded great. I had just written a FORTRAN subroutine and ran around to find somebody who was willing to read and comment on it. I finally persuaded a colleague to do so.

All the benefits mentioned in the Datamation article were attained in this first exercise. First, my colleague pointed out that a certain statement could be improved by using a FORTRAN feature I was not aware of. Second, my colleague asked me to explain the exact meaning of another statement that he was unfamiliar with. And finally, my colleague found a bug I would never have found by blind testing. The program worked beautifully for N<1000. It failed gracefully for N>1000. But it crashed for N=1000. Careful reading of the code might have highlighted the number 1000 as critical so that it should have a special test. But such reading would have revealed the bug and the test would have been superfluous.

The outcome of this first attempt at peer review was that both my colleague and I learnt something new in addition to the main result of a bug-free subroutine. All this achieved at the cost of 15 minutes of proof-reading.

We used peer review in all our work from that day on. Every subroutine had two comments: One identified the original programmer and another identified the reader. The important feature was that it was the reader who was responsible for the correctness of the code. In the rare case of a bug, the original programmer could point at the reader and say: "your fault!"

When I read my own code, I know what it is supposed to say and naturally assume that I have written what I intended. My colleague has no such pre-conception and he knows perfectly well that I am fallible. His chance of finding a deficiency is far better than mine when we read the same code.

I said above that code should primarily be written for the human reader. With peer review, there is an immediate check the code is indeed readable. We can be reasonably certain that future maintainers can read and understand the code since the reviewer has already done so.

Conclusion

Program testing can never show the absence of bugs. Indeed, *the more bugs we find during testing, the more bugs remain in the shipped product.* (Because a given test regimen can only find a certain percentage of all bugs). Contrast with a competent reviewer who reads all the code and can reveal bugs, glitches, clumsy code, and potential traps for a future maintainer.

Effective code reading is only feasible if the code is partitioned into reasonably independent chunks and if the remaining dependencies are well defined. I have tried using peer review in object-oriented programming, but have as yet not succeeded because I have not been able to partition the system into reasonable chunks. I expect that some changes to my programming method will help:

- Subclassing must be kept to a minimum both to reduce system complexity and to make it less vulnerable to the inevitable program evolution.

- Subclassing can often be replaced by delegation.
- Chunking objects into components with a corresponding chunking of the code is essential.
- Literate programming is tempting for an example educational program, but is too rigid for general programming.
- Pair programming is powerful but may not lead to chunked and readable code.

My pet idea is peer review. May it become an essential element in the creation of quality programs.

References

[1] Andersen, J. *Queries on sets in an Object-Oriented Database*; Cand. Scient. Thesis; Department of informatics, University of Oslo; 1991.
[2] Gamma, E,; Helm, R,; Johnson, R; Vlissides, J. *Design Patterns*; ISBN 0-201-63361-2; Addison-Wesley, Reading, MA. 1995.
[3] See my chapter on *Programming with roles and classes* in this book.
[4] Reenskaug, T.; Skaar, A. L. *An environment for literate Smalltalk programming*; OOPSLA 1989; ISBN: 0-89791-333-7; ACM Press; New York, NY 1989; pp. 337–345.
[5] For more Dijkstra contributions to computing, see *E. W. Dijkstra Archive;* University of Texas; [web page] http://www.cs.utexas.edu/users/EWD/

RESEARCH AND REVIEW STUDIES

In: Computer Software Engineering Research
Editor: Ari D. Klein, pp. 11-44

ISBN: 1-60021-774-5

Chapter 1

Action Research in Software Engineering: Using a 3D Analogy to Analyze the Implementation of Agile Software Development in Software Teamwork

Yael Dubinsky *

Department of Computer Science,
Technion – Israel Institute of Technology

Orit Hazzan **

Department of Education in Technology & Science,
Technion – Israel Institute of Technology

Abstract

This chapter deals with implementing agile software development methods in software projects. It focuses on aspects that expose the problems of the software engineering field that mainly concern customer requirements, software defects, management of software projects, and characteristics of the actual development work. Action Research is the research paradigm that we used. Using this paradigm, researchers perform a rigorous, systematic, and criticized process on their own work in the research field. The research is iterative when each research cycle is composed of planning – action – collection of data available as a result of the action – data analysis – reflection – refinement of the results.

We present a conceptual model that has emerged as part of a comprehensive qualitative research that deals with the implementation of the agile approach in software teamwork. The model is composed of a three-dimensional analogy of the following concepts: action research, agile software development method, and teaching the agile approach. Using the analogy, we analyze findings from our research settings in both industry and academia. For clarity of what such a research setting means, we focus in this chapter on the academic research setting.

* E-mail address: yael@cs.technion.ac.il
** E-mail address: oritha@tx.technion.ac.il

The main contribution of this chapter is the 3D analogy that is suggested as a tool to analyze software processes. Illustrating its usage provides a better understanding of the implementation of the agile approach in software processes.

1. Introduction

Software processes are complicated and composed of technical aspects, as well as organizational, managerial, cognitive, and social aspects (Hamlet and Maybee, 2001; Highsmith, 2002; Berry, 2002; Tomayko and Hazzan, 2004). Though few decades of experiencing software processes have passed, there is no agreed standard method for software development. Further, the software engineering community still seeks to solve the cost and quality problems that occur in most software projects. One of the solutions to these problems is the agile approach that has received more attention in the last few years when more software organizations are interested in checking if it is suitable for their projects. In this chapter, we examine the implementation of the agile approach in software teamwork based on our research of the implementation of agile processes in both academia and industry. For clarity, we focus on the academic research setting in which we implement the agile approach in a project-based Computer Science course.

We present a conceptual model that has emerged as part of a comprehensive qualitative research that deals with the implementation of the agile approach in software teamwork. The model is composed of a three-dimensional analogy of the following concepts: action research, agile software development method, and teaching the agile approach. Using the analogy, we analyze findings from our research settings. Since the development environment is characterized by frequent changes, we further analyze the findings to see how they relate to known ways of coping with changes (Plotkin, 1997).

In what follows in this section we briefly describe the agile approach and its implementation in a project-based course. In Section 2, the research framework is detailed with respect to the research paradigm, method, and tools. During the analysis of the research findings a theoretical framework in the form of an analogy was defined. The analogy is presented in Section 3, and is used as a tool to discuss the research findings. The teaching framework that includes the practices and principles for teaching software development methods is detailed in (Dubinsky, 2005). In Section 4, the concept of dealing with changes is presented, and in light of this concept, the research findings are discussed by applying the analogy as presented in Section 3. Section 5 is a summary.

1.1. The Agile Approach

Agile software development methods have emerged over the past decade as a response to the above-mentioned unique problems that characterize software development processes (Highsmith, 2002). In general, agile software development methods emphasize customer needs, communication among team members, short releases and heavy testing throughout the entire development process. These emphases are defined in the Manifesto for Agile Software Development[1], as follows:

[1] The agile manifesto at http://agilemanifesto.org/

- **Individuals and interactions** over processes and tools
- **Working software** over comprehensive documentation
- **Customer collaboration** over contract negotiation
- **Responding to changes** over following plans

It is stated that while there is value in the items on the right, agile practitioners value the items on the left more.

The agile principles are implemented quite differently by different agile methods (Highsmith, 2002; Abrahamsson, Salo, Ronkainen and Warsta, 2002). Fowler explains that "agile methods have some significant changes in emphasis from heavyweight methods" (Fowler, 2002). For example, he mentions that "agile methods are people-oriented rather than process-oriented". Specifically, there are seven main agile methods: Extreme Programming (XP) (Beck, 2000; Beck and Andres, 2004), Scrum (Schwaber and Beedle, 2002), Crystal (Cockburn, 2002), Feature Driven Development (FDD) (Palmer and Felsing, 2002), Dynamic Systems Development Method (DSDM) (Stapleton, 1997), Adaptive Software Development (ASD) (Highsmith, 2000), and Lean Software Development (Poppendieck and Poppendieck, 2003).

1.2. Implementing the Agile Approach

One of the advanced courses offered by the Department of Computer Science at the Technion, and taught by the first author for more than ten years, is the project-based capstone course "Projects in Operating Systems". The Department of Computer Science is considered to be comparable to the ten leading Computer Science departments in the US[2]. Approximately 1,300 undergraduate students and about 200 graduate students are currently studying at the Department. In addition to its general B.Sc. program, the Department offers 4 special undergraduate tracks in Software Engineering, Information Systems Engineering, Computer Engineering, and Bioinformatics. The Technion in general, and the Department of Computer Science in particular, are one the main suppliers of (software) engineers to the Israeli hi-tech industry.

The course "Projects in Operating Systems" is offered three times a year (winter, spring and summer semesters), and approximately 150 students participate each year. The course has been taught in a studio-oriented format since the summer semester of 2002. The "studio" is the basic learning method used in architecture schools. In such studios, students develop projects, closely guided by a coach and while performing on-going reflection, both on what is created and on the creation process itself (Kuhn, 1998; Tomayko, 1996). Analysis of how the studio can be implemented into software development environments is presented by Hazzan, 2002. Extreme Programming, commonly abbreviated XP (Beck, 2000) is the agile development method chosen to be introduced into the studio in that course.

Since the summer semester of 2002, the studio format has been applied in the Operating Systems Projects course in 31 projects. The initiative is highly supported by the Department of Computer Science, which, among other things, provides the required resources and

[2] This is according to an international Review Committee that has reviewed the Department of Computer Science in January 2000 and has submitted a report to the President of the Technion (taken from http://www.cs.technion.ac.il/GeneralInformation/AbouttheDepartment/index.html).

equipment. Thus, each team of 10-12 students works on a specific operating system project during the entire semester, in its own studio, which is equipped with computers, tables and white boards. Each team has an academic coach who guides the development process.

Attendance of all students at all of the weekly 2-4 hour sessions is compulsory. In these meetings, XP practices are taught and employed. In between sessions, communication is conducted via an electronic forum, which is part of the course web-based environment. Although the new format of the Operating Systems Projects course also includes the teaching of a software development method, the operating systems-related material traditionally taught in the course has remained unchanged. Furthermore, the introduction of XP into the course has been found to enrich the development environment with respect to topics such as customer needs and process management (Dubinsky and Hazzan, 2005; Dubinsky and Hazzan, 2006).

To illustrate the change that has been introduced with the new approach, several facts were added about the teaching method that was employed in the course prior to the introduction of the studio approach with teams of 10-12 students that work according to a specific software development method. Prior to the introduction of XP into the course, projects were performed in teams of 2-3 computer/software engineering students. The students were required to submit documentation, mid-semester and final presentations and to participate in a project fair. The academic staff consisted of two instructors, who coordinated the teaching and administration of the course, and of several academic coaches. If questions or other issues arose, the students could meet with the academic coaches during their regular office hours. Usually projects were not completed at time and were continued into the examination period or even to next semester. In groups of three students and sometimes even in pairs the "free riders" phenomenon was evident many times but for some reasons students bear with it. Since summer 2002, when the studio approach was introduced, all projects are completed in the last week of the semester which is partially a result of tight time management that is part of the XP planning game practice. In addition, the "free riders" phenomenon was significantly reduced due to the role scheme that was activated and reflected in the grade policy, and due to group stand up meetings at the beginning of every weekly session. The academic coaches, who are present in the weekly sessions of the studio with the group of 10-12 students, are updated regularly with the status of the project.

2. Research Framework

2.1. The Course as the Research Field

In this Section the research field description is elaborated by adding the details about the actual implementation and integration of Extreme Programming (XP) in the course schedule and its main activities. The focus in the following description is placed on one team consists of 12 students which is supervised by one academic coach. We note that the course schedule and activities described in this Section are part of the teaching framework that was constructed in the course of the research and are elaborated in (Dubinsky, 2005) where the teaching framework is presented.

The studio is a kind of computers laboratory that is equipped to serve as a project development center. There is a discussion table in the middle of the room and computers tables around. There are boards that contain the project stories and management material such as measures that are taken regularly.

In a 14-week semester, the team task is to develop the first release of a software product in the subject matter of operating systems. The project subject, as well as a brief description of the software development method to be used, is introduced in the first meeting of the semester. In fact, in this meeting the first iteration (out of three iterations that comprise a release) starts. As XP guides, each iteration includes the following activities: listening to customer stories, planning the work, programming and testing, presentation of the intermediate product and reflection on the iteration activities. The first iteration is 7-week long and includes, in additional to the above activities, the launching of the project development environment, the learning of the project subject, and roles distribution among teammates. Since after the first iteration the students are more experienced, the second and third iterations long together half of the semester.

The detail course schedule, together with a short description of the main activities conducted in each lesson, is presented in Appendix I. The information for each week includes the purpose of the meeting, the main activities of the academic coach and of the students, and the XP practices and values that are conveyed during these activities. The academic coaches use this table regularly and update it occasionally based on their reflection.

In what follows an example of a second iteration is described. The second iteration is the most typical one since it does not include the launching of the project as occurs in the first iteration, and does not include the final release presentation as happens in the third and last iteration. Table 1 lays out part of the complete course schedule (Appendix I), and it presents the entries of the second iteration weeks – from the eighth to the eleventh weeks. All activities are guided by the academic coach. In what follows, a detailed description of each meeting is presented together with what XP practices and principles are expressed.

The Eighth Meeting

The eighth meeting starts, as all the other meetings, with a stand-up meeting. The students stand and one after the other describe in few sentences what s/he was doing in the last week since the previous meeting took place and what s/he is going to work on during the coming week. This meeting longs about ten minutes and its main goal is information sharing.

The practice of planning game, in which the iteration is planed and tasks are allocated to all the students, is the leading activity of this meeting. It is played after the product, that was developed during the first iteration, had been presented in the seventh meeting and the customer (in most cases one of the students) decided, with all the other students, about the stories to be developed during the second iteration.

During the week between the seventh and eighth meetings the students should prepare a design for the decided new stories and a pile of cards with the relevant development tasks. During this meeting (the eighth) the students estimate the development time for the development tasks and check if the total development time matches the development time that available during the second iteration. The calculation is based on the following two facts: each student should dedicate 10 hours per week in a regular week and 15 hours per week in a week before presentation; the iteration longs 3 weeks. Accordingly, each student should work 35 hours during the 3 weeks of the iteration. Since each student has a personal role which includes responsibility on a specific aspect of software development (Dubinsky and Hazzan,

2006), 20% of the accumulative time of all students is dedicated to the carrying out of the personal roles and the rest 80% for development tasks. As part of the evaluation process, the academic coach uses the activities of stories analysis and time management to learn about the team and the individuals work. At the end of the planning game every student knows his/her tasks for the next three weeks.

Table 1. Schedule of Second Iteration

#	Purpose of Meeting	Main Activities (academic coach and students)	XP Practices and Values
8	Lessons learned and planning game for Iteration 2 - Phase II	- Reflect on the lessons learned - Play customer: Develop customer stories and make customer decisions	-Communication - Feedback - Courage - On-site customer - Planning game - Metaphor - Small releases - Sustainable pace
9	Development activities and test-first exercise	- Test-first and refactoring exercise - Design - Develop code	- Testing - Refactoring - Simple design - Collective ownership - Pair programming
10	Development activities, preparations for the presentation next week of Iteration 2	- Design - Develop code	- Simple design - Collective ownership - Pair programming - Continuous integration
11	Presentation of Iteration 2, feedback, planning game of Iteration 3 - Phase I	- Presentation - Customer stories - Make customer decisions	- Communication - Feedback - Courage - On-site customer - Planning game - Metaphor - Small releases - Sustainable pace
		End of Iteration 2	

Although a feedback was given at the previous meeting (the seventh) after the intermediate product of first iteration had been presented, part of the eighth meeting is dedicated too to teammates discussion about lessons learned and their implementation during this iteration. This discussion is significant since it is performed one week after the first iteration product is presented, when students get a more remote perspective about the first iteration process.

As all the other meetings, the eighth meeting ends with a request to fill a reflection about the meeting activities which is posted on the web. The reflection is open right after the activity and stays open for a week till the next activity starts.

During the eighth meeting several XP values and practices are conveyed. The value of communication is expressed in all activities, and the feedback value is mainly expressed in the lessons-learned discussion. The courage value is mainly expressed in the stand-up meeting and in the planning game when known problems in the product should be raised for the sake of time estimation.

Within the planning game activity, additional practices are expressed such as the customer-on-site practice (when decisions are made) and metaphor (when requirements are described and discussed). The small releases practice is also expressed when a fixed date for the second iteration delivery is announced, and the sustainable pace practice is considered for time calculation.

The Ninth Meeting

As all other meetings, this meeting starts with a stand-up meeting. The focus in this meeting is placed on the topic of test-driven-development. Specifically, students learn about the testing technique and about refactoring as part of test-driven-development, and exercise it on their personal development task. Since the students are not familiar with this testing approach, in order not to overload the first iteration in which the project is launched, this approach towards testing is introduced only in the second iteration.

In addition, this meeting is dedicated to actual software development, meaning detailed design of the code that is about to be developed, programming, and testing. The ninth meeting ends with filling a reflection on the web.

During the ninth meeting several XP practices are conveyed. The main practices conveyed are testing and refactoring which are parts of test-driven-development. The practice of simple design is also expressed while working on the details of the current design of the development tasks which are going to be developed. In addition, programming is performed in pairs (an expression of the pair programming practice) and the code that is integrated is owned by all teammates (an expression of the collective ownership practice).

The Tenth Meeting

The tenth meeting starts with stand-up meeting. As in the ninth meeting, in this meeting the focused is also placed on development activities, but in addition part of the meeting is dedicated for the preparation of the presentation for next week in which the intermediate product of the second iteration will be presented.

Usually, students are not used to perform presentations for customers. Therefore, all team members discuss, based on their reflection on the presentation of the first iteration, what improvements can be made. Students delve into the details of how long the slide presentation be and how and when to interweave the demonstration of the application itself.

Specifically, the students prepare the list of customer stories together with the appropriate automatic acceptance tests that were developed to ensure the existence of every customer story. In addition, students deal with presenting the roles' products, such as different measures taken by the tracker, or process documentation prepared by the documenter. The tenth meeting ends with filling a reflection on the web.

In addition to the practices that are expressed in the ninth meeting, in the tenth meeting the continuous integration practice is also expressed, which indeed it usually starts effecting towards the end of an iteration when more work is completed and the pressure on the integration environment increases.

The Eleventh Meeting

In the eleventh meeting the product of the second iteration is presented. Specifically, students present their software product and the customer gives feedback. The academic coach facilitates open feedback conversation and gives his/her own feedback too.

The customer presents his/her stories for the last and third iteration and the students are asked to design and distribute to development tasks towards the next meeting (as was done towards the eighth meeting).

The eleventh meeting ends with filling a reflection on the web which its subject is the evaluation of the teamwork and the individual work. All students are asked to evaluate verbally and in a 0-100 scale the way the team met the customer stories and the defined time estimations. In addition, each student is asked to summarize his/her role activities and evaluate it on a 0-100 scale. This evaluation is part of the evaluation process performed by the academic coach.

Some of the XP values and practices that are conveyed during this meeting are the same as the ones expressed in the eighth meeting. In addition, the value of communication is expressed by presenting to the on-site customer, the feedback value is expressed during the discussion that follows the presentation, and the value of courage is expressed by presenting both problems and successful aspects related to the software product and to the software process.

To summarize this part, the continuation of the semester consists of a third iteration which is very similar to the second iteration. The students are familiar with the subject matter of the project and with the applied software development method. The students gradual learning proceeds and can even improve during the third iteration. At the same time, the academic coach observes the process regularly and gains rich data based on which to evaluate the team as a whole and the individuals (Dubinsky, 2005).

2.2. Research Paradigm: Action Research

Action Research is the research arena in which researchers study the domain within which they work, employing a systematic and criticized process. This research approach is usually adopted in cases in which researchers wish to improve their understanding of an action they perform, identify problems, find solutions to these problems and examine these solutions in order to improve the process undergone in the research field. The origin of this research perspective is in the work of Kurt Lewin (Lewin 1946, reproduced in Lewin 1948), whose approach involves a spiral of steps, 'each of which is composed of a circle of planning, action and fact-finding about the result of the action' (p. 206).

The discussion of Action Research tends to fall into two distinctive camps (Smith, 1996). The British tradition tends to view Action Research as research that is oriented toward the enhancement of direct practice, and largely associates it with educational research. The second tradition, more accepted in the USA, conceives of Action Research as 'the systematic collection of information that is designed to bring about social change' (Bogdan and Biklen 1992, p. 223). It seems that our research touches on both traditions.

As can be observed, Action Research inspires an inductive method of research in which a framework is developed by means of an iterative process, in which the researcher develops a theory while simultaneously testing it and gathering additional data in the course of the research itself. When a study is conducted within the paradigm of Action Research, there is a continuous interplay, which is an integral element of the on-going research process, between data collection, data analysis and the application of intermediate results.

The Action Research paradigm was deemed suitable for our research because it was possible to apply it in a very natural manner. The research field, in this case, an academic environment, enabled us to establish an iterative process, during which our proposed teaching framework was shaped in an inductive process, while the results obtained so far were constantly applied, and the suitability of the developed framework was continually examined and compared to newly gathered data and findings.

2.3. Research Method

The research paradigm (i.e., Action Research) is applied in the research by the use of a measured-qualitative research method, i.e., a qualitative research method that is accompanied by a set of measures which provides complementary quantitative data with respect to predefined factors. In what follows the main characteristics of the qualitative research method are described, along with an explanation regarding its suitability to the research presented in this chapter. This analysis is based on Cook and Reichardt, 1979; Strauss, 1987; Patton, 1990.

Qualitative research is interpretive. Its objective is to explain situations and processes. Indeed, in the presented research, the aim is to describe the process of teaching software development methods.

The qualitative researcher feels a relative lack of control. Indeed, at the start of this research, the feeling was that the integration of XP into the course activities might reveal interesting and important findings that, eventually, would help in the construction of a desired framework. Although at that time there was neither an initial hypothesis nor a complete design for the study, the fact that the adoption of the Action Research paradigm for the research will help navigate the vague and unclear first steps of the course of research.

Qualitative research is inductive. In other words, categories and theories emerge from the data. Indeed, our teaching framework has evolved based on data analysis and is, in fact, still undergoing refinement.

Qualitative research is also process oriented and insider centered. In the research described here, the researcher works in the research field, guiding a team of students each semester, working in parallel to three other academic coaches who each guide their own team of students. The research supervisor observes studio activities and participates in meeting of the academic coaches, and is also involved in the investigation of human aspects of software engineering (Tomayko and Hazzan, 2004).

The application of the research paradigm (Action Research) using the measured-qualitative research method led to the establishment of an iterative process that consists of data gathering, data analysis, reflection, refinement of the framework constructed so far, action and so on and so forth (data gathering, data analysis...).

Such iterations reoccurred during the research at various intervals, and had different cycle times. Some iterations were long (a full academic year); other iterations were shorter (one semester); yet, there were even shorter cycles, such as those that were performed in order to improve the understanding of a specific topic. From the accumulative interpretations obtained during all iterations of all lengths, a framework was gradually formulated and conclusions were derived.

The above process was applied during the past 9 semesters (summer of 2002 through spring of 2005) in 31 projects, developed by more than 300 students who worked in teams of 10-12 students each.

2.4. Research Tools

This section describes the research tools that were used in this research for the purpose of data gathering.

***Videotapes*:** Each semester, all of the meetings held by one team were videotaped. The videotapes were viewed during, as well as after, the semester in which the data were gathered. Focus was placed mainly on the discourse that took place during the meetings, in order to find repeated discourse patterns.

***Student reflections*:** After each weekly meeting, the students reported their reflections using the web-based tool that was used for course management. These reflections referred to subjects addressed and dealt with at the most recent meeting.

***Electronic forum*:** In between the weekly meetings, the students complemented their communications using an electronic forum. Analysis of the forum messages revealed the story of the group in general, and the group dynamics and status of the project development in particular.

***Interviews*:** In order to improve our understanding of specific issues, whether they emerged from observations, videotapes or student reflections, open interviews and semi-structured interviews with students and academic coaches were conducted.

***Questionnaires*:** Questionnaires were used in order to learn about new topics, and enabled us to examine the responses of a relatively large number of people. Usually, after the questionnaire results were gathered and analyzed, the findings were refined by means of interviews. Questionnaires were also used in some instances in preparation for a retrospective process.

***Researcher's diary*:** The researcher kept a researcher's diary, which included personal observations, reflections, thoughts, short notes made on different occasions, etc.

The data gathered using these research tools provided a multi-faceted picture of the process of teaching (and learning) software development methods. It enabled to see the development environment, hear the voices of the students and coaches, and read their reflections and questionnaire answers. In addition, the data were used for the measures required for the assessment of the development process.

2.5. Data Analysis Methods

The data gathered using the above research tools were analyzed using common qualitative research methods (see upper part of Table 2) as well as quantitative data analysis that fits our set of measures (see lower part of Table 2). In what follows, each of the data analysis methods is described.

Table 2. Data Analysis Methods and Their Corresponding Research Tools

Approach	Data Analysis Method	Research Tools
Qualitative	Constant comparison	- Interviews of students - Interviews of coaches - Observations - Questionnaires
	Hermeneutical analysis	- Questionnaires - Electronic text Electronic forum Students' online reflections
	Discourse analysis	- Videotape of studio sessions - Record of coaches' training - Electronic text Electronic forum
	Narrative analysis	- Electronic text Students' online reflections
Quantitative	Measuring quantitative data analysis	- Questionnaires - Electronic text Electronic forum Students' online reflections

Constant comparison is a data analysis method in which the researcher examines the data, codes (transcribes) events and behaviors, and then begins an analysis process based on the comparison of different pieces of data with the objective of identifying consistencies that may reveal categories. In this research, for example, interviews with the course's academic coaches were transcribed and findings that emerged from them were constantly compared in order to reveal categories that later influenced the construction of the coaching practice (Dubinsky, 2005).

Hermeneutical analysis is a data analysis method in which the researcher makes sense of a written text while looking for its meaning from the perspective of the people involved in the situation (Manen, 1990). The researcher uses the people's own words to tell their stories and to describe social interactions among them. In this research, for example, this method was used to analyze students' written reflections, in which they described their perception of their individual role in the software project (Dubinsky, 2005).

Discourse analysis is a linguistic analysis of an ongoing flow of communication (Gee, 1992). The researcher refers to linguistic aspects, while considering the way people conceive a specific topic and the influence this conception has on their behavior. In this research, for example, discourse analysis was used to study videotapes of studio activities. Results obtained from this analysis were used in the construction of the course.

Narrative analysis is the study of the speech or narrative of the individual (Reisman, 1993). Unlike discourse analysis, in which the interaction among individuals is at the focus of the analysis, in narrative analysis the focus is placed on the story as it is told by the individual. This kind of analysis was used in this research in different ways. For example, narrative analysis was used in order to examine students' personal narratives that were presented as reflections using the web-based tool. This kind of analysis was also used in the analysis of videotapes.

Measuring analysis provides a way to assess activities that occur during the development process by quantitative means. The measuring is performed after the activities have been conducted by using quantitative data. In this research, quantitative data is gathered from questionnaires, students' communication using the course electronic forum and students' reflections after each activity (Dubinsky, 2005).

3. The Three Dimensional Analogy

As the research progressed and the teaching framework was started being shaped and refined, the question of when to stop the research cycles was considered. Specifically, questions such as the following were raised: How does one know if nine research cycles are sufficient? Maybe six cycles are enough, or maybe, alternatively, the process should continue till no refinement is required? Attempts to answer this question clarified that a teaching framework cannot be formulated as a final version ready to be used by others unless it would have a dynamic nature. In other words, it was clear that such a teaching framework can not be static; Changes in technology, in software engineering methods and in teaching and learning approaches will go on affecting the proposed teaching framework. In practice, the dynamic nature of the teaching framework will provide future instructors as well as practitioners who will use it, with the ability to refine and maintain it according to their needs.

An examination of the previous paragraph reveals that this kind of questions also emerges with respect to software development. Specifically, with respect to software development questions such as the following are asked: How does one know when the software is ready to be delivered to customers and shipped to end users? How many features will be developed before the software product is started to be sold for use? In fact, it is a well known fact that the life cycle of software does not end when it is shipped to the users, and that the maintenance phase enables users to introduce and ask for changes in the software tool according to their needs (Hughes and Cotterell, 2002; Sommerville, 2001).

This similarity in the two processes led to the formulation of an analogy, described in what follows, between action research and an agile software development method. This analogy is expanded later to a 3D analogy (Section 3.2) within which the research findings are analyzed. An example of such analysis is presented in Section 3.3. In Section 4, the 3D analogy is utilized for the analysis of findings from our research of implementing software development methods in the academia.

3.1. The Action Research-Agile SDM Analogy

It seems that the paradigm of Action Research (AR) has much in common with agile software development method (ASDM). Specifically, the process of AR and some of its major activities have the same rationale and are performed in a similar fashion to that of an ASDM. There are, of course, different aspects that distinguish between AR and ASDM processes; still, the resemblance is very clear. In other words, there is no claim here that a research process is a software development process, or vice versa; however, as is illustrated in what follows, the resemblance of the two processes is used to improve the understanding of an ASDM process, and in the sequel, with its teaching.

In what follows, three major categories of this analogy (abbreviated by AR-ASDM analogy) are elaborated: Origin and Goals (Table 3), Process Perspective (Table 4) and Participant Perspective (Table 5). Relevant keywords of the analogy entries are emphasized in italics-boldface font.

The first category is the Origin and Goals presented in Table 3. At the beginning of our research, AR was referred to, as it is commonly used, for the enhancement of a direct practice (Zeichner and Gore, 1995; Newman, 2000). Indeed, the typical problems of software engineering constituted (and still form) a good reason to enhance the practice of software engineering as well as its teaching. In other words, at that early stage of the research, the primary origin of using AR seemed to be more suitable for its engineering aspect rather than for its social-anthropology aspect. However, along the way, when research findings related to human and social aspects started taking an increasing part among all findings, the ASDM started to be conceived as a method that requires a conceptual and social change by itself (Somekh, 1995; Zeichner, 1993). As it is described in Table 3, the founder of XP, Kent Beck, also conceived of XP in this way (Beck and Andres, 2004). Thus, the origin of AR, which deals with social changes, forms the heart of this category of the AR-ASDM analogy.

Table 3. The AR-ASDM Analogy – Origin and Goals

Action Research	Agile Software Development Method
The origin of AR is considered as a systematic collection of information that is designed to bring about **social change.** As it has been developed, AR is used for the **enhancement of a direct practice.**	The origin of ASDM is rooted in the problems that characterize the software engineering field. ASDM fosters **individuals and interactions, collaboration among participants,** and work that aims at providing **quality software** while continually **responding to customer introduced changes.** Illustratively, the first sentence in Beck and Andres (2004) is “XP is about **social change**”.

The second category of the AR-ASDM analogy is Process Perspective presented in Table 4. Its five sub-categories refer mainly to the characteristics of the AR and of ASDM processes.

Table 4. The AR-ASDM Analogy – Process Perspective

Action Research	Agile Software Development Method
1. An iterative process with short cycles	
The research **is composed of iterations** (Lewin, 1946) that each is composed of the action plan, the action performance, data collection, data analysis, reflection on action (Schön, 1983; Schön, 1987) and the next iteration plan. **The duration of each cycle is relatively short** in order to refine action in a reasonable manner. The relatively short cycles and the activities in each cycle raise the notion of **flexibility, adaptability to the researched process**.	The development **is composed of iterations** that each contains plan of work (including understanding the customer requirements and an initial design), testing and coding, data tracking, data analysis, reflection on iteration and the next iteration plan. **The duration of each cycle is relatively short** in order to respond to customer changes periodically. The relatively short cycles and the need to adhere and **respond to the customer requirements and changes** in each iteration are the essence of **agility**.
2. Initialization of the process	
The beginning of the first iteration of an AR is not a simple task. In most cases, the researcher **isn't familiar yet** with the field, **doesn't understand** the participants' **problems or desires**, and is **uncertain** about the results of **the executing the action for the first time**.	The beginning of the first iteration of a software project is not a simple task. The developers **are not familiar yet** with the development environment and specifically with the integration and testing environment, **aren't familiar yet (don't understand)** with the **customer requirements**, and are **not sure** about the results of the **first iteration**.
3. A systematic process accompanied with validated tools and methods	
The action researcher **uses validated tools and methods** in order to learn about the research domain. Each of the research activities is supported by well-defined tools, like interviews, questionnaires, and videotaped sessions, and by data anaysis methods such as constant comparison and interpretive analysis. During this process the researcher is engaged with a **learning process** of the research field.	The development team **uses validated tools and methods** in order to learn about the software domain. Each of the project activities is supported by well-defined tools like e.g., Integrated Development Environments (IDEs) and their components, and by methods like, e.g., testing techniques that increase the software quality, and refactoring that improve design and provide a clearer well-structured code. During this process the team is engaged with a **learning process** of the software product to be created.
4. A criticized process and the reflection activity	
The researcher **constantly reflects in and on action** (Schön, 1983; Schön, 1987) in order to improve understanding with the action itself and with the field of research. This is performed based on specific **measures** taken during the action and on the researcher own perspective.	The development team **constantly reflects in and on action** using tracking **measurements** and face-to-face activities, in order to improve understanding with respect to the product requirements and the project progress.
5. Inductive outcome	
The outcomes of an AR process are **inductively formed** during the process into one comprehensive **research product** that meets the **research purpose**.	The outcomes of ASDM process are **inductively formed** during the process into one comprehensive **software product** that meets the **customer requirements**.

The third category of the AR-ASDM analogy is the Participant Perspective. This category includes three sub-categories by which it is suggested to draw the analogy. The sub-categories are: environmental features, cultural aspects, and insider roles. This category is presented in Table 5.

Table 5. The AR-ASDM Analogy – Participant Perspective

Action Research	Agile Software Development Method
1. Insider roles	
The people involved in the action research, namely the researcher and the research participants, are the **inside players** of the research process. In AR processes, **special roles**, such as the customer role, are performed by the researcher in order to better investigate the environment.	The people involved in the development process, namely analysts, testers, developers, customer, and all business people in the organization, are the **inside players** of the development process. In ASDM processes, **special roles** are performed by the teammates.
2. Environmental features	
The researcher relates to the **environment resources** when preparing the required research tools, such as videotapes or questionnaires. The researcher is part of such an **environment**. This environment dictates the **research pace** and **provides research data.**	The project leader coordinates the **environment resources**, such as the project room, as well as all required equipment, such as computers. The ASDM developers work in the **project room environment**. This environment dictates the **work pace** and **provides information** with respect to the project progress.
3. Cultural aspects	
The researcher experiences a **cultural situation** during the investigation process.	The project leader deals with a **cultural situation** when implementing agile practices. Another **cultural situation** is when the project leader, as well as the organization management, must **form teams** that are to be productive.

3.2. The 3D Analogy: Action Research–Agile SDM–Teaching SDM

So far the analogy addresses the research approach of action research and the agile approach towards software development method. As it turns out, this analogy fits also as a basis for the action performed within the described action research – teaching and guiding agile. Analysis of the emerged teaching framework revealed that it fits and, in fact, extends the above analogy, and thus provides a 3-dimensional analogy between AR, ASDM, and teaching SDM (abbreviated by TSDM). Beyond the clear contribution of such an analogy as a means that may help us in the understanding of analogous objects (Lakoff and Johnson, 1980; Holyoak and Thagard, 1995; Vosniadou and Ortony, 1989), as is illustrated in Section 3.3, it also guides the finding analysis, presented in Section 4.

In order to present the extension of the analogy with the TSDM dimension, a third column for the TSDM dimension could be added to the two columns of the AR-ASDM analogy. As it turns out, such a description is difficult to grasp. Therefore, the third dimension is presented in a way that provides a complete picture of the teaching framework. Specifically, the ASDM column is reused in order to give the perspective of the students who work according to it for the development of their course software project; the TSDM column is added to present the teacher, i.e., the academic coach's perspective. Thus, the two columns form together a complete teaching framework. In what follows the analogy is extended by laying out the main characteristics of the TSDM process. The complete teaching framework is presented in (Dubinsky, 2005).

Table 6 extends the analogy with respect to the category of Origin and Goals.

Table 6. Extending the Analogy - Origin and Goals

Agile Software Development Method	Teaching SDM
The origin of ASDM is rooted in the problems that characterize the software engineering field. ASDM fosters **individuals and interactions, collaboration among students,** and work that aims at providing **quality software** while continually **responding to customer introduced changes.** Illustratively, the first sentence in Beck (2004) is "XP is about **social change**".	The original need for the teaching framework is the problems that characterized the field of software engineering and the academia role with respect to this situation. The teaching framework **promotes the SDM principles**; thus enables **students** to **practice software development** in a supported academic environment.

In what follows TSDM is illustrated from the organization and the students' perspective. The implementation of an ASDM as part of an AR in an academic institute involves a social and cultural change in the organization. From an organizational perspective, as aforementioned, the project-based course which constitutes the research field takes place in four different rooms in the building of the Department of Computer Science of the Technion, allocated for this purpose, and equipped with computerized equipment for the project development. Each team of 10-12 students gets a room and keys are provided to all students. Clearly, such allocation for project-based courses is not common in many universities.

Table 7. Extending the Analogy - Process Perspective

Agile Software Development Method	Teaching SDM
1. An iterative process with short cycles	
The development **is composed of iterations** that each contains plan of work (including understanding the customer requirements and an initial design), testing and coding, data tracking, data analysis, reflection on iteration and the next iteration plan. **The duration of each cycle is relatively short** in order to respond to customer changes periodically. The relatively short cycles and the need to adhere and **respond to the customer requirements and changes** in each iteration are the essence of **agility**.	The course schedule **is composed of iterations** each contains work plan which includes the teaching and guidance of studio sessions, evaluation, reflection, and planning of the teaching activities for next iteration. **The duration of each cycle is relatively short** (3-4 weeks); it enables 3 teaching iterations. The schedule format is presented in Appendix I. The schedule seems to be **flexible, responsive, and agile**.

Table 7. Continued

Agile Software Development Method	Teaching SDM
2. Initialization of the process	
The beginning of the first iteration of a software project is not a simple task. The students **are not familiar yet** with the development environment and specifically with the integration and testing environment, **aren't familiar yet (don't understand)** with the **customer requirements**, and are **not sure** about the results of the **first iteration**.	It is not a simple process for an academic coach to start the first iteration of a software project in the course. S/he **is not familiar yet** with the students and do not know the level of knowledge and commitment they bring into the project. Further, when there is an external customer, the academic coach **needs to better understand** together with the students what are the **customer requirements** and to make sure that the project scope remains reasonable. The academic coach is **uncertain** about the results of **the first iteration.**
3. A systematic process accompanied with validated tools and methods	
The development team **uses validated tools and methods** in order to learn about the software domain. Each of the project activities is supported by well-defined tools like e.g., Integrated Development Environments (IDEs) and their components, and by methods like, e.g., testing techniques that increase the software quality, and refactoring that improve design and provide a clearer well-structured code. During this process the team is engaged with a **learning process** of the software product to be created.	The academic coach **uses validated tools and methods** in order to guide and evaluate the students during the semester. Each of the teaching activities is supported by well-defined tools and methods. For example, the personal reflections that students fill give the academic coach a feedback about the teaching and project progress. Another example is that by guidance of the practice of stand-up meetings s/he gains weekly information about professional and social aspects of the group and teammates. This is part of the evaluation process. During this process the academic coach is engaged with **learning processes** of the individuals, team work, and the software that is created.
4. A criticized process and the reflection activity	
The development team **constantly reflects in and on action** (Schön, 1983; Schön, 1987) using tracking **measurements** and face-to-face activities, in order to improve understanding with respect to the product requirements and the project progress.	As a reflective practitioner, the academic coach constantly **reflect in and on action** (Schön, 1983; Schön, 1987) using tracking **measurements** and face-to-face compulsory activities, in order to improve understanding with respect to the teaching activities, the students' work, and the progress of the project.
5. Inductive outcome	
The outcomes of ASDM process are **inductively formed** during the process into one comprehensive **software product** that answers the **customer requirements.**	The outcomes of the course are **inductively formed** during the semester into one comprehensive **learning product** that meet the **pedagogical requirements** of the project-based course with respect to the subject matter itself (e.g., operating systems, information systems, etc.) as well as to the taught SDM used for the project development.

From the student perspective, one social change is expressed by the fact that the students should attend weekly 4-hour meetings that take place in the project lab, participate in the course activities and reflect on the main activities. In other project-based courses that take place in the Department of Computer Science of the Technion, students usually develop the software projects in teams of 2 or 3 students and meet the academic coaches only several times during the semester. Such a social change introduced by the teaching framework reflects in fact a change of the didactic contract (Tall, 1991) both between the academic staff and the students and among the students themselves.

Table 7 extends the analogy with respect to the category of the Process Perspective.

Table 8 expanded in what follows to include also the TSDM dimension with respect to environmental features, cultural aspects, and insider roles.

Table 8. Extending the Analogy - Participants' Perspective

ASDM	Teaching SDM
1. Insider roles	
The people involved in the development process, namely analysts, testers, developers, customer, and all business people in the organization, are the **inside players** of the development process. In ASDM processes, **special roles** are performed by the teammates.	The people involved in the training aspects of the agile development process: learners, customer, and facilitator, are the **inside players** of the development process. Specifically, each learner has a **special role** in managing the software development process.
2. Environmental features	
The project leader coordinates the **environment resources**, such as the project room, as well as all required equipment, such as computers. The ASDM developers work in the **project room environment**. This environment dictates the **work pace** and **provides information** with respect to the project progress.	The facilitator coordinates the **environment resources** for the entire learning period, as well as all required equipment. The learners experience working in such an **environment**. Working in this environment dictates the **training pace** and **provides information** with respect to the learners and the project progress.
3. Cultural aspects	
The project leader deals with a **cultural situation** when implementing agile practices. Another **cultural situation** is when the project leader, as well as the organization management, must **form teams** that are to be productive.	The facilitator guides the learners in the use of the agile practice while observing the benefits and problems it brings. Solving the problems that arise makes the facilitator part of a **cultural situation**, and in a position that requires the expression of an opinion and guiding of the team accordingly. Another **cultural situation** exists when the facilitator must **form teams** during the training process.

It is important to add that the 3D analogy does not imply, neither that a researcher is a teacher is a developer, nor any other permutation of this kind. Rather, the analogy should be conceived of as a tool for the analysis of the research findings as is illustrated in what follows (Section 3.3).

3.3. Findings Analysis Using the 3D Analogy

The detailed research findings are described in (Dubinsky, 2005) in the form of a teaching framework. In this subsection, the way the 3D analogy is used for the interpretation and the analysis of the research findings is described and illustrated. The analysis is presented in Section 4.

Two main activities are used when a specific finding is analyzed by using the 3D analogy. The first activity is characterization and connectivity in which the finding is examined on both axes of the analogy. Specifically, (a) the category of the finding is determined, that is, whether it is a process-oriented finding or a participant-oriented one, and (b) its relationship to the other analogous subjects is described. A TSDM finding can be for example, a process-oriented finding which relates both to AR and ASDM. Another example is a TSDM finding that has both process and participant orientations and relates only to ASDM.

The second activity is interpretation and implication in which the perspective of the specific finding is provided in the context of teaching software development methods - TSDM (the research topic), and if exists, its implication to the global context of software engineering.

In order to illustrate the two activities, consider the following finding.

A research finding: Using a role scheme according to which each student has a special role in the project management besides being a developer, increases the communication among teammates.

Characterization. The finding indicates an increase in communication when a role scheme is used. This finding is both process- and participant-oriented. This is because each student has a special role (participant-orientation) in the project management (process-orientation) besides being a developer who is responsible only for his/her development tasks. Accordingly, it is related to the Participant Perspective category of the analogy and in particular to the insiders' roles sub-category. In addition, this finding deals with measuring the level of communication the role scheme is used. This part is related to the Process Perspective category of the analogy and, in particular to the sub-category that describes the process as a criticized process which is controlled by measures. The measure in this case is the level of communication with respect to each role.

Connectivity. The role scheme (Dubinsky and Hazzan, 2006) is one of the actions that were performed and refined by the researcher. It is connected both with AR and ASDM. With respect to AR, this finding is connected in two different ways. First, when reflecting on this finding, the researcher increased her awareness with respect to her level of communication with the students, or in research-oriented terminology, to the level of her participation in the research. This occurs because when the role scheme is shaped, the researcher different roles were shaped too. Thus, as students communication is measured according to their specific roles, so does the communication level of the researcher. Second, the ability to measure the level of communication is used as a tool by the researcher in order to evaluate the role scheme itself, for example, by assessing the need of a specific role over others.

Here are two relations that this finding has with ASDM. First, there is no standard with respect to what is a winning role scheme (see Appendix II for the different agile role schemes). Second, there is a continuous study about which measures should be taken in order to control a software process (Mayrhauser, 1990; Putnam and Myers, 1997; Pulford and Combelles and Shirlaw, 1996).

Interpretation. The role scheme that is used in the course strengthens the notion of action learning (Revans, 1983) of the teaching framework. Each student should communicate and collaborate with the other students in the team in order to perform successfully his/her role to contribute to the project progress. Specifically, the main purpose of action learning (Revans, 1983 according to Weinstein, 2002) is 'to develop the capacity to ask fresh questions rather than to communicate technical knowledge', all with a view to improve future actions. In the teaching framework (Dubinsky, 2005), this concept is illustrated in checking how many original forum messages versus responses were used by each role holder. This kind of information together with the messages context helped in the personal evaluations of the students.

Implication. The implication of this finding is expressed by questioning who is in charge of the process of software development and how collaboration can be achieved among all parties involved. In his book The Invisible Computer (Norman, 1999), the author relates to the subject of the development process ownership saying that "The human-centered development team itself has to consist of a team of equals, all contributing their own areas of expertise", and later with respect to the same subject, he says: "Who owns the product? Everyone."; "The end result is always a tradeoff. Engineering emphasizes different aspects of the product than does marketing, which in turn has different emphases from user experience. They are all valid, all important. The development process is one of continual tradeoffs: marketability, functionality, usability. That's life in the world of business."(pp. 219-221). It is suggested that one implication of this research finding is that the role scheme provides a mechanism to improve the control of the inner tradeoffs exists in a software project, like simple design and exhaustive testing, and to do so in an equal communicative setting.

The analogy between the ASDM process and the TSDM process revealed that the framework which is constructed for the teaching of a specific SDM has the shape of the SDM itself. Specifically, it is not a coincidence that an analogy can be drowned between ASDM and the teaching framework that aims to teach it. In practice, during the construction of the TSDM framework, it was shaped more and more like the ASDM it tries to convey. This idea will be further elaborated in the findings analysis (Section 4).

4. Finding Analysis – The Notion of Change

The complete research findings presentation (Dubinsky, 2005) includes a detailed description of the principles and practices that constitute the teaching framework. In the spirit of action research, the research findings, at the same time, are derived from and support the teaching framework. In this section, the notion of change is introduced, and specific findings, derived from the teaching framework, are discussed in the context of dealing with changes. Specifically, the principles and practices that these findings are connected to, are specified. The 3D analogy, presented in Section 3, is then used for analysis elaboration.

The notion of change is presented in Henry Plotkin's book "Darwin Machines and the Nature of Knowledge" as part of the chapter about the evolution of intelligence. In this section it is used as the main motif that inspires the discussion about the research findings.

> "Change is a universal condition of the world. ... Nothing stands still, and the very occurrence of evolution is both a force for change itself and proof positive for its existence" (Plotkin, 1997, p. 139).

Changes are all around us. In software development processes many changes occur, among them the one with which we are most familiar is the change in customer requirements. Still, this is not the only change that occurs in software development processes. Changes in different areas like technology, economy, and society, constantly take place. The main question Plotkin poses is how we can solve the uncertainty introduced by changes. He describes two main sets of solutions to deal with the change phenomenon, and explains how it can be coped with. None of the solutions is exclusive of the others (Plotkin, 1997, pp. 145-152).

The first set of solutions concerns with 'reducing the amount of significant change', thus reducing the change scope (see left branch in Figure 1). One way to do it is by reducing the period of time (see T branch in Figure 1) between conception and reproductive competence; Meaning, to keep the ratio 'life-span length to numbers of offspring' low, i.e., to maintain high reproductive output in a relatively short period of time. This way, the change is coped by keeping updated as far as possible the genetic instructions of each individual. Plotkin's examples in this chapter are taken mostly from animals' life. The second way to reduce the amount of significant change according to Plotkin is to live in a relatively isolated and unpopulated place (see P branch in Figure 1). A variation of this idea is parents' protection on their offspring by isolating them.

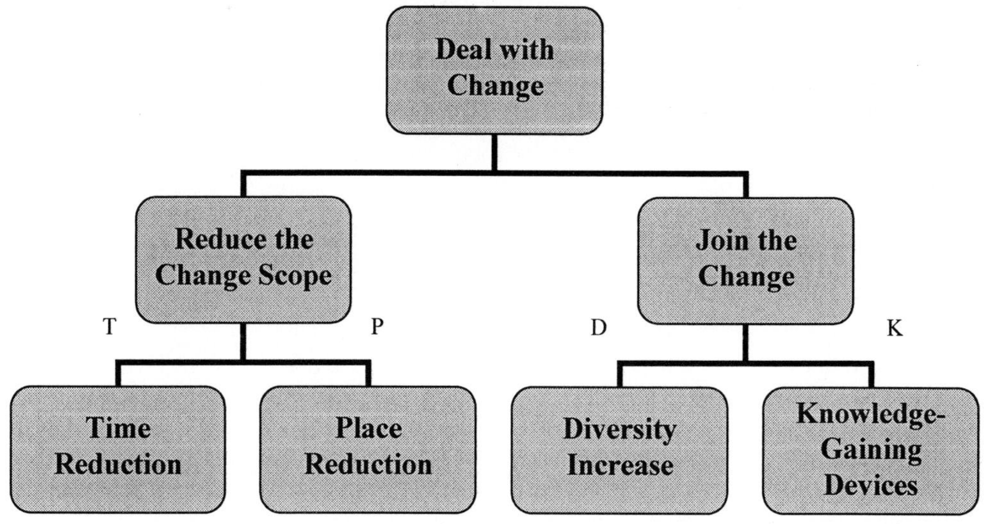

Figure 1. Solutions for Dealing with Change (Plotkin, 1997).

The second set of solutions to the phenomenon of change takes the form of 'if you can't beat it, join it', i.e., change the phenotypes so that they can change with and match the changing features of the world (see right branch in Figure 1). The first strategy to accomplish it is to produce large numbers of different offspring in order to increase the chance that this approach will lead to a situation in which at least some individuals will be able to face the change (see D branch in Figure 1). The second strategy, named the 'tracking option', is to give rise to a change within phenotypes, i.e., by producing phenotypes that change in response to changes in the world (see K branch in Figure 1). The tracking option is performed by using knowledge-gaining devices which, according to Plotkin, are the immune system and the intelligence mechanisms of the brain. And thus, the immune system operates in the sphere of chemistry, while the brain mechanisms, known as rationality or intelligence, operate in the sphere of the physical world of temporal and spatial relationships of events and objects.

Sections 4.1 and 4.2 discuss in more details the first and second set of solutions respectively, and illustrate how they can be projected on the research findings.

4.1. Reducing the Amount of Significant Change

This section presents six specific research findings that are derived from the teaching framework principles and practices (Dubinsky, 2005), and fit the first set of solutions suggested for coping with change by the reduction of the change scope.

According to Plotkin, reduction in the amount of a significant change can be expressed in terms of time and place (Plotkin, 1997). In Table 9, three research findings T1-T3 are formulated with respect to time reduction, and three research findings P1-P3 are formulated with respect to place reduction.

Table 9. Research Findings that Reduce the Change Scope

Reduce Change Scope	#	Research Findings
Time Reduction	T1	A complete software release which is composed of three iterations can be accomplished in a 14-week semester.
	T2	Students and coaches prefer and appreciate tight time management.
	T3	The project-story is composed in the 10-minute stand-up meetings held at the beginning of each weekly session.
Place Reduction	P1	The Studio environment and the activities performed in it increase the level of students' involvement.
	P2	Academic coaches prefer to have a clear and well-structured teaching framework (principles and practices).
	P3	The focus on only specific customer-selected stories each iteration enables to meet deadlines.

For illustration, in what follows, the research finding P2 is elaborated and analyzed by using the 3D analogy presented in Section 3.

P2 – "Academic coaches prefer to have a clear and well-structured teaching framework (principles and practices)" – belongs to the 'place reduction' category of coping with change since it provides the academic coaches with a relatively isolated framework that settles the teaching borders (Hazzan and Dubinsky, 2003). In practice, the course schedule (presented in Appendix I) which guided the academic coaches with specific weekly activities as well as home tasks, is based on the structure of the teaching framework with respect to its principles and practices. Accordingly, P2 is a global finding that by definition relates to all principles and practices.

Therefore, using the 3D analogy terminology, P2 is characterized as both process-oriented with respect to the systematic process characteristic and as participants-oriented with respect to all characteristics, e.g., working in the project room, the studio. A systematic process is referred to a process which its goals and procedures are detailed and clear, and accordingly layouts a well-structured teaching framework, its time schedule is reasonably planned and known to all participants, and measures are taken to provide confidence with the process progress.

The connectivity of P2 to ASDM is reflected by the fact that the teaching framework is formulated by principles that are analogue to the XP structure which consists of values, from which practices, that are analogue to the XP practices, are derived (Hazzan and Dubinsky, 2003; Dubinsky and Hazzan, 2005).

The connectivity of P2 to AR is reflected by the fact that an analogy can be drawn between the principles of the teaching framework and the AR principles of research e.g., 'explain by doing – research as an insider' or 'reflect on teaching activities – reflect on the research actions'. The analogy can be extended in the sense of practices e.g., 'evaluate teaching activities – analyzing research data that is gathered'.

The interpretation of P2 is reflected by the fact that through the analogy lens the TSDM schedule is presented in a similar way to the iterations of a software development project. In other words, the ASDM project projects its shape on the teaching framework, or, as it can be put from the TSDM perspective, the teaching framework inherits the shape of the ASDM.

It is not the first time that someone draws the attention to this similarity. Here are several examples. Bianco and Sassaroli (2003) propose an agile approach for teaching Software Engineering in introductory courses based on strict collaboration of students and teachers in design activities. Chun (2004) proposes an agile teaching manifesto formulated in a parallel fashion to the agile manifesto (presented in http://www.agilemanifesto.org): "Agile Teaching/Learning Methodology values students/teachers and their interactions rather than a particular approach to teaching/learning; working knowledge rather than rote-learning; communication rather that negotiation; and responding to changes rather than just following a schedule". Chun presents a method for agile teaching and learning and states that it is used in technology-related courses. Laster (2004) uses the characteristics of different software development models, including the Waterfall SDM, for the purpose of curriculum design. Birkhoelzer, Navarro and van der Hoek (2005) present the idea that "The students built the model [of a game-based simulation environment] as an extended waterfall model [emphasis added] that incorporates hardware aspects as well as software, using the following basic flow: starting from system requirements, hardware, software, and supply components are pursued in separate paths (with the associated artifacts) and finally integrated into the product."

However, our main contribution with respect to this similarity is expressed in several ways. First, a comprehensive teaching framework was constructed for project-based CS and SE capstone courses. Second, the analogy was presented in detail and used as a tool for the analysis of the research findings. Third, the presented analogy has three dimensions, one of them is action research. The dimension of action research can guide researchers in the planning of their research by basing the actual research on the process they are trying to explore. The full analogy can help them in the analysis of their findings with respect to all three dimensions.

The implication of P2 is that developers, like students and researchers, prefer to have a clear and well-structured frame of work. In such a working mode they know how to act at different situations, they know what is expected from them and is appreciated by their organization, and their confidence with the process, as well as with themselves, increases.

4.2. Joining the Change

This section presents seven specific research findings that are derived from the teaching framework principles and practices (Dubinsky, 2005), and fit the second set of solutions suggested to cope with change by embracing it.

According to Plotkin, instead of reducing the change impact as the first set of solutions aim at (presented in the previous section), the second set of solutions does not try to change the change but rather aims at accepting the change and joining the new way the change brings with (Plotkin, 1997).

With respect to software engineering, it may be of no surprise that Extreme Programming (XP), the agile software development method, published internationally five years ago, included the sub-title Embrace the Change (Beck, 2000). There are several meanings to the embracement of change by using XP. The first one and the most important meaning is the acceptance and the reaction to changes in customer requirements. A common statement among software practitioners is that 'customers usually do not know what they want'. The embracement of change idea means to accept the idea that customers do know what they want, and even if sometimes it seems otherwise, developers should follow customers' changes in requirements, collaborate with the customer on a regular daily basis, and still feel that they do the right thing. Some practitioners report that by doing it they feel a kind of a relief simply because they should not envision anymore the customer's needs. It is suggested that this relief is one outcome of the embracement of a change.

Table 10. Research Findings that Join the Change

Join the Change	#	Research Findings
Diversity Increase	D1	Using a role scheme in which each student has a special role in the project management besides his/her development tasks, increases communication among teammates.
	D2	Using the teaching framework introduces women students as equally-communicative.
	D3	The planning game as a multi-participants multi-ideas discussion contributes to the understanding of the project issues and requirements.
Knowledge-Gaining Devices	K1	Using metaphors increase understanding of the project issues and requirements.
	K2	Using a balanced grading policy contributes to the reduction in the free-rider phenomenon.
	K3	Reflection in general (and potentially a new suggested kind of reflection – the towards reflection activity) improve communication among team members and among coaches and team members.
	K4	Students increase their cognitive awareness when they prepare their stand-up meeting words.

In Table 10, three research findings D1-D4 are formulated with respect to diversity increase, and four research findings K1-K4 are formulated with respect to knowledge-gaining devices.

In what follows, the research findings D1, D2, and K3 are elaborated and analyzed using the 3D analogy presented in Section 3.

According to Plotkin, the first way to accept the change can be referred to as increase in diversity which part of it (this diversity) will probably be able to deal with future changes (Plotkin, 1997). Diversity is expressed in several ways in this research.

First, with respect to D1 – "using a role scheme, in which each student has a special role in the project management besides his /her development tasks, increases the communication among teammates" – it (D1) was already analyzed in Section 3.3 using the 3D analogy. Using the change notion presented in this section, it is suggested that since the role scheme aims at covering all aspects of project management, D1 implies in fact a diverse management. This implication is also expressed in the second edition of Extreme Programming Explained (Beck and Andres, 2004) which, according to the author, has the same scope as the first edition but uses a different tone and a different perspective. In the new edition, a new principle is added named diversity. "Teams need to bring together a variety of skills, attitudes, and perspectives to see problems and pitfalls, to think of multiple ways to solve problems, and to implement the solutions. Teams need diversity" (Beck and Andres, 2004, p. 29). The rest of D1 analysis using the analogy is described in Section 3.3.

Another example for diversity is D2 – "Using the teaching framework introduces women students as equally-communicative". D2 is characterized as participants oriented and specifically as a culture aspect. The connectivity to ASDM is clear as women contribute to the variety of skills and attitudes with their own personal style and power (Fisher, 2000, p. 32). The connectivity to AR is expressed by paying attention to cultural aspects as part of its origin. D2 is interpreted in the sense that within the studio environment and the course setting, women take an equal part as men, so diversity is empowered. The implication of D2 is expressed by increasing awareness of software practitioners to the notion of diversity. "Diversity is expressed in the practice of Whole Team, where you bring together on the team people with different perspectives" (Beck and Andres, 2004, p. 29).

The second way to embrace the change can be referred to as the creation of brain mechanisms in such a way that they will help dealing with future changes (Plotkin, 1997). With respect to our research, the reflection activity (Schön, 1983; Schön, 1987) that was one of the activities conducted as part of AR, ASDM and TSDM, is discussed. The performance of this activity by software practitioners in the studio environment is a rewarded practice and may help in the assessment of the process itself (Tomayko, 1996; Hazzan, 2002). The use and the teaching of the reflection activity and the conduction of a retrospective process have led us to a new idea with respect to reflection.

Specifically, listening to software practitioners, it was found that teammates who learn the reflection activity tend not to continue using it on a regular basis for future activities. One can easily observe a similar problem with respect to the testing: developers tend not to write tests after the code is completed (Hutcheson, 2003). In the case of testing the solution was the introduction of the test-first development technique (Beck, 2002). In a similar way, it is suggested to introduce the term toward-action reflection for the activity of reflection that is performed prior to the performance of the action. Such a toward-action reflection should be done by all participants involved in the process and should include thinking about future changes that may occur and a preparation toward them. The shape of the term toward-action reflection is similar to the other two kinds of reflection introduced by Schön – reflection-in and reflection-on – conducted respectively during and after the performance of the activity (1987).

In what follows the finding K3 - "Reflection in general (and potentially a new suggested kind of reflection– the towards reflection activity) improve communication among team members and among coaches and team members" - is analyzed by using the 3D analogy. The finding K3, is characterized as a process-oriented item related to the criterion of a criticized measured process. The activity is part of the learning process and it is performed by each teammate individually and in addition it is performed collectively by the team. It should be emphasized that the academic staff perform reflection during and after teaching activities, and the towards-action reflection is also intended to extend their reflection (see Dubinsky, 2005 for reflection activities performed by the academic coaches).

The connectivity of K3 to ASDM is expressed by referring to reflection as it is expressed in Beck and Andres, 2004. "Reflection comes after action. Learning is action reflected. To maximize feedback, reflection in XP teams in mixed with doing" (Beck and Andres, 2004, p. 30). The connectivity of K3 to AR extends the concept of reflection as described in each AR cycle, with the idea that this kind of activity helps the researcher as an insider with raising the communication among research participants and among the researcher and researcher participants.

The interpretation of K3 is done by using the notion of knowledge-gaining devices as presented in Plotkin, 1997. In order to be ready to face the change we aim at building a device which will enable us to gain knowledge before changes occur, in a way that will enable us to cope with the change. In other words, the knowledge gained from previous activities of reflection in general, and from the suggested toward-action reflection in particular, may provide us with an appropriate mechanism to deal with future changes. The implication of the toward-action reflection is expressed by the following words: "Good teams don't just do their work, they think about how they are working and why they are working" (Beck and Andres, 2004, p. 29).

5. Summary and Future Implications

This section is the closing of the research presented in this chapter and at the same time an opening for implications to be further investigated.

The contribution of this chapter is composed of two parts as follows:

- The 3D analogy that can be used as a tool for the analysis of the research findings, as presented in Sections 3.3.
- The use of the notion of change in order to further analyzing the research findings with respect to their role in coping with changes within teaching process, as presented in Section 4.

Using analogies improves our understanding (Lakoff and Johnson, 1980). The analogy presented in this chapter has three dimensions, and is discussed in nine different analogous subjects arranged in 3 categories, as presented in Section 3. The dimensions are AR, ASDM, and TSDM which are the main processes performed in this research. The researcher is involved with the AR process; the students are involved in the ASDM process; and the academic coaches as well as the researcher, who is the instructor and an academic coach too, are involved in the TSDM process.

Therefore, the analogy provides a tool that enables a discussion of the three processes in general and to analyze the research findings in particular, as presented in Section 3.3.

The future implications of this analogy that can be further investigated relate to teaching and research. With respect to teaching, the implication is expressed by the fact that a teaching framework that aims at implementing a specific process can be deliberately shaped by the process it aims to implement, in order to convey the process ideas and practices. With respect to research, the dimension of action research can guide researchers in the planning of their research by basing the actual research on the process they are trying to explore. The complete analogy can help them in the analysis of their findings with respect to all three dimensions which are the action research, the process that is explored, and the teaching framework this process can be taught by.

It is a challenge for designers of a teaching framework to be able to establish and refine it. It is even more challenging to be able to establish a kind of niche within this framework that enable us to cope with future changes that may occur in the framework surrounding, e.g., changes in technology and in teaching and learning methods, while keeping the framework principles.

Using the notion of change (Plotkin, 1997) provides us with the ability to cope with changes that are going to occur by reducing their effect or by embracing them, as presented in Section 4.

The process of software development is highly complicated (Hamlet and Maybee, 2001; Tomayko and Hazzan, 2004) and so is the teaching of the process. When describing the ways to cope with changes, Plotkin (1997) encourages us to buttress the use of one way with the others, meaning to make sure we did all we can to cope with the change to come.

As a future implication, the use of the change notion both in teaching software development methods as well as in the world of software development is suggested as a means to reduce their complexity and to reach a kind of consensus regarding their implementation.

Appendix I. The Course Schedule

#	Purpose of Meeting	Main Activities (academic coach and students)	XP Practices and Values
1	Opening of course and getting acquainted	- Introduce the studio environment - Create a team - Introduce the project subject and gather relevant materials - Present student XP roles	- Communication
2	Planning game of Iteration 1 - Phase I	- Assign student XP roles - Play customer: Develop customer stories and make customer decisions	- On site customer - Planning game - Metaphor - Courage

Appendix I. Continued

#	Purpose of Meeting	Main Activities (academic coach and students)	XP Practices and Values
3	Planning game of Iteration 1 - Phase II	- Design - Write development tasks	- Planning game - Simple design - Small releases
4	Coding and testing	- Estimate time for the development tasks - Balance students' development work loads - Teach/learn unit testing	- Sustainable pace - Pair programming - Testing
5	Integration, coding standards, presentation and documents	- Establish the integration machine - Agree on coding standards - Prepare the structure of the presentation - Document process	- Continuous integration - Coding standards - Collective ownership
6	Test-first and refactoring	- Teach/learn the test-first and refactoring practices - Develop code	- Test-first - Refactoring
7	Presentation of Iteration 1, feedback, planning game for Iteration 2 - Phase I	- Present Iteration 1 - Provide feedback - Play customer: Develop customer stories and make customer decisions	- Feedback - On-site customer - Planning game - Courage
End of Iteration 1			
8	Lessons learned and planning game for Iteration 2 - Phase II	- Reflect on the lessons learned - Play customer: Develop customer stories and make customer decisions	-Communication - Feedback - Courage - On-site customer - Planning game - Metaphor - Small releases - Sustainable pace

Appendix I. Continued

#	Purpose of Meeting	Main Activities (academic coach and students)	XP Practices and Values
9	Development activities and test-first exercise	- Test-first and refactoring exercise - Design - Develop code	- Testing - Refactoring - Simple design - Collective ownership - Pair programming
10	Development activities, preparations for the presentation next week of Iteration 2	- Design - Develop code	- Simple design - Collective ownership - Pair programming - Continuous integration
11	Presentation of Iteration 2, feedback, planning game of Iteration 3 - Phase I	- Presentation - Customer stories - Make customer decisions	- Communication - Feedback - Courage - On-site customer - Planning game - Metaphor - Small releases - Sustainable pace
End of Iteration 2			
12	Lessons learned and planning game for Iteration 3 – Phase II	- Reflect on the lessons learned	- Continuous integration - Coding standards - Collective ownership
13	Development activities	- Design - Code	- Simple design - Collective ownership - Pair programming - Continuous integration
14	Presentation of Release 1, feedback, Project fair, end of course	- Present Release 1 - Give feedback	- Feedback - On-site customer - Planning game - Courage
End of Release 1 (three iterations)			

Appendix II. Roles in Agile Software Development Methods

SDM	SDM Roles
XP (Beck, 2000)	**Seven roles in Extreme Programming (XP):** The **programmer** analyzes, designs, tests, programs, and integrates. The programmer writes tests and refractors the code; working as part of a pair. The programmer communicates and coordinates closely with other programmers in order to ensure the project's success. The programmer integrates the code and shares it with the others. The **customer** tells and writes stories to be implemented and decides when they will be implemented. The customer defines tests to verify the correct functionality of the stories. The customer receives feedback from the team, and makes decisions to help the team best benefit the project. The **tester** uses the customer's viewpoint in order to determine which items most require verification. The tester must consider the system through the eyes of the customer (Crispin and House, 2002). The **tracker** measures progress quantitatively, by comparing estimations with actual results. He or she is responsible for monitoring the big picture and informing the teammates about their progress. The tracker is the team historian, and keeps log of tests results and reported faults/defects. The **coach** is responsible for the process as a whole. He or she keeps track of the project's process and helps other teammates in their decision making. The coach pairs off with programmers, identifies/looks for refactoring tasks, and sees to their execution. The coach also explains the process to upper-level managers. The roles of **consultant** and **boss** are external and are filled by people from outside the team.
DSDM	**Eleven roles in Dynamic Systems Development Method (DSDM):** The **executive sponsor** is a high-level executive who is responsible for the system and for its fast development progress. The **ambassador user** represents the entire user community. The **visionary user** makes sure that the vision of the product is not lost. The **advisor user** brings daily business knowledge to the development team. The **project manager** is responsible for ensuring project delivery, coordinating and reporting to the management. The **technical coordinator** reports to the project manager and assists all development teams. The **team leader** ensures that the team functions as a whole, and that the objectives are met. The **senior developer** interprets user requirements into prototypes and deliverable code. The **developer** assists with these tasks as part of DSDM skills development. The **facilitator** is responsible for managing the workshop process, an interactive communication technique for making decisions. The **scribe** records requirements, agreements and decisions reached.
Scrum	**Four roles in Scrum:** The **scrum master** reviews the team's progress team and ensures time estimations are updated. The **product owner** writes user stories and defines acceptance tests. The **scrum team** estimates task durations and develops stories and unit tests. The **manager** provides directions to keep the work going according to plan and removes obstacles.

Appendix II. Continued

SDM	SDM Roles
Crystal Clear	**Eight roles in Crystal Clear:** Distinct roles: The **sponsor** provides the mission statement. The **senior designer** produces the system design. The **user** helps with use cases and screen drafts. The **designer-programmers (designers**) design, code and test. Four additional merged roles are identified in Crystal Clear, which means that they can come from the people filling the above-mentioned roles: The **business expert** can come from the sponsor, user, or senior designer. The **coordinator** can come from the senior designer and is responsible for the schedule and the release sequence. The **tester** can come from the designers and is responsible for test results and defect reports. The **writer** can come from the designers and is responsible for the user manual.
FDD	**Six [core] roles in Feature-Driven Development (FDD):** The **project manager** leads the team and reports on its progress. The **chief architect** is responsible for system design. The **development manager** is responsible for the development activities. The **chief programmers** provide technical leadership to the smaller teams. The **class owners** are developers who each own one class and are responsible for making all changes in it. The **domain experts** are the users.
Lean Development	**Six roles in Lean Development:** The **customer** provides the requirements. The **master developer** is responsible for system design. The **expertise leader** is responsible for specific technical areas such as GUI design, database development, and security. The **project leader** is responsible for time estimations and the team's progress. The **observer** takes notes on the team's process. The other team members are the **programmers**.
ASD	Adaptive Software Development (ASD) promotes the leadership-collaboration model, which focuses on work states rather than on processes, on creating a collaborative environment, and on creating accountability for results (Highsmith, 2002). **Six roles are mentioned in ASD:** The **executive sponsor** is responsible for the product being developed. The **developer** and **customer** representatives. The **facilitator** plans and leads the development sessions. The **project manager is** responsible for product delivery. The **scribe** records requirements, agreements and decisions reached.

References

Abrahamsson, P., Salo, O., Ronkainen J. and Warsta J. (2002). Agile Software Development Methods – Review and Analysis, VTT Publications 478.

Beck, K. (2000). Extreme Programming Explained: Embrace Change, Addison-Wesley.

Beck K. and Andres C. (2004). *Extreme Programming Explained: Embrace Change*, 2nd Edition, Addison-Wesley.

Berry, D. M. (2002). The inevitable pain of software development: Why there is no silver bullet, Monterey Workshop 2002, *Radical Innovations of Software and Systems Engineering in the Future.*

Bianco, V.D. and Sassaroli, G. (2003). Agile Teaching of an Agile Software Process, 4th International Conf. on eXtreme *Programming and Agile Processes in Software Engineering,* pp. 402-405.

Birkhoelzer, T. Navarro, E.O., van der Hoek, A. (2005). Teaching by Modeling instead of by Models, *In Proceedings of the 6th International Workshop on Software Process Simulation and Modeling*, St. Louis, MO.

Bogdan, R. C. and Biklen, S. K. (1992). Qualitative Research for Education, Boston: Allyn and Bacon.

Chun, H.W. (2004). The Agile Teaching/Learning Methodology and its e-Learning Platform, In *Lecture Notes in Computer Science* - Advances in Web-Based Learning, Volume 3143, Springer-Verlag Heidelberg, pp. 11-18.

Cockburn, A. (2000). Writing Effective Use Cases, *The Crystal Collection for Software Professionals*, Addison-Wesley Professional.

Cook, T.D., and Reichardt C.S. (1979). *Beyond qualitative versus quantitative methods: Qualitative and quantitative methods in evaluation research*, Sage Publications, London.

Dubinksy, Y. (2005). *Teaching Software Development Methods*, Ph.D. Research Thesis, Technion – Israel Institute of Technology.

Dubinsky, Y. and Hazzan, O. (2005). The construction process of a framework for teaching software development methods, *Computer Science Education*, 15:4, December 2005.

Dubinsky, Y. and Hazzan, O. (2006). Using a Role Scheme to Derive Software Project Metrics, *Journal of Systems Architecture*, 52, pp. 693–699.

Fisher, H. (2000). *The First Sex: The Natural Talents of Women and How They Are Changing the World*, Random House.

Fowler, M. (2002). The New Methodology, published in martinfowler.com, http://www.martinfowler.com/articles/newMethodology.html.

Gee, J.P. (1992). *Discourse analysis*. In M. LeCompte et. al., The Handbook of Qualitative Research in Education. San Diego: Academic Press.

Hamlet, D. and Maybee, J. (2001). *The Engineering of Software*, Addison-Wesley.

Hazzan O. (2002). The reflective practitioner perspective in Software Engineering education, *The Journal of Systems and Software* 63(3), pp. 161-171.

Hazzan, O. and Dubinsky, Y. (2003). Bridging cognitive and social chasms in software development using Extreme Programming, *Proceedings of the Fourth International Conference on eXtreme Programming and Agile Processes in Software Engineering*, Genova, Italy, pp. 47-53.

Highsmith, J. (2000). *Adaptive Software Development*, Dorset House Publishing.

Highsmith, J. (2002). *Agile Software developments Ecosystems*, Addison-Wesley.

Holyoak, K.J., and Thagard, P. (1995). *Mental leaps: analogy in creative thought*, Cambridge, Mass.: MIT Press.

Hughes, B. and Cotterell M. (2002). Software Project Management, 3rd edition, McGraw-Hill.

Kuhn, S. (1998). The software design studio: An exploration, *IEEE software* 15(2), pp.65-71.

Lakoff, G. and Johnson M. (1980). Metaphors we live by, Chicago : University of Chicago Press.

Laster, S. (2004). Model-Driven Design: Systematically Building Integrated Blended Learning Experiences, In *Elements of Quality Online Education*: Into the Mainstream, Edited by Bourne J. and Moore J.C., Volume 5 in the Sloan-C Series, pp. 159-177.

Lewin, K. (1948). Resolving Social Conflicts; *Selected Papers on Group Dynamics*. Gertrude W. Lewin (ed.). New York: Harper & Row.

Manen M.V. (1990). *Researching Lived Experience*. New York: State University of New York Press.

Mayrhauser, V.A. (1990). Software Engineering Methods and Management, Academic Press.

Newman, J.M. (2000). Action research: A brief overview, Forum: *Qualitative Social Research*, 1(1). Available at: http://qualitative-research.net/fqs

Norman, D.A. (1999). *The Invisible Computer: why good products can fail, the personal computer is so complex, and information appliances are the solution*, The MIT Press.

Palmer S.R. and Felsing J.M. (2002). A Practical Guide to Feature-Driven Development, Prentice Hall PTR.

Patton, M. Q. (1990). *Qualitative Evaluation and Research Methods*, 2nd. ed. Newbury Park, Cal.: Sage Publications.

Plotkin, H. (1997). *Darwin Machines and the Nature of Knowledge*, Harvard University Press.

Poppendieck, M. and Poppendieck, T. (2003). *Lean Software Development*: *An Agile Toolkit*, Addison-Wesley.

Pulford, K. and Combelles, K.A. and Shirlaw, S. (1996). *A quantitative Approach to Software Management – The ami Handbook*, Addison-Wesley.

Putnam, L.H. and Myers, W. (1997). *Industrial Strength Software – Effective Management Using Measurement*, IEEE Computer Society Press.

Reisman, C.K. (1993). *Narrative analysis*, Newbury Park, Cal.: Sage.

Revans, R. (1983). *The ABC of Action Learning*, republished 1998. London: Lemos & Crane.

Schön, D. A. (1983). *The Reflective Practitioner*, BasicBooks,

Schön, D. A. (1987). *Educating the Reflective Practitioner*: Towards a New Design for Teaching and Learning in The Profession, San Francisco: Jossey-Bass.

Schwaber, K. and Beedle, M. (2002). *Agile Software Development with Scrum*. Prentice Hall.

Smith, M. K. (1996). *Action research: A guide to reading*, http://www.infed.org/research/b-actres.htm.

Somekh, B. (1995) The Contribution of Action Research in Social Endeavours: a position paper on action research methodology, *British Educational Research Journal*, 21, pp. 339–355.

Sommerville, I. (2001) *Software Engineering*, 6th edition, Addison-Wesley.

Stapleton, J. (1997). *Dynamic Systems Development Method*: The Method in Practice, Addison-Wesley.

Strauss, A.L. (1987). *Qualitative Analysis for Social Scientists*. New York: Cambridge University Press.

Tall, D. (1991). *Advanced mathematical thinking*, Dordrecht: Kluwer Academic Publishers.

Tomayko, J. E. (1996). Carnegie-Mellon's software development Studio: A five-year retrospective, *SEI Conf. on Software Engineering Education*.

Tomayko, J. and Hazzan O. (2004). *Human Aspects of Software Engineering*, Charles River Media.

Vosniadou, S. and Ortony A. (1989). Similarity and analogical reasoning, Cambridge: Cambridge University Press.

Wenstein, K. (2002). *Action Learning: The Classic Approach, In 'Action Learning Worldwide: Experiences of leadership and organizational development'*, Edited by Boshyk Y., Palgrave Mackmillan, New York.

Zeichner, K. M. (1993) Action Research: personal renewal and social reconstruction, *Educational Action Research*, 1, pp. 199–220.

Zeichner, K. M. and Gore, J. M. (1995) *Using Action Research as a Vehicle for Student Reflection*, in S. Noffke & R. B. Stevenson (Eds) Educational Action Research. New York: Teachers College Press.

In: Computer Software Engineering Research
Editor: Ari D. Klein, pp. 45-88

ISBN: 1-60021-774-5

Chapter 2

PROGRAMMING WITH ROLES AND CLASSES: THE BABYUML APPROACH

Trygve Reenskaug
Dept. of Informatics, University of Oslo

Abstract

The goal of the BabyUML project is to increase my confidence in my programs. The keywords are simplicity and leverage. Simplicity helps me to think clearly and a reader to understand and audit my code. Leverage lets me say more with less. The end result shall be a new interactive development environment with appropriate languages and tools for supporting high level abstractions.

The essence of object orientation is that objects interact to produce some desired result. Yet current programming languages are focused on individual objects as they are specified by their classes; there are no explicit language constructs for describing communities of interacting objects. In BabyUML, I will zoom back from the classes and let my code specify the roles that objects play in collaborations and interactions.

The BabyUML project is experimental; its ideas and concepts are explored and their feasibility demonstrated with actual code and running programs. One experiment is completed, it explores an old and a new paradigm for organizing objects in clear and explicit structures. The old is MVC, the Model-View-Controller paradigm that describes the objects bridging the gap between a human mental model and the corresponding data stored in the computer. The new is DCA, the Data-Collaboration-Algorithm paradigm where the collaborating objects are explicitly identified by the role they play in an interaction, and where the interaction pattern is explicitly defined in terms of these roles.

Another experiment shall lead to BabyIDE, an integrated development environment that exhibits a balance between classes and roles. BabyIDE will be part of a new discipline of programming where programmers can work consistently at a high conceptual level throughout coding, debugging, testing, and maintenance. It will be implemented in a corner of Smalltalk that I have called the BabyIDE Laboratory. In the last part of this chapter, I describe the laboratory and how it will support new programming paradigms and tools. I finally indicate the future direction towards a workable BabyIDE.

1. Introduction

On the 9th September 1945, a moth was found trapped between the contact points on relay #70, Panel F, of the Mark II Aiken relay calculator. The event was entered in the calculator's log book as the word's first recorded computer bug. [1] This first bug was an "act of God"; most of the later bugs are blunders of our own making and the fight against them has been an essential part of software engineering ever since. The following quotes from the first NATO Software Engineering conference [2] could have been uttered today: [1]

> David and Fraser: Particularly alarming is the seemingly unavoidable fallibility of large software, since a malfunction in an advanced hardware-software system can be a matter of life and death.
>
> Dijkstra: The dissemination of knowledge is of obvious value -- the massive dissemination of error-loaded software is frightening.

The needs of society are still beyond us. An insatiable software market ever wants more, and we keep promising more than we can deliver. Major projects are delayed and even cancelled. Delivered software is buggy and hard to maintain. In his 1980 Turing Award lecture, Tony Hoare succinctly stated our choices [3]:

"There are two ways of constructing a software design: One way is to make it so simple that there are obviously no deficiencies and the other is to make it so complicated that there are no obvious deficiencies."[2]

The other way is the easy way. We get it by default when we fail to find a simple design. Maybe the time available is unreasonably short. Or maybe our concepts, languages, and tools do not match the challenges posed by the requirements. We end up relying on testing to get most of our blunders out of our systems. But any given test method can only find a certain percentage of all the errors. So keeping the test method fixed, *the more errors we find during testing, the more errors are probably left in the shipped software.* To quote Dijkstra: [3]

> "Program testing can be used to show the presence of bugs, but never to show their absence!" [4]
>
> "One of the reasons why the expression "software industry" can be so misleading is that a major analogy with manufacturing fails to hold: in software, it is often the poor quality of the "product" that make it so expensive to make! In programming, nothing is cheaper than not introducing the bugs in the first place." [5]

Hoare's first way is the hard way. It is also the only way to get quality software, because no industry has ever been able to work quality into an inferior product by testing it. I have been programming for half a century and *simplicity* has always been my holy grail. The simple structure is not only the key to mastery by my brain, but also the key to a correspondence between user requirements and system implementation and thus to habitable systems.

---

[1] Quoted with permission from NATO, CBP.
[2]©ACM 1981. Quoted with permission.
[3] Quoted with permission from Hamilton Richards, Univeristy of Texas.

Through the years, requirements have escalated from the simple computation to distributed systems with complex data and powerful algorithms. My brain has remained roughly the same, so I have had to rely on better tools for thinking, designing, coding, and maintenance. My tools have been ahead of the requirements some of the time, and I have had the deep satisfaction of running tests merely to check that I haven't made any serious blunders. At other times, requirements have been ahead of my tools, and I have shamefully been forced to rely on testing to get some semblance of quality into my programs.

Requirements have been ahead of my tools for quite some time now, and Hoare's other way has been my way. I started the *BabyUML project* in an attempt to remedy this deplorable situation, hoping once again to experience the pleasure of following Hoare's first way. The goal of the project is to increase my confidence in my programs. The keywords are simplicity and leverage. Simplicity helps me to think clearly and a reader to understand and audit my code. Leverage lets me say more with less. The end result shall be a new interactive development environment with appropriate languages and tools for supporting high level abstractions.

The essence of object orientation is that objects interact to produce some desired result. Yet current programming languages are focused on individual objects as they are specified by their classes; there are no explicit language constructs for describing communities of interacting objects. In BabyUML, I will zoom back from the classes and let my code specify the communities with abstractions taken from OOram role modeling [6] and the concepts of collaboration and interaction from the OMG Unified Modeling Language®. [7]

The abstractions need to be represented as computer programs. I need new tools that bridge the gap between my brain and those programs. I want my code to be effectively chunked and self documenting so that other people can read it and grasp the system architecture and operation. I want to be able to write a piece of code and give it to a colleague so that she can audit it and take responsibility for its correctness. The BabyUML success criterion is that programmers shall be happier and more effective when they use its results. Programmer happiness is closely coupled with powerful concepts, responsive environments, exploration, evolution, and excellence.

The *Baby* was the world's first electronic, digital, stored program computer. It executed its first statements on the 21st June 1947 at the University Of Manchester, England. [8] BabyUML is, somewhat whimsically, named after this computer because it is based on the idea of a *stored program object computer* such as it is pioneered in Smalltalk. [9] The other part of the name, *UML*[4], reflects that I see UML as a gold mine of concepts and ideas that are unified into a fairly consistent metamodel, many of them applicable to my project.

Most of my almost 50 years in computer programming have been devoted to creating tools for people. My success criteria have been the happy and effective user rather than the weighty scientific paper. This chapter is an engineering status report on the project. Most of the chapter is about harnessing known principles for the purposes of the project. Some of the chapter is about new ideas; the most important are identified in the conclusion (section 7).

The BabyUML project is experimental because I need to use a tool in order to understand how to improve it. The result of the BabyUML series of experiments shall be a new discipline of programming that includes abstractions, processes, and computer tools. One or more new programming languages may or may not be required. I expect to find many useful concepts in

---

[4] UML is a registered trademark of Object Management Group, Inc. in the United States and/or other countries.

UML. I do not commit to applying UML concepts correctly according to the specification, but will merely let them inspire my engineering solutions. One important simplification is that BabyUML is limited to sequential programming while UML also caters for parallel processes.

In section 2A, I describe a simple example taken from activity network planning that will be used to illustrate the concepts presented in this chapter. In section 2B, I use this example to illustrate why my old programming style can fail when scaled up to large problems.

In section 3, I have selected some fundamental ideas that have proven their worth in the past and discuss them from a BabyUML perspective. Section 3A stresses that BabyUML see the *object* as an entity that encapsulates state and behavior; it can be more than a simple instance of a class. Section 3B describes the *class* as a descriptor of individual objects. Section 3C describes the *role model* or *collaboration.* This is an ensemble of objects that interact to realize certain functionality. A *role* is a link to an object that makes a specific contribution in a collaboration. The link is dynamic; it is only valid at a certain time and in a certain execution of a collaboration. The BabyUML project shall achieve its goal by creating BabyIDE, an interactive programming environment where there is a balance between the *classes* that describe what the objects *are* and the *roles* that describe what the objects *do* when they interact at runtime.

The chunking of run-time objects is critical to the mastery of large systems. Section 3D describes a *BabyComponent* as a "monster object" that looks like a regular object in its environment. This object is completely characterized by its provided interface and encapsulates *member objects* that are invisible from outside. Different components can structure their member objects according to different paradigms. Two examples called MVC and DCA are discussed in depth in later sections. The notion of a BabyComponent is recursive; its member objects can turn out to be components in their own right without this being apparent from their external properties. The partitioning of the total system into components is an important contribution to system simplicity.

Aspect oriented programming is a technology for capturing cross cutting concerns in code that spans several classes. In section 3F, I speculate if similar techniques can be used to write code for roles so that the code spans all classes implementing these roles. Finally, in section 3G, I show that packages are not applicable to the clustering of run time objects.

I cannot device a new discipline of programming before I understand what I want to achieve, i.e. the run-time structure of interacting objects. BabyUML will provide leverage with a programming environment that supports an extensible set of object structuring paradigms. Section 4 and section 5 describe my old MVC and my new DCA programming paradigms together with a demonstration implementation in Java [5], [6] . Both paradigms answer the essential questions: *What are the objects*, *How are they interlinked*, and *How do they interact*. Both are important stepping stones in my pursuit of the utmost simplicity. Both paradigms exemplify the kinds of object structures I envisage for BabyUML. Both paradigms demonstrate a balance between classes and roles in the code.

Section 4 describes *MVC*, my old Model-View-Controller paradigm [10] that has survived for more than 30 years. The MVC bridges the gap between the human brain and the domain data stored in the computer. Its fundamental quality is that it separates model from

[5] Java is a trademark of Sun Microsystems, Inc. in the United States and other countries.

[6] The program is given in full on the enclosed CD.

view, i.e., tool from substance. The ideal Model is pure representation of information, while the ideal View is pure presentation:

- The domain data are represented in an object called the *Model.*
- The human user observes and manipulates the data through a *View.* The view shall ideally match the human mental model, giving the user the illusion that what is in his mind is faithfully represented in the computer.
- The *Controller* is responsible for setting up and coordinating a number of related views.

Section 5 describes *DCA*, my new Data-Collaboration-Algorithm paradigm. The essence of object orientation is that objects collaborate to realize certain functionality. Many object oriented designs distribute the specification of the collaborations as fragmentary information among the domain objects. In the DCA paradigm, the collaborating objects are explicitly identified by the role they play in an interaction, and the interaction pattern is explicitly defined in terms of these roles as follows:

- The *D* for *Data* part is a simple "micro database" that manages the domain objects.
- The *C* for *Collaboration* part is an object that defines the roles that objects play in an ensemble of interacting objects. The collaboration also binds the roles to objects by executing queries on the set of Data objects.
- The *A for Algorithm* part is a method that specifies an interaction. The method is expressed in terms of the roles objects play in the interaction; the binding from role to object is done in the collaboration.

The MVC/DCA experiment reported in sections 4 and 5 is completed. It has revealed the kind of high-level structures that shall be supported by the BabyUML discipline of programming.

The next major step in the BabyUML project is to create *BabyIDE*, an integrated development environment for BabyUML. The experiment will be done in a *BabyIDE laboratory* where I will try out novel semantics for classes and metaclasses together with tools for design, compilation, and inspection.

Section 6 describes a rudimentary BabyIDE laboratory together with its core concepts. The laboratory is embedded within a Smalltalk stored program object computer. Its main feature is that it gives the systems programmer full control over the semantics of classes and metaclasses. Its foundation is a deep understanding of the implementation of objects, classes, instantiation and inheritance.

The laboratory will initially be used to create a BabyIDE for the DCA and MVC paradigms. I will clearly need to harness imperative, algorithmic programming as well as the declarative definition of data structures. I will need class oriented programming to define the nature of the objects as well as role models to define their collaboration. I will also need new debuggers and inspectors to create an integrated environment. The prospects are challenging, and I look forward to dig into them.

The BabyUML project will be completed when it has produced a BabyIDE working prototype that can act as a specification for a commercial, generally applicable software engineering product. Most products will not need the flexibility of a laboratory and can be written in any language.

2. An Example and a Problem

2A. An Activity Network Planning Example

Project planning and control is frequently based on the idea of *activity networks*. A piece of work that needs to be done is described as an activity. The work done by an architect when designing a house can be broken down into activities. The work of erecting the house likewise. Example activities: drawing a plan view, digging the pit, making the foundation, erecting the frame, paneling the walls, painting these walls.

Some of the activity attributes are *name*, *duration*, a set of *predecessor* activities, a set of *successor* activities, *earlyStart* time, and *earlyFinish* time. Predecessors and successors are called *technological dependencies*. The *earlyStart* of an activity is when all its predecessors are finished. The *earlyFinish* is most simply computed as *earlyStart* + *duration*. There are more sophisticated forms of technological dependencies. For example, it is possible to start the painting of one wall before the paneling of all walls is finished. Such cases are catered for with various kinds of *activity overlap*.

Frontloading is the calculation of the *earlyStart* and *earlyFinish* times of each activity given the earlyFinish times for their predecessors. The example chosen for this experiment is the rudimentary activity network shown in figure 1. The activity *duration*, *earlyStart* and *earlyFinish* times are shown in parenthesis.

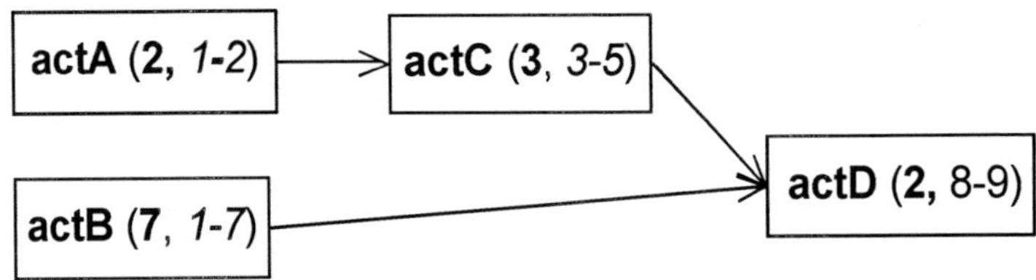

Figure 1. The experimental activity network.

Activities may be tied to *resources*. The creation of the design of a house requires some hours of work by an architect and a draftsman. The digging of the pit requires machinery and the efforts of some workers. *Resource allocation* is to reserve resources for each activity. It is a non-trivial operation; one can easily end up with unimportant activities blocking the progress of critical ones. (We cannot dig the pit because the workers are busy leveling the garden.) There is a single resource in this illustrative network example, say a pool of workers. The resource has unlimited capacity and an activity employs a single worker for its duration.

The example has been programmed in Java as an illustration of the concepts discussed in this chapter[7]. The user interface (GUI) is shown in figure 2. It is partitioned into four strips. The top strip has three command buttons: *First Network* that creates the network shown in figure 1. *Frontload* the network and allocate resources. *Second Network* that creates another

[7]The complete Java code can be found on the enclosed CD.

network in order to demonstrate that the program works for more than one network. The second strip shows the dependency graph. The third strip is a Gantt diagram showing when the different activities will be performed. Time along the horizontal axis, activities along the vertical. The bottom strip shows how the activities are allocated to the resource. Time along the horizontal axis, resource loading along the vertical. The snapshot in figure 1 has been taken when *actA* has been selected.

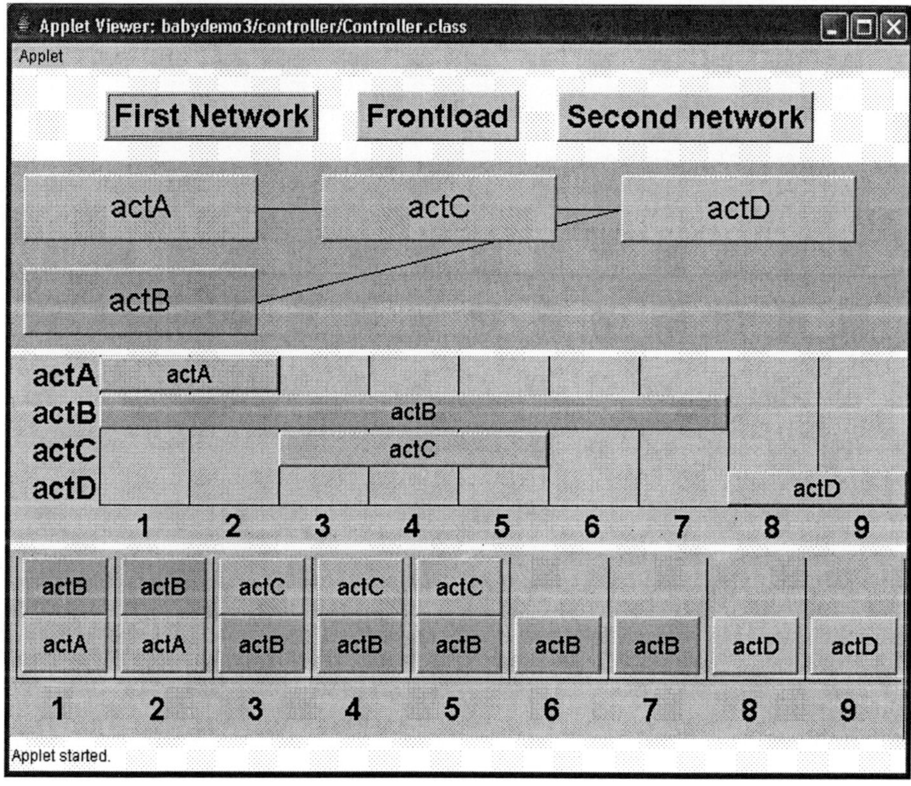

Figure 2. The Java program user interface.

The network example could be programmed in many different ways. I use it to illustrate the MVC and DCA paradigms, pretending that I'm working on a non-trivial, comprehensive planning system.

2B. My Old Style Doesn't Always Scale

A potential problem with my usual programming style is easily demonstrated. Figure 3 illustrates how I would normally implement the network example. The rounded rectangles denote objects, the solid lines denote links between them, the white rectangles denote classes, and the dashed arrow denotes «instanceOf».

The activity objects are shown bottom right with heavy outlines. The idea is that planning is realized by negotiation; internally between the activity objects themselves and externally between activity objects and their required resources. The technicalities of the user interface have been separated from the domain objects in conformance with the MVC paradigm; the View and Controller objects are shown on the left.

My usual implementation style tends to give fairly small objects in a distributed structure and with distributed control. This leads to a large number of links and interaction patterns. An activity uses a certain resource; let the activity object negotiate directly with the resource object to establish a mutually acceptable schedule. A symbol on the computer screen represents a certain activity; let the symbol object interrogate the activity object to determine how it is to be presented, and let the activity object warn the symbol object of significant changes. This works fine in simple cases, but it can degenerate into a bowl of spaghetti for very large systems.

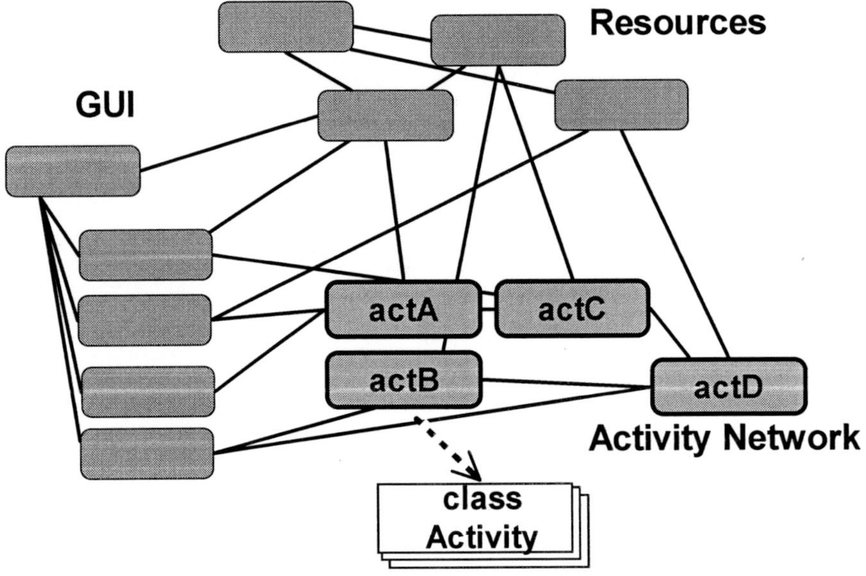

Figure 3. A typical application.

Every object is an instance of a class written in a language such as Simula, Java, or Smalltalk. The structure and domain logic is distributed among the methods of the classes with their superclasses. This fragmentation makes it hard to see the system as a whole. Any spaghetti that may be in the design will effectively be chopped into noodles in the classes. The structure is in the mind of the beholder and not explicit in the code; so my beauty can be your noodles.

3 Some Fundamental Concepts and Their Use in BabyUML

3A. The Object

The notion of objects was introduced by Nygaard and Dahl with the Simula language. [11] The concepts were considerably refined in the Smalltalk language and run-time system. [9]

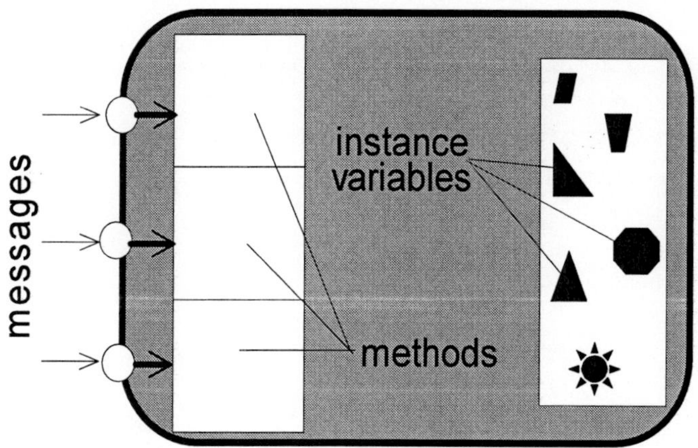

Figure 4. The object.

Objects are entities that encapsulate state and behavior. In this chapter, I use Smalltalk's pure object model as illustrated in figure 4. The *state* of an object is defined by the values of its *instance variables*. Its *behavior* is defined by its *methods*. Neither state nor behavior is directly visible from outside the object; they can only be accessed through messages to the object. A message is intention-revealing; it specifies *what* is required, but not *how* this is to be produced[8]. When an object receives a message, it looks up a *message dictionary* to find the appropriate method for handling the message. A method can read and change the value of the instance variables, and it can send messages to itself or other objects. Different objects can thus handle identical messages in different ways.

In some contexts, an object is defined as an instance of a class. A more conceptual definition is preferred in BabyUML: *An object is an entity that encapsulates state and behavior.* This allows me to focus on the objects and work with different abstractions for different purposes. The class abstraction discussed in section 3B describes the nature of a set of objects. The role abstraction discussed in section 3C describes an object's contribution made by a set of objects in a structure of collaborating objects.

The concept of an object is specialized in the *BabyComponent* that is introduced in Section 3D.

3B. The Class

In most object oriented languages, an object is an instance of a class. The class defines all features that are common to the instances of the class, notably their methods and the specification of their instance variables. Note that the class was not mentioned in the above description of the object because it is the object that holds the state and the methods are executed in the context of the object.

A class inherits all the features of its superclasses, it can add features of its own, and it can override methods defined in the superclasses. A class with its superclasses can always be flattened into a single class with no superclass. This means that the actual distribution of

[8]This in contrast to a procedure call that uniquely identifies the procedure body. Also in contrast to Java where the instance variables are visible from outside the object.

features between the superclasses does not in any way influence the semantics of the object, and I see class inheritance mainly as a very powerful device for code sharing.

The class concept is important in BabyUML, but its use is restricted to describing isolated objects. The state and behavior of ensembles of collaborating objects are described by the role models of the next section.

3C. The Role Model

Prokon was to be a comprehensive system for planning and control [12] that we worked on in the early seventies. The system architecture was based on objects negotiating on behalf of the line managers and depended on global control of the object interaction patterns. The line managers should own their objects with the corresponding classes. Objects playing the same roles in the interactions could, therefore, be implemented by different classes owned by different managers. We tried implementing the system in Simula [11], but failed because the Simula language insisted on our knowing the class of every object. Indeed, there was no notion of an object with an unknown class.

The Prokon project lost its funding and died, but the vision has stayed with me. The transition to Smalltalk was a major step forward because the Smalltalk dynamic typing let me focus on object interaction independently of classes and class hierarchy. The MVC paradigm discussed in section 4 was a result of thinking in terms of objects rather than classes, but there was still no construct for explicitly programming the interaction patterns.

The experience with MVC led me to search for a new abstraction that let me work explicitly with the interactions. The result was *role modeling*, an abstraction that describes how an ensemble of objects interact to accomplish some desired result. Each object has a specific responsibility in an interaction[9]; we say that it plays a specific *role*.

We developed role modeling tools for our own use in the early eighties. Our tools were demonstrated in the Tektronix booth at the first OOPSLA in 1986. The first mention in print was in an overview article by Rebecca Wirfs-Brock and Ralph Johnson. [14] Our own report was in an article in JOOP in 1992. [15] My book, *Working with Objects* [6], explains role modeling in depth. A theory of role modeling is given in Egil P. Andersen's doctoral thesis. [16]

Some of the role modeling concepts have made it into the UML Collaborations and Interactions packages as follows (my emphasis):

Collaborations[10]

> Objects in a system typically cooperate with each other to produce the behavior of a system. The behavior is the functionality that the system is required to implement.
>
> A behavior of a collaboration will eventually be exhibited by a set of cooperating instances (specified by classifiers) that communicate with each other by sending signals or invoking operations. However, to understand the mechanisms used in a design, it may be important to

[9]More about responsibility driven design and roles in [13].

[10] Extract from section 9.1 in OMG document formal/2007-02-03. Reprinted with permission. Object Management Group, Inc. (C) OMG. 2007.

describe only those aspects of these classifiers and their interactions that are involved in accomplishing a task or a related set of tasks, projected from these classifiers. ***Collaborations* allow us to describe only the relevant aspects of the cooperation of a set of instances by identifying the specific roles that the instances will play.** Interfaces allow the externally observable properties of an instance to be specified without determining the classifier that will eventually be used to specify this instance. Consequentially, the roles in a collaboration will often be typed by interfaces and will then prescribe properties that the participating instances must exhibit, but will not determine what class will specify the participating instances. [7]

A role model is analogous to a stage production. *Hamlet* is a tragedy written by William Shakespeare. In a certain production; the role of Hamlet may be played by the actor Ian, Ophelia by the actress Susan. Outside the stage, Ian and Susan live their regular lives. Other productions of the same play may cast different actors. Role modeling sees a system of interacting objects as a stage performance:

- A set of objects is like a set of available actors.
- An object interaction is like a stage performance and objects play roles just as actors do.
- A role model corresponds to a drama. Both describe what shall take place in terms of roles and their actions. Neither specifies objects, classes or specific actors.
- *A BabyUML discovery is that the selection and assignment of objects to roles can be done by a query on the objects just as the selection and assignment of actors to roles is the task of casting.*
- A role may be seen as an indirect link to one or more objects.
- A role really exists only while it is being played, i.e., when it is bound to one or more objects. At other times, there may be no object or actor assigned to the role. Therefore, the role concept is a dynamic concept.

As a role model example, we will consider the *Observer Pattern* as described in the *Design Patterns* book. [17] A design pattern describes a solution to a general problem in such a way that it can be realized in many different ways and made to fit under many different circumstances. The *Observer Pattern* is described in the book with a textual description, a class diagram, and a kind of collaboration diagram. I will here describe it with a role model.

The essence of object orientation is that objects collaborate to achieve some desired objective. Three questions need to be answered: *What are the roles? How are they interlinked? How do they interact?* The answer to the first two questions is the structure of roles that work together to reach the objective and the links between these roles.

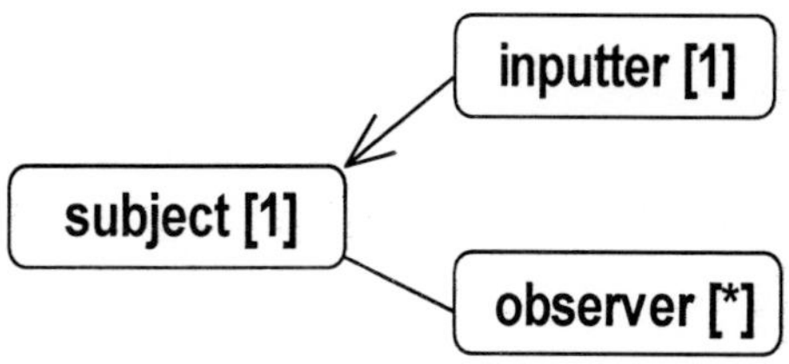

Figure 5. The Observer role model.

Figure 5 show the Observer pattern as a role model. We see three roles. There is one object playing the subject role. There is one object playing the inputter role. There is any number of objects playing the observer role. They are all linked to the single subject, and the subject is linked to them all.

Every object has a unique identity. A role name such as subject is an alias for one or more objects, it can be seen as indirect addressing with dynamic binding between role and objects. We use a role name as an abbreviation of: *"the object or objects that play this role at a certain time and in a certain context"*.

Figure 6 specifies how the objects interact when synchronizing subject and observer. We see that inputter sends setState () to subject, presumably changing its state. subject then sends an update () message to all observers. The observers finally interrogate the subject to get the new state.

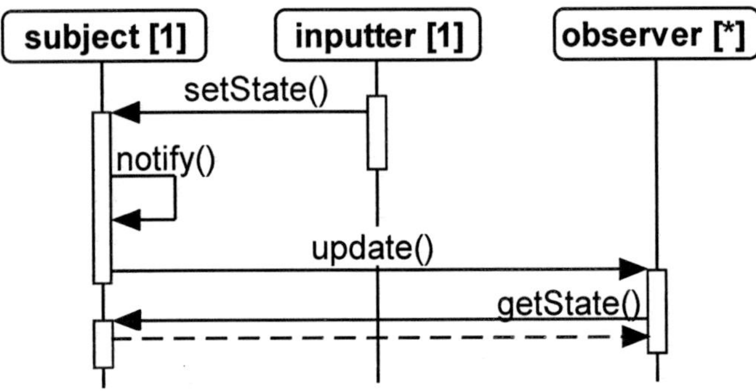

Figure 6. An Observer interaction[11].

Note that many objects may play the observer role in different contexts and at different times, but we are only concerned with the objects that play the observer role *in an occurrence of the interaction.* Also note that a role may be played by many objects and an object may play many roles. In this example, an object playing the inputter role could also play the observer role. The collaboration diagram in *Design Patterns [17]* mandated this by showing two objects called aConcreteObserver and anotherConcreteObserver respectively; the first also playing the inputter role.

A role modeling tool called *OOram* was put on the market, but the interest was not sufficient to sustain it as a product.

The reason for the OOram failure could be that I had not found a conceptual bridge between roles and classes. I have recently found this bridge; *a role is bound to a set of objects through a query.* The relations are illustrated informally in figure 7. Object interaction is specified by an algorithm. The algorithm references the interacting objects indirectly through their roles. A query binds a role to one or more objects. An object is an instance of a class. There is no restriction on the formulation of a query. Its results may vary over time so that the

[11] This BabyUML sequence diagram describes sequential interaction. A filled arrow is a method call. A thin, vertical rectangle denotes a method execution. The objects bound to the observer[*] role work in lock-step; their updates appear to occur simultaneously.

role is a dynamic notion. The nature of an object does not change over time so that the class is a static notion.

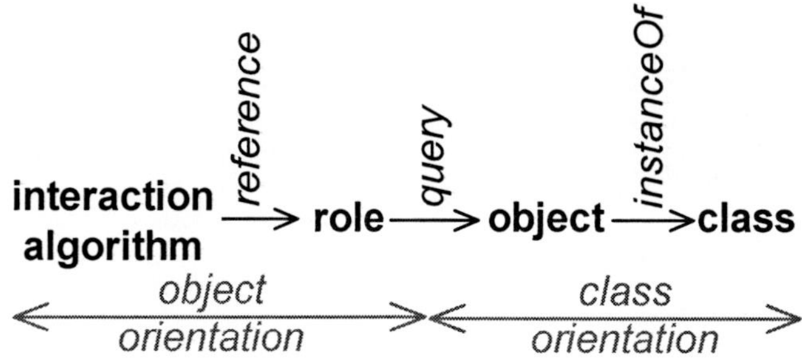

Figure 7. Bridge between roles and classes.

An implementation of this unification is described in section 5 on the DCA paradigm.

3D. The BabyComponent

Section 2B demonstrated my need for injecting some sort of object clustering into my systems. The instance variables in the objects are in themselves less than useful for this purpose. Some of them may point to what can be considered peers in a cluster, e.g., an activity predecessor. Some of them may point out of a cluster, e.g., from an activity to its resource. And some of them may point to sub-objects that may be considered as parts of the object itself, e.g., from an activity to its name. Well chosen variable names can help a knowledgeable reader understand the semantics, but it is a weakness that we only see the object structure from the perspective of a single object, we do not see the structure as a whole.

The UML definition of *Composite Structures* provides the idea. In [7], we find the following[12]:

> **9.1. Overview**
> The term "structure" in this chapter refers to a composition of interconnected elements, representing run-time instances collaborating over communications links to achieve some common objectives.
>
> **Internal Structure**
> The InternalStructure subpackage provides mechanisms for specifying structures of interconnected elements that are created within an instance of a containing classifier. A structure of this type represents a decomposition of that classifier and is referred to as its "internal structure."

A *babyComponent* is an object that encapsulates other objects and can loosely be described as an instance of a UML Composite Structure. A *babyComponent* looks like a regular object seen from its environment and is characterized by its provided interface.

[12] Extract from section 9.1 in OMG document formal/2007-02-03. Reprinted with permission. Object Management Group, Inc. (C) OMG. 2007.

Regular objects and components can be used interchangeably. Inside a component, we find a bounded structure of interconnected Member Objects.

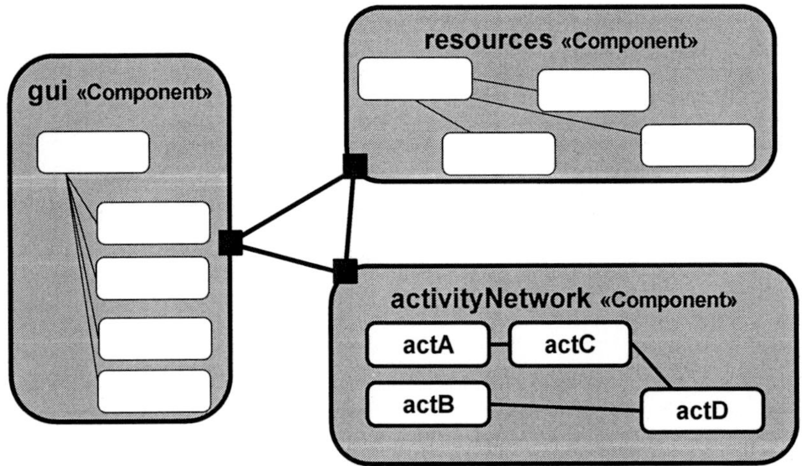

Figure 8. A Component is an object that encapsulates other objects.

Figure 8 illustrates how the spaghetti of figure 3 can be replaced by a simple structure of three interacting components. The notion of a BabyComponent is recursive; I can organize several hundred thousand objects in a component structure so that I can deal with a manageable number at each level.

There are many advantages of an architecture based on the BabyUML components:

- My brain can better visualize how the system represents and processes information. My code can specify how components are interconnected and how they interact. The code can thus document the high level system architecture.
- The notion of components makes it easier to ensure correspondence between the user's mental model and the model actually implemented in the system.
- The component boundary forms a natural place to put firewalls for security and privacy. Indeed, it is hard to see how privacy and security can be achieved without some form of enforced component architecture.

The notion of a BabyComponent is useful in many contexts. A specialization is the DCA component described in section 5.

3E. The Database

An early idea for system structuring was the idea of separating system state and system behavior. From the first, 1963 version, our Autokon CAD/CAM ship design system [24] was structured as a number of application programs arranged around a central data store that held information about the ship, its geometry and the arrangement of its parts. Different application programs accessed the store through special access routines that transformed the store's data structure to an apparent structure suitable for the application as illustrated in figure 9.

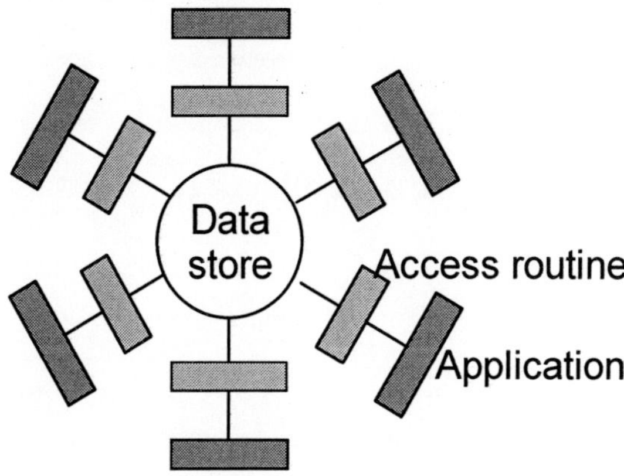

Figure 9. Separating data and procedure.

This separation of state and behavior is very useful for our purposes. Consider the roles and classes illustration in figure 7. Put the objects of figure 7 in the data store and you get the Data of the DCA paradigm. Put the role definitions with their queries into the access routines and you get the Collaboration of the DCA paradigm. Put the interaction methods into the applications and you get the Algorithms of the DCA paradigm. The DCA paradigm is discussed further in section 5.

3F. Aspect Oriented Programming

Some programming problems cannot easily be captured by procedural or object oriented code because they cut across procedures and objects. Aspect Oriented Programming, AOP, [23] was introduced to handle such cross-cutting aspects of the problem. Examples are aspects related to security and performance.

At a first glance, it seems that roles and interactions can be such aspects since they cut across class boundaries. A technology similar to AOP should be able to support methods that are defined for a particular role and thus shared among all classes that implement this role. These classes may specialize the role methods as needed. There is an appealing symmetry here: A class defines methods that are common to all its instances. What if a role defines AOP-like methods that are common to all objects that play this role? An interesting thought for a future experiment.

3G. The Package

A UML *package* is used to group model elements. A package is a namespace for its members, and may contain other packages. A package can import either individual members of other packages, or all the members of other packages. In Java, similar packages are used to group classes and interfaces.

An object is an instance of a class. The classes in its superclass chain are typically members of different packages. An object is thus related to several packages. The notion of a package relates to compile-time issues and is irrelevant in the context of interacting, run-time objects.

4. MVC: The Model-View-Controller Paradigm

How can we build a system that is experienced as an extension of the user's brain? How can we put the user in the driver's seat so that he can not only run the program but also understand and even modify its operation? How can we structure a system so that it presents an image of the world that corresponds to the user's own conception of it?

MVC was first conceived as a means for giving human users control of the computer resources. MVC bridges the gap between the users' mental model and the information represented in the computer. The idea is illustrated in figure 10.

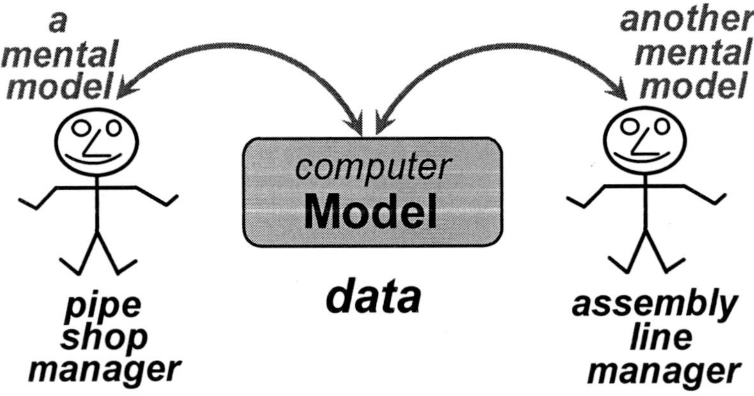

Figure 10. Bridge the gap between the user's mind and the stored data.

The domain of my first MVC was shipbuilding. The problem was project planning and control as described in section 2A. A manager was responsible for a part of a large project. His department had its own bottlenecks and its own considerations for planning. Other departments were different; a pipe shop was very different from a panel assembly line which was again very different from a design office. How could each manager have his own specialized part of the planning system while preserving the integrity of the plan as a whole?

The answer was to replace the "dead" activity records in traditional, procedure oriented planning systems with interacting objects. The objects would represent their owners within the universe of interacting objects. The objects would be specialized according to the needs of their owners, yet they could all interact according to a common scheme.

I implemented the first MVC while being a visiting scientist with the Smalltalk group at Xerox PARC. [10] The conventional wisdom in the group was that objects should be visible and tangible, thus bridging the gap between the human brain and the abstract data within the computer. This simple and powerful idea failed for the planning systems for two reasons. The first was that a plan was a structure of many activity and resource objects so that it was too limiting to focus on one object at the time. The second was that users were familiar with the planning model and were used to seeing it from different perspectives. The visible and tangible object would get very complex if it should be able to show itself and be manipulated in many different ways. This would violate another Smalltalk ideal; namely that code should be visible, simple, and lucid.

4A. The MVC Model

The terms *data* and *information* are commonly used indiscriminately. In the Stone Age, IFIP defined them precisely in a way that I still find very fruitful when thinking about the human use of computers [19]:

> **DATA**. A representation of facts or ideas in a formalized manner capable of being communicated or manipulated by some process.
> **Note**: The representation may be more suitable either for human interpretation (e.g., printed text) or for internal interpretation by equipment (e.g., punched cards or electrical signals).
> **INFORMATION**. In automatic data processing the meaning that a human assigns to data by means of the known conventions used in its representation.
> **Note**: The term has a sense wider than that of information theory and nearer to that of common usage[13].

So the user's mental model is *information,* information does not exist outside the human brain. But *representation of information* can and do exist outside the brain. It is called *data.* In the network example, the Model is the data representing the activity network and the resources. The Model data may be considered *latent* because they need to be transformed to be observable to the user and related to the user's mental model of the project.

I will discuss the Java implementation of the View and Controller below, and the Model with its links to the View-Controller pair in section 5.

4B. The MVC View

The *View* transforms the latent Model data into a form that the human can observe and convert into *information* as illustrated in figure 11.

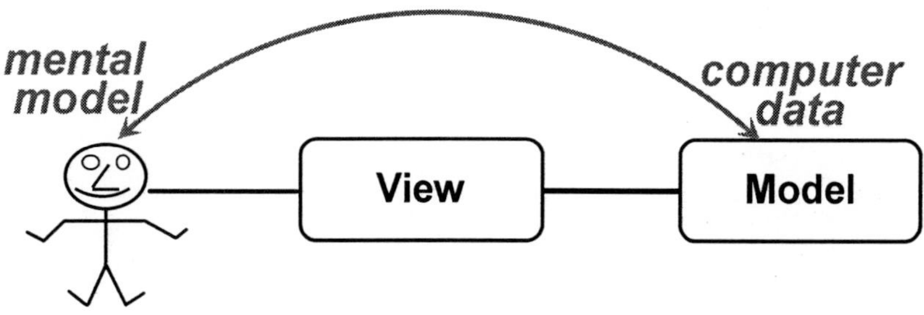

Figure 11. The View couples model data to the information in the user's brain so that they appear fused into one.

I will discuss the Java implementation in section 5E.

4C. The MVC Controller

The Controller is responsible for creating and coordinating a number of related Views. I sometimes think of the Controller-View combination as a *Tool* that the user employs to work with the system's latent information.[14] [15]

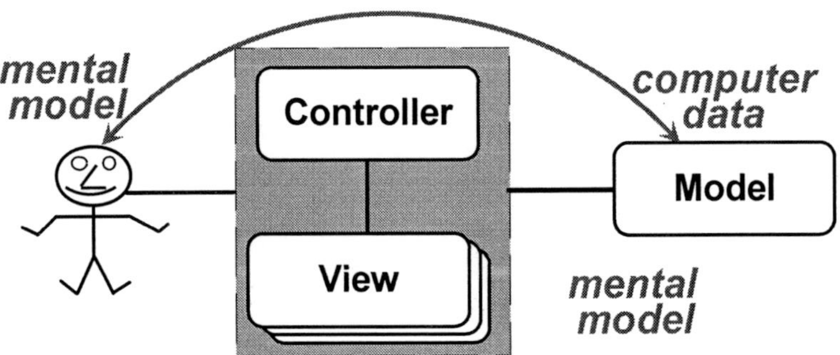

Figure 12. The Controller creates and coordinates multiple Views.

Looking back to section 3C on role models, we realize that *Model*, *View*, and *Controller* are *roles* played by objects. Their classes are unspecified and irrelevant to the MVC paradigm.

4D. The Anatomy of the Java User Interface Code

The GUI for the network example was shown in figure 2. Figure 13 shows the same GUI annotated with the implementation class names for its main parts. We see that the four strips of the tool are

1. The top strip is an instance of class ButtonStrip; it contains command buttons.
2. The second strip is an instance of class DependencyPanel; it is a view that shows the activities with their technological dependencies.
3. The third strip is an instance of class GanttPanel; it is a bar chart showing the time period for each activity.
4. The fourth strip is an instance of class ResourcePanel; it shows the activities that are allocated to the resource in each time period.

---

[13] ©IFIP 1966. Quoted with permission.

[14] Note that a Smalltalk 80 Controller is only responsible for the input to a single view. It is thus different from the one discussed here, see [18].

[15] Also note that some so-called MVC structures let the controller control the user interaction and thus, the user. This idea is fundamentally different from MVC as described here. I want the user to be in control and the system to appear as an extension of the user's mind.

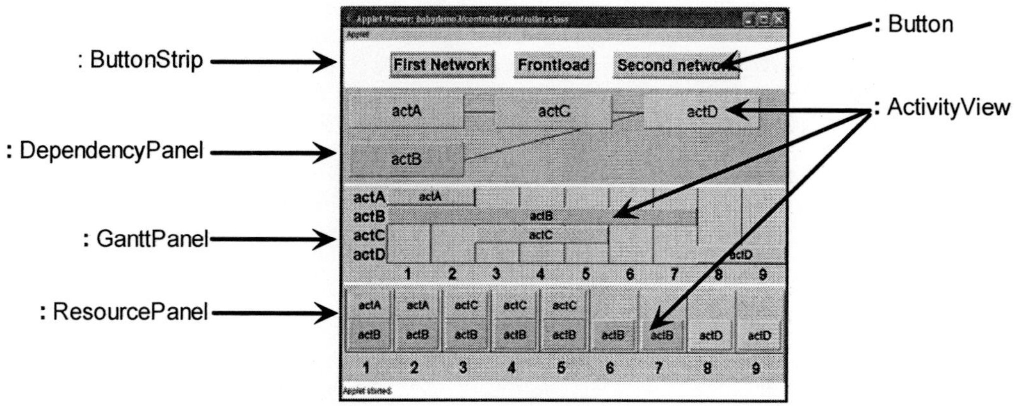

Figure 13. The anatomy of the MVC Java tool. *(: ButtonStrip means an instance of class ButtonStrip)*

An overview of the implementation is shown in the class diagram of figure 14. In my traditional programming style, the views would all be associated with the model. In this implementation, I reduce the number of associations in order to get a simpler and cleaner structure. The views are now subordinated the controller by being enclosed in a controller-managed component. This is indicated by a dashed line in figure 14. The *Model* and *Controller* are shown in heavy outline to indicate that they are the main collaborators in this implementation. The *Views*, being subordinate in this implementation, are shown in light outline. The Java library superclasses are shown dashed along the top of the diagram.

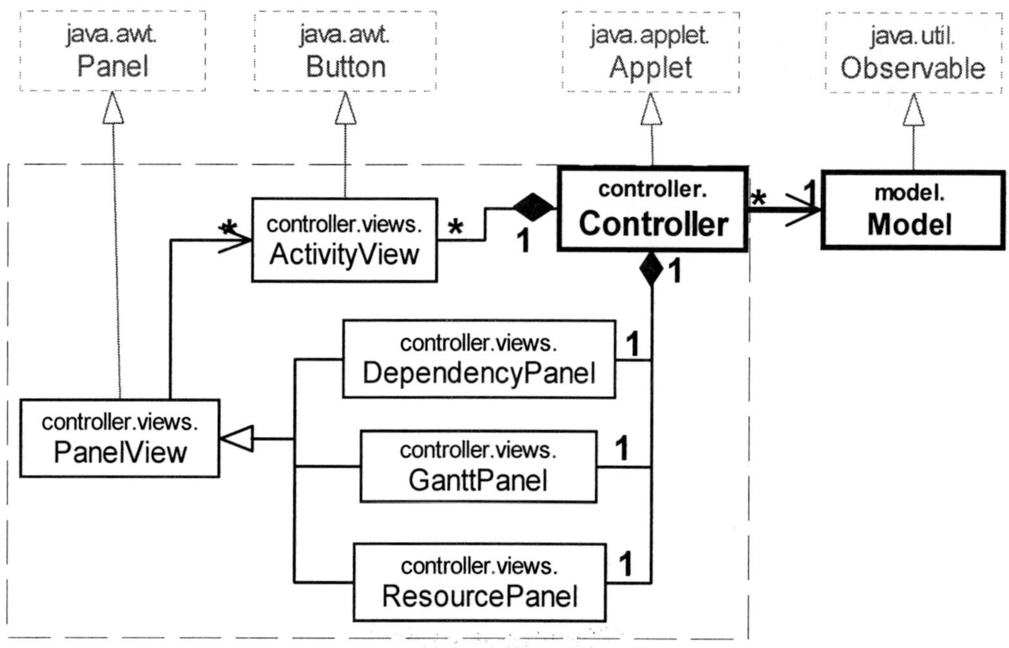

Figure 14. Java class diagram.

I will go into more details when I discuss the Model internals and system behavior in section 5.

4E. Controller Code Coordinates Selection

I will now take the *selection* function as an example of how the controller coordinates the behavior of the views.

Figure 15 shows the tool after the user has clicked on any of the actA activity views. The key to simplicity and generality is that the view being clicked only reports this event to the controller object. The controller decides that this is indeed a selection command, and that it shall be reflected in the appearance of all activityViews, including the one that was clicked. This behavior is illustrated in the BabyUML sequence diagram of figure 16.

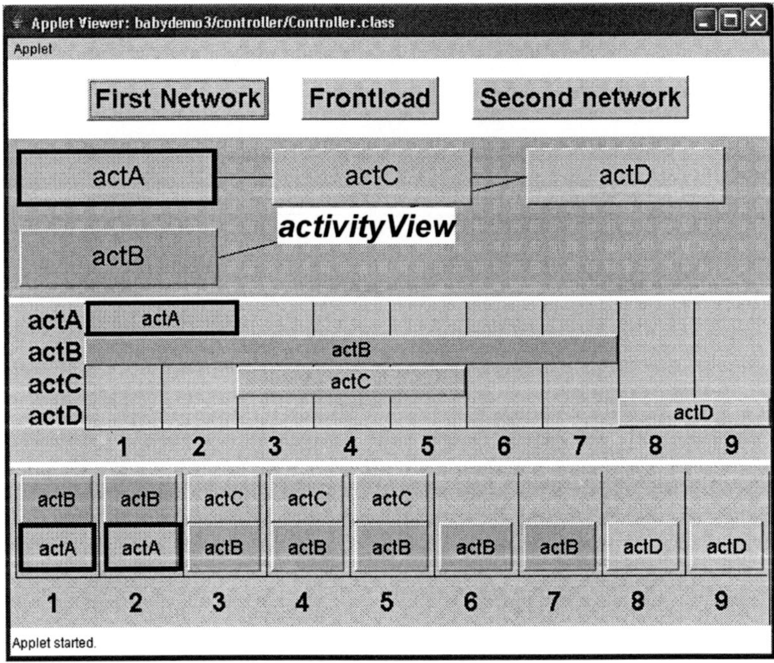

Figure 15. actA is selected in all views where it appears.

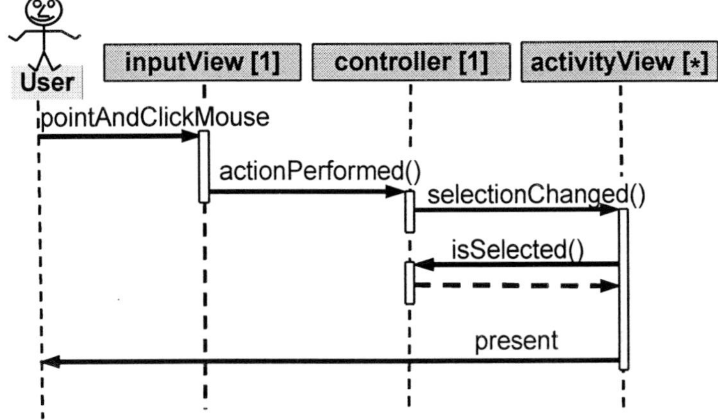

Figure 16. The selection interaction.

In this program, the inputView role happens to be played by an instance of class ActivityView. We see from figure 14 that ActivityView is an awt.Button, so it sends an actionPerfomed event to its actionListener. All activityViews are created to let the controller be their actionListener.

Discussion 1. A variant of the selection interaction could use the Observer pattern[16] to let the controller alert the views about a changed selection. On the face of it, this is very flexible, extensible, and so on. But in this case, it would merely be an obfuscator. The observer pattern is useful when the subject should be decoupled from its dependents. But here, the controller knows its views since it created them. The direct solution is the simplest and does not restrict flexibility and extensibility.

Discussion 2. We see from figure 14 that the controller knows both panels and activityViews. An alternative could be to let the controller know the panelViews only. Each panelView could then act as a local controller for its activityViews. The programmer of the top level controller would then not need to know the inner workings of the panels. I did not choose this solution because I wanted to keep the experimental program as simple as possible.

5. DCA: The Data-Collaboration-Algorithm Paradigm

I now come to the Model part of MVC. Seen from the Controller, it looks like an ordinary object. But a single object that represents all activities and resources would be a monster. My new *DCA paradigm* tells me how to master a monster object by clearly separating roles from objects and by creating bridges between them as illustrated in figure 7.

The Model of the MVC paradigm is implemented as a *DCAComponent*. It looks like a regular object from the outside, characterized by its provided operations. Inside, there is a well ordered and powerful object structure partitioned into three parts, *Data*, *Collaborations*, and *Algorithms*. I hinted at the nature of these parts in the introduction and will now go into the details.

5A. The MVC Model Part as a Single Object

The Java tutorial [20] describes an object as a number of variables (state) surrounded by methods (behavior) as illustrated in figure 17(a). This is actually a better illustration of the Smalltalk object than the Java object. In Smalltalk, the variables are invisible from outside the object; all access has to be through the methods.[17]

Figure 17(b) shows an alternative illustration that I use as a starting point for discussing DCA. Borrowing terminology from UML, I use the term *owned attributes* to denote the object state (fields, instance variables). I use the UML term *derived attributes* to denote attributes that are computed rather then stored. For example, a person object could have

[16]See *section 3C*.

[17] The Java object is different; the fields *are* visible from the outside. I write x = foo.fieldX; to access a field directly, and I write x = foo.getFieldX(); to access it through a method.

birthDate as an owned attribute, while age could be a derived attribute. Other methods implement the object's provided operations.

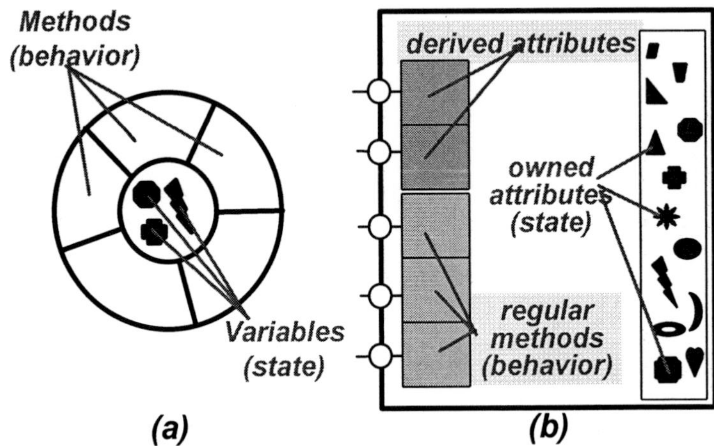

Figure 17. The object as an instance of a class. a) The object as depicted in the Java tutorial. (b) A more accurate object model

Behavior is activated in an object when it receives a message. The message is dynamically linked to the appropriate method, and the method is activated. This link is symbolized by a small circle on the object boundary in figure 17(b).

5B. The DCA Component; a Well-Structured Monster Object

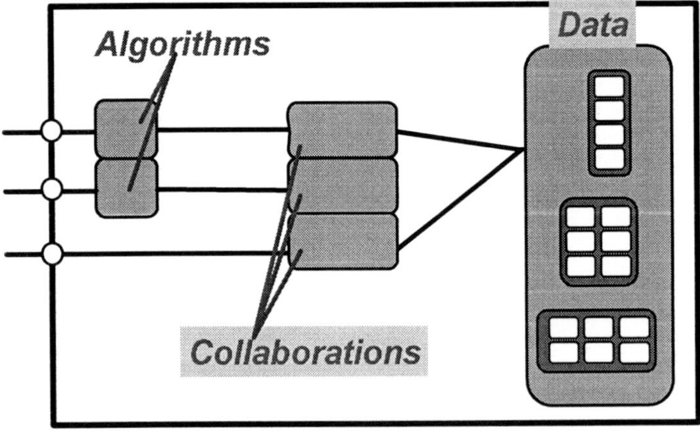

Figure 18. The DCA component.

Figure 17 shows an object as an entity that encapsulates state and behavior. Figure 18 illustrates the *DCA component*. It looks like the object of figure 17 when seen from its environment. Inside, there are a number of specialized parts: Data, Collaborations, and Algorithms.

5B.1. The D stands for Data

The Data part corresponds to the variables (owned attributes) of the regular object. The variables are replaced by a "baby database" that holds the component's domain objects and their structure. The term "database" is used in a restricted sense; it is a set of domain objects organized according to a conceptual schema. The schema can be read and understood independently of the system around it; an important step towards system simplicity:

- The domain objects are organized in a number of relations in the first normal form, ensuring referential integrity.
- The structure is represented in explicit relations. Contrast with my traditional representation where structure information is fragmented among the domain objects. The DCA domain objects are correspondingly simplified.
- The code for the Data part should ideally be declarative in the form of a *conceptual schema*, but I merely implement some Java classes in the network example.

I do not assume persistence, concurrency, access control, security, or any other goodie usually associated with databases. There is also an addition to mainstream database technology; the DCA data are encapsulated within a component so that the system as a whole can include a hierarchy of independent "micro databases".

5B.2. The C stands for Collaboration

DCA *Collaborations* correspond to the derived attributes of the regular object. Algorithms access the domain objects through the roles these objects play. Collaborations bind roles to domain objects through queries as illustrated in figure 7. A role can be seen as indirectly addressing one or more domain objects, making it possible to address different objects at different times without changing the algorithm code. The notion of Collaborations is derived from the OOram role model [6] and corresponds to the external views used in database technology.

In this experiment, collaborations are coded as classes that have the collaboration roles as attributes and the database queries as methods. A *DCA Collaboration* is an instance of such a class where the results of the queries are assigned to the role variables, thus binding roles to actual domain objects. A binding is only valid in a certain context and at a certain time and realizes a kind of dynamic, indirect addressing, [18]

Objects using a Collaboration see the Data in a perspective optimized for their needs. Note that these user objects can be internal or external to the Model.

5B.3. The A stands for Algorithm

Algorithms occur in two places in the DCA paradigm. Some are local to the domain objects and are coded as methods in the domain classes. Other algorithms describe domain object interaction and are properties of the inter-object space. The interaction algorithms are coded

[18] The DCA Collaboration corresponds to the UML *CollaborationUse*. My choice of name reflects my focus on objects rather than classes.

in separate classes in BabyUML, distinct from the domain classes. This ensures that object interaction is specified explicitly and makes it easier to check the code for correctness and to study the system dynamics.

5C. The MVC Model Part as a DCA Component

The Model part of the network example is implemented as a DCA component. Some important objects are shown in figure 19. For illustrative purposes, I have separated the Data into two sub-parts. The netBase holds the activity network in two relations. The activities relation is a list of Activity objects. The dependencies relation is a list of Dependency objects, each having a predecessor and successor attribute. The resourceBase has a single relation, *allocations*, that is a list of Allocation objects, each having a time and an Activity attribute.

We have previously seen that the GUI is split into a controller object and three panelView objects, each with a layout algorithm that creates its display. In addition, the *frontload* command button activates the frontload Algorithm. The Algorithms are users of the DCA Data and access them through suitable Collaborations.

In the following, I will discuss the code for the dependencyPanel and frontload buttons together with their algorithms and data access collaborations as illustrated in figure 19.

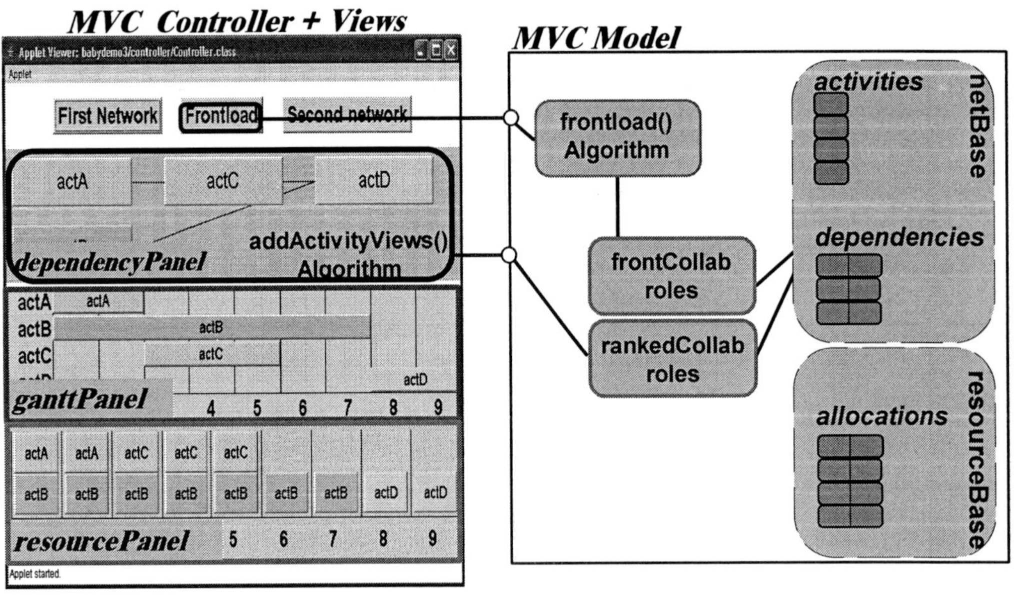

Figure 19: The MVC Model part as a DCA model.

5D. The Data Structure Defined by a Schema

The Data parts are defined by their schemas. Figure 20 shows the netBase schema expresses as a UML class diagram.

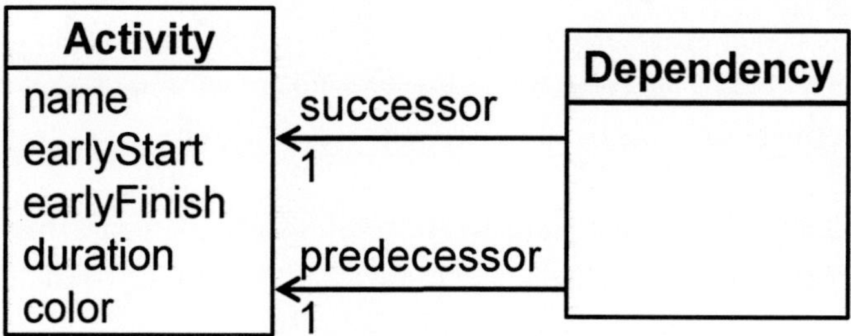

Figure 20. The *netBase* schema as a UML class diagram.

The corresponding Java class declarations are trivial.

5E. Example 1: Panel layout

Figure 21 illustrates that the unit on the horizontal axis in the DependencyPanel is the activity *rank*; i.e., the max length of the activity's predecessor chain from the activity to the start of the network. Activities having the same rank are stacked vertically.

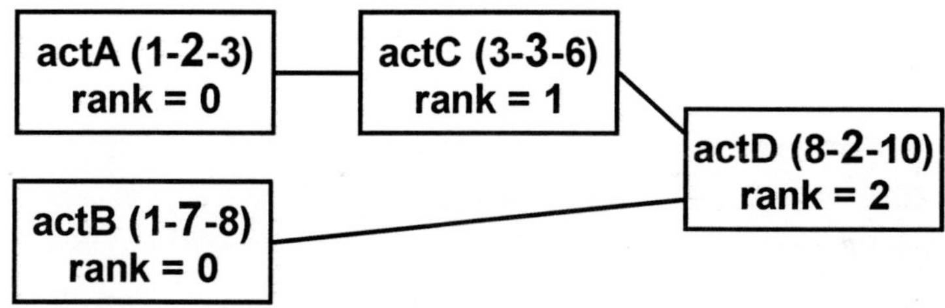

Figure 21. The ranked activities.

The DependencyPanel layout Algorithm is as simple as can be. (Too simple, actually, it will often lead to overlapping dependency lines.) The most interesting statements in the DependencyPanel class are as follows:

```
DependencyPanel::private void addActivityViews() {
        ....
        for (int rank=0; rank <= rankedCollab.maxRank(); rank++) {
            ....
            for (Activity act : rankedCollab.activityListAtRank(rank)) {
                ActivityView actView = new ActivityView(controller, act, 24) ;
                ....
                add(actView);
                ....
            }
        }
}
```

This layout algorithm accesses the activity objects through the rankedCollab, an instance of the RankedCollab class. This collaboration presents the data in a table with two columns: *rank* and *activity*. The table is accessed through the call to activityListAtRank () in the fifth line of the above code.

The rankedCollab object has a simple recursive method for computing the rank of all activity objects. The rankedCollab object could safely cash the results because it is an observer of the network as a whole and can recompute the rank when necessary.

```
RankedCollab::public List<Activity> activityListAtRank(Integer rank) {
    List<Activity> activityListAtRank = new ArrayList<Activity>();
    for (Activity act : netBase. activities()) {
      if (rankOf(act) == rank) {
        activityListAtRank.add(act);
      }
    }
    // Hack. Sort to ensure always same diagram.
    Collections.sort(activityListAtRank, NAME_ORDER);
    return activityListAtRank;
}
```

5F. Example 2: Frontloading

Frontloading is the calculation of the earlyStart and earlyFinish for each activity given the start time of its predecessors. We see from figure 21 that actA and actB can both start when the project starts, e.g., in week 1. actA then finishes in week 2 and actB in week 7. We can now compute earlyStart and earlyFinish for actC. actD can finally be computed since we know the earlyFinish for both actC and actB. The result of the frontloading is shown in the Gantt diagram of figure 2.

The frontloading operation is traditionally distributed among the activity objects. A default method could look like the following:

```
Activity :: public void frontloadSimple (Integer projectStart) {
    earlyStart = projectStart;
    for(Activity pred : predecessors()) {
      earlyStart = Math.max(earlyStart, pred.earlyFinish() + 1);
    }
}
```

The problem with this simple solution is that the method cannot be triggered in an activity object before the earlyFinish of all predecessors are known. This means that the frontload network operation belongs in the inter-activity space and should be treated at a higher system level.

The common frontload logic could be in a method in the Model class, but I feel that this would be overloading a class that should be clean and simple. So the top level frontload () method is coded in a separate FrontloadAlgorithm class. Three problems need to be resolved:

1. Identifying activities that are ready to be planned is essentially a query on the Data objects. This work properly belongs in a collaboration class, here the FrontloadCollab class.
2. The earlyStart of an activity depends on all its predecessors and all modifiers such as activity overlap etc. This logic belongs in the inter-activity space and is here coded in the FrontloadAlgorithm class.
3. The earlyFinish of an activity once its earlyStart is known depends on the activity alone. The code, therefore, belongs in the Activity class.

I will discuss the coding of these actions in turn.

5F.1. FrontloadCollab, the Frontloading Collaboration

I have chosen a query-based solution to illustrate how a query result changes through the frontloading process. An activity is *ready to be loaded* if it is not yet loaded and if all its predecessors have been loaded. Here is the query that finds a candidate activity for frontloading expressed in an unspecified language:

```
define frontloader as
        (select act
        from Activities act
        where act.earlyStart == null and (
            for all pred in predecessors
                (pred.earlyStart != null )
        ) someInstance
```

The FrontloadCollab code is not trivial, but it is nicely isolated giving an attractive separation of concern. The complete code for class FrontloadCollab can be found on the enclosed CD.

5F.2. FrontloadAlgorithm, the Frontloading Interaction Algorithm

The frontload algorithm can be expressed in terms of the frontloader role and can loop until frontCollab fails to bind that role to an object. I can give the code to a colleague and ask her to audit and sign it. The frontloading interaction is implemented in the FrontloadAlgorithm class:

```
FrontloadAlgorithm::public void frontload (Integer startWeek) {
    .....
        Activity frontloader;
        while ((frontloader = frontloadCollab.frontloader()) != null) {
            Integer earlyStart = startWeek;
            for (Activity pred : frontloadCollab.frontPredecessors()) {
                earlyStart = Math.max (earlyStart, pred.earlyFinish() + 1);
            }
            frontloader.setEarlyStart(earlyStart);
        }
}
```

We see that frontCollab defines two roles; frontloader is the activity object being loaded, and frontPredecessors are its predecessor objects. The frontload code is pure algorithm with no confusing side issues. It is thus a good starting point for dealing with more complex situations.

5F.3. The Frontloading earlyFinish Algorithm in the Activity Class

The activity object is responsible for all activity properties and can compute its earlyFinish when the earlyStart is known:

```
public class Activity {
    private Integer earlyStart, earlyFinish, duration;
    ...
    public void setEarlyStart(Integer week) {
        earlyStart = week;
        earlyFinish = earlyStart + duration - 1;
    }
    ...
```

6. The BabyUML Laboratory

I am now entering upon a new stage in the BabyUML project and find it opportunely to restate the project goal:

The goal of the BabyUML project is to increase my confidence in my programs. The keywords are simplicity and leverage. Simplicity helps me to think clearly and a reader to understand and audit my code. Leverage lets me say more with less. The end result shall be a new interactive development environment with appropriate languages and tools for supporting high level abstractions.

The results reported in the previous sections have revealed the kind of abstractions that shall be parts of *BabyIDE*, the BabyUML integrated development environment

My completed experiments have clarified the notions of a *class* to describe the nature of an object and the notion of a *role* to describe its place in an interaction. I also have the notion of a *collaboration* to select the objects that play certain roles at certain times and in certain contexts. It is now time to turn to the tool. What does it take to create a tool that implements roles and classes on an equal level? The notion of a class is well covered in current programming languages, but the notion of a role is more elusive. I need to lift the role to the same level as the class; I already know how to bridge the gap between them.

The next stage is to experiment and try out novel semantics for classes and roles together with tools for design, compilation, debugging, and inspection.

In the Java network example, the roles were represented as attributes in collaboration classes and the queries were coded as regular methods in those classes. The notion of a role was in my head, not in the code. Another weakness was that the language for defining the DCA Data schema was regular Java where I would have preferred a declarative language. I need to experiment with different notions of classes, roles, components, and other concepts in my next move towards the BabyUML goal. I need a *BabyUML laboratory*.

The nature of an object is specified by the object's class; the object is an *instance of* that class. Different kinds of objects are instances of different classes. But the concept of a class is rigidly defined in the language specification of common object oriented languages such as Java. Contrast this with the Smalltalk stored program environment. Classes are here represented as regular objects. This means that the concept of a Smalltalk class is defined by *its* class, a metaclass. Classes and metaclasses come in pairs, the metaclass being responsible for static methods and variables. The notions of classes and metaclasses are defined in the default Smalltalk class library. I can complement them with my own versions by implementing my own ideas. The extreme flexibility of Smalltalk makes it an ideal foundation for my BabyIDE laboratory. This does not mean that a future BabyIDE product need be written in Smalltalk; the product can be written in any language based on a specification expressed as a Smalltalk prototype.

BabyIDE starts from a simpler basis where an object is an instance of a class, a class is an instance of *MetaSimpleclass*, this metaclass is an instance of *MetaMetaclass*, and *MetaMetaclass* is an instance of itself. Other kinds of classes will later be added by adding new metaclasses. The *instantiation hierarchy* is essential for understanding the nature of all objects.

A class may be subclass of another class that may be subclass of some other class, etc. This *class inheritance hierarchy* is useful for code reuse and, to a certain extent, for organizing the programmer's thoughts. The nature of an object is not influenced by the actual ordering of classes in a chain of superclasses because the chain can always be refactored into a single class as described in section 3B.

The instantiation and inheritance hierarchies are orthogonal. The human brain does not seem well equipped to deal with two hierarchies simultaneously, and the instantiation and inheritance hierarchies have been confused by better brains than mine. Yet progress in the BabyUML project depends upon alternative definitions of the concepts of class and metaclass. As a start, I have implemented the core objects of a BabyUML laboratory including my own versions of class and metaclass as a foundation for further experiments.

Section 6A describes what I mean by an integrated development environment as distinct from a modeling tool equipped with code generators. Section 6B introduces the BabyUML object notation. This is a notation for the run-time objects as distinct from the well known notation for compile-time classes as they appear in UML class diagrams. Section 6C describes the BabyUML laboratory as it is embedded within the Smalltalk stored program object computer. This section is somewhat detailed because I find that its careful attention to run-time objects is an excellent antidote to the potential confusion of instantiation and inheritance.

6A. The Integrated Development Environment

Nusse, the first Norwegian computer, was deployed in 1953. Its smallest addressable unit was a *word* of 32 bits. When I started programming in 1958, I met a computer where data and operations were indistinguishable in the computer memory; my programs typically modified themselves. I moved a word to the *accumulator register* and the computer treated it as an operand in an operation. I moved the same word to the *operation register* and the computer executed it. My mind-set was binary, my programs were written in binary, and I ran and inspected the programs from the binary console. There was an exact correspondence between the program in my mind and the bits in the computer. Figure 22 illustrates the situation. The man-machine system was harmonious because the same conceptual framework applied throughout my thinking, coding, debugging, and inspecting.

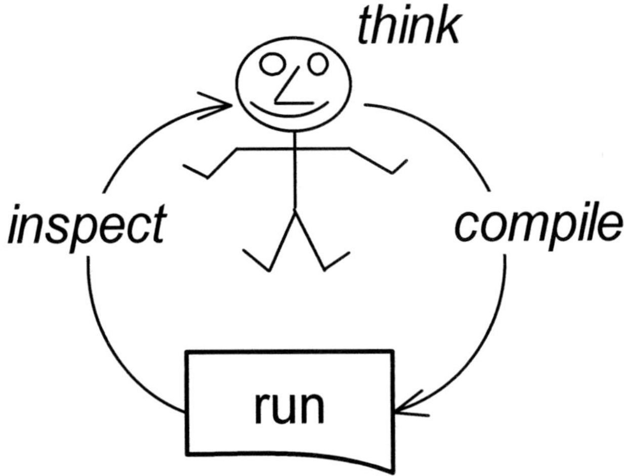

Figure 22. The programmer's mind and the computer.

I moved to larger computers and higher level languages. A gap opened between my mind and the realities of the computer. I thought in FORTRAN, I coded in FORTRAN, a compiler translated my code into binary, but the inspect path remained binary. Harmony was lost; I have spent innumerable hours debugging my FORTRAN programs by manually decoding pages of hexadecimal dumps.

The loop in figure 22 was again closed when the plain compilers grew into *integrated development environments*. First for FORTRAN, today I use the Java NetBeans IDE[19]. I think, code, inspect, debug, and even refactor a program within the conceptual framework of Java.

I introduced a new mismatch when I began thinking in terms of MVC and DCA. I had to translate my mental models into Java code, and then compile, inspect, and debug within the Java environment. My mental model was in my head only, and a Java expert reading my code couldn't possibly guess my models. I could comment the code, but the comments would clutter the code and often be misleading. Extensive documentation could help, but I can never promise to maintain exact correspondence between documentation and code. I am highly motivated to improve the code; comments and documentation can be fixed later.

I tried using an advanced UML modeling tool for creating the demo program. There were several difficulties that hindered me working exclusively in UML. The three most important were:

- The tool only implemented parts of the UML 2.0 definition. The first stumbling block was that it lacked a necessary feature in the UML sequence diagram.

[19] http://www.netbeans.org/

¤ The code generator was incomplete. The generated code was a mere skeleton; I had to fill in most of the code in Java. So much so that there was very little gain from using the additional tool for my simple problem and I quickly abandoned it.

These two difficulties can, in principle, be overcome with a more complete tool implementation. But the third is inherent in the idea of a model with a code generator:

¤ The code generator only transforms the model from UML to Java. I still have to inspect and debug in terms of Java. The correspondence with my MVC and DCA models is far from simple. Harmony is lost.

6B. The BabyIDE Object Notation

The BabyIDE is centered on objects and their interaction. Interacting objects can only see the *provided operations* of their collaborators. Conceptually, an object appears to encapsulate state and behavior. BabyIDE introduces new notations for objects. A notation for the external properties of an object is described in section 6B1. A notation for the object as a conceptual entity is described in section 6B2. The object implementation with class and superclasses is discussed in section 6C.

The notations presented here symbolize concrete objects with their identity, state, and behavior. The notations will later be modified to symbolize roles.

6B.1. The Encapsulated Object Notation

An object is encapsulated; it can only be accessed through its *provided operations*. Its attributes and methods are invisible from its environment. BabyIDE uses the *encapsulated object* notation shown in figure 23 to denote an object seen as a black box.

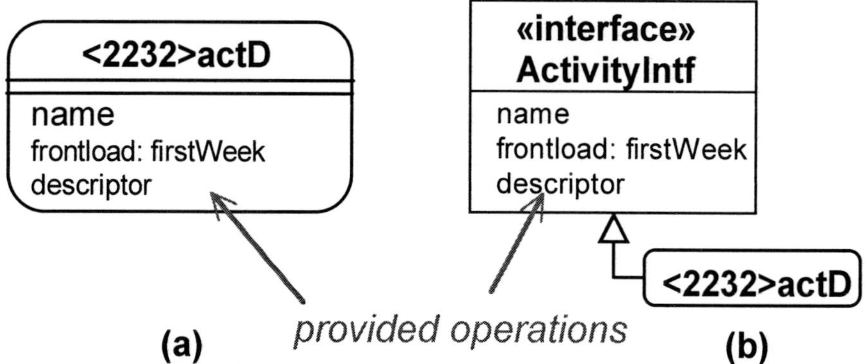

Figure 23. Examples of the encapsulated projection.

The BabyIDE notation for an object is a rounded rectangle; its corners are rounded to distinguish it from the UML classifier. An object has a unique identifier, the objectID that is shown in angle brackets <...>. Some objects have a name; this is then shown after the objectID. There are two equivalent notations. The inline form in figure 23 (a) is useful in simple diagrams. The compact form of figure 23 (b) uses the UML symbol for an interface to show provided operations. A tool can pop up the interface dynamically so as to save screen acreage.

Note that I use the Smalltalk syntax throughout this section. For example, name is equivalent to the Java name() method call.[20] The Smalltalk frontload: firstWeek is equivalent to the Java frontload(firstWeek).

The encapsulated object notation is useful in "wiring diagrams" showing structures of interlinked objects as illustrated in figure 24.

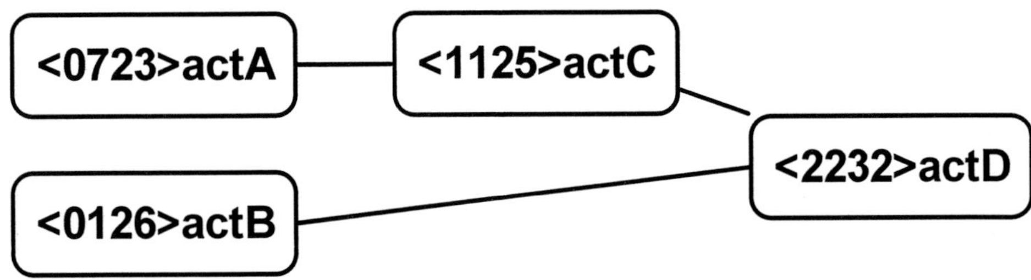

Figure 24. "Wired" objects implementing the planning network example.

6B.2. The Conceptual Object Notation

An object encapsulates state and behavior. We all know that many of the object's features are specified by its class and superclasses, but we shall not let it confuse us. It is the object that has state and behavior; it is the object that interacts with other objects. So we hide the classes and pretend that the object itself holds all that it encapsulates. The result is the *conceptual object*; very effective as a concept and very inefficient if naïvely implemented. We again use a rounded rectangle to denote an object and get the white box view of figure 25. We see selected object features, but we do not see how they are implemented. The conceptual object has three compartments:

- The top compartment shows the objectID <2232> together with a possible name.
- The middle compartment shows some or all of the names and values of the object's instance variables.
- The bottom compartment shows some or all of the operations. A tool could also show the code that implements a selected operation so that it can be inspected and edited.

[20]In Java, name is a reference to the corresponding instance variable. Instance variables are invisible from outside the object in Smalltalk, so name must here necessarily be an operation.

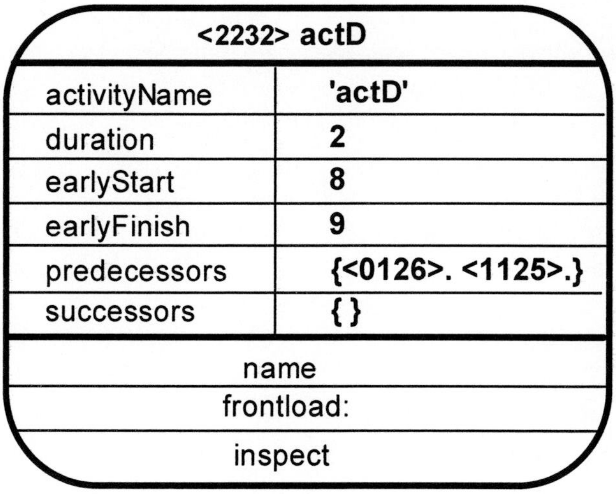

<2232> actD
activityName
'actD'
duration
2
earlyStart
8
earlyFinish
9
predecessors
{<0126>. <1125>.}
successors
{}
name
frontload:
inspect

Figure 25. Example conceptual, white box object projection.

6C. The Smalltalk Stored Program Object Computer

Smalltalk [9] is the ideal proving ground for BabyIDE. The Smalltalk notions of class, method, programming language and programming tools are all realized by objects. A new class is created by sending the message new to its *metaclass*; another object. The code for a method is translated from its text form to byte codes by a compiler method that is part of the class object. This means that BabyIDE can implement its own notions of programs, programming languages and tools by simply replacing the Smalltalk library classes with alternative ones.

In this section, I give a detailed description of how objects and classes are implemented in the default Smalltalk class library. I need this deep understanding of the default Smalltalk way before I can safely create my own variants of almost any of the Smalltalk library classes for the purposes of my new BabyIDE.

Smalltalk Object Space (Image)
<1>object1
<2>object2
<3>object3
<4>class1
<5>metaclass3
Smalltalk
Virtual Machine (VM)

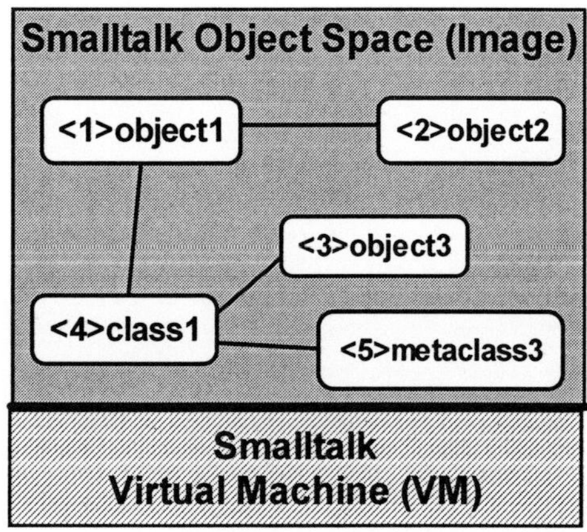

Figure 26. The Smalltalk stored program virtual object computer.

Figure 26 shows Smalltalk as a virtual, stored program, object computer. *Object*, because all data are represented as objects; even Booleans, numbers, and characters; classes and methods; stacks and activation records; inspectors and debuggers. *Virtual*, because it is realized in software by the *Smalltalk Virtual Machine (VM)*. *Stored program* because programs are represented as regular objects.

Smalltalk objects are stored in the Object Space, the *image*. The VM creates a new object when told to do so by a class method; returning the objectID of the new object so it can later be the receiver of messages. The VM also removes objects as they become unreachable (garbage collection).

The bytes representing an object are stored on the computer's memory heap. It would be ridiculously inefficient if all the features of an object should be stored in every object. The <2232>actD object only stores its state values as indicated on a white background in figure 27. In addition, the object has a number of hidden values, the most important being its identity and a link to the class object. The rest is delegated to the class and superclass objects as illustrated in the figure.

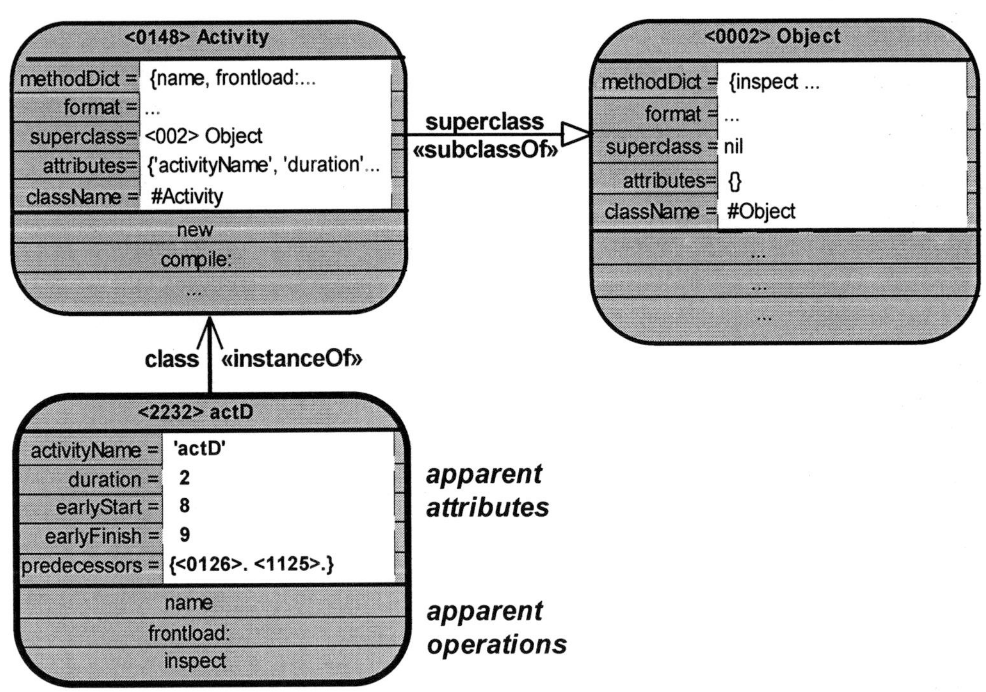

Figure 27. Implementation of the example object.

The objects in figure 27 are as follows:

- The object that is in the center of our interest has objectID=<2232> and stores the values 'actD', 2, 8, 9, {<0126>. <1125>.}
- The <2232>actD object is an instance of class *Activity*, represented in the <0148>Activity object. This class object has a link to its superclass, <0002>Object. The superclass of <0002>Object is nil, thus terminating the superclass chain.

- ¤ The names of the object's attributes are the union of the attributes attribute of the class and all its superclasses. They are shown on a gray background in the middle portion of the <2232>actD conceptual object.
- ¤ The object's operations are a union of the operations defined in the methodDict attribute of the class and all its superclasses. The operations are shown in the bottom portion of the <2232>actD object. A tool can display the corresponding methods.
- ¤ The figure shows clearly how the «instanceOf» relation essentially defines the object's semantics, while the exact distribution of feature definitions along the «subclassOf» relations is irrelevant to the object and thus is in the nature of a comment.

A class object has a methodDict attribute that binds operations (selectors) to the corresponding CompiledMethod objects. A CompiledMethod object contains a sequence of VM instructions (byte codes) and also a link to the corresponding source code. There are byte codes for getting and setting attribute values as well as for sending messages to specified objects.

Object behavior is activated when an object receives a message. The message is an object with attributes for sender, receiver, message selector (operation) and actual parameters. The VM locates the receiver's class object and looks up its methodDict dictionary to find the corresponding CompiledMethod. If not found, it recursively tries the methodDict of the superclasses. If this search fails, the VM starts the search anew with the default selector doesNotUnderstand: aMessage. The search will never fail because the doesNotUnderstand:-method is defined in the root class. Once the search has succeeded, the VM creates an activation record (an object) and puts it on the stack (another object). It then begins executing the method's byte codes in the context of the activation record. The method's byte codes can send a message to an identified receiver object, and the story repeats itself.

The <2232>actD object responds to the frontload: operation. The corresponding method is stored in the methodDict attribute of the <0148>Activity class object. The <2232>actD object also responds to the inspect method that is stored in the <0002>Object class object. Both of them are visible to the collaborators of the <2232>actD object as bona fide operations on that object.

There are two important kinds of relationships in figure 27; the «instanceOf» and the «subclassOf» relationships. The implementation of an object consists of one «instanceOf» relation to its class object, followed by any number of «subclassOf» relations up the superclass chain. The two kinds of relations can easily be confused by the unwary. For example, the features of the <2232>actD object are stored in attributes in its class object, <0148>Activity with its superclasses. Correspondingly, the features of the <0148>Activity class object are stored in attributes of *its* class object, its *metaclass* (not shown in figure 27). I look at an object; its features are in the attributes of its class object. I look at the class object; *its* features are in the attributes of the metaclass. This characteristic of "everything is stored somewhere else" is a potential source of extreme confusion. It is here that the BabyUML conceptual object notation proves its worth by showing state and behavior where they belong conceptually, rather than where they happen to be stored.

It is hard to see where the UML class symbol fits in. It does not symbolize the instance, because the instance is a merger of all classes in the superclass chain. It is does not symbolize the class object, because the features shown in the UML symbol are not the features of the class object.

In my first BabyIDE experiment, I tried to realize a stored program object computer by simply instantiating the UML metaclasses to get my stored program class objects. I failed because there is a fundamental difference between UML class diagram and the corresponding run-time objects. Take the notion of a *link*. In UML, it is defined by three interlinked elements: anAssociationEnd, anAssociation, and anotherAssociationEnd. These three model elements form the high level description of a run-time binary link that can be realized as a pair of instance variables. The model elements must be compiled into the run-time objects; instantiating UML metaclasses to get run-time objects simply does not work. I abandoned this first, naïve approach and accepted that I must clearly distinguish between compile-time and run-time in my experiments.

The conclusion was that the UML class symbol represents the source code and is inappropriate for describing run-time objects in a stored program object computer. The motivation for introducing the BabyIDE object notation discussed in section 3B was to resolve this difficulty.

The <0148>Activity class object has its own provided operations with the corresponding methods. In the default Smalltalk implementation, it responds to the message compile: sourceCode. The corresponding method is a compiler that translates the sourceCode into a CompiledMethod and installs it into the methodDict for later execution by an instance of this class. In BabyIDE, I will use this feature to provide different compilers for different languages, new or old. The CompiledMethod object has a link to its sourceCode, thus making it feasible to close the loop of figure 22.

6D. The BabyUML Laboratory Implementation

I argued for the choice of Smalltalk for implementing BabyIDE in section 6C. The choice of its Squeak dialect [25] was harder. It is fairly easy to learn the semantics and syntax of the Smalltalk programming language, but it can be frustrating to become familiar with its pragmatics and class libraries. Squeak is even more frustrating because it is evolving very rapidly and any release includes a large number of undocumented features in different states of completion. But the advantages far outweigh the objections:

- The most important argument is that there is a very active and creative community around Squeak. Many ideas that can be applied to BabyIDE are to be found in the Squeak mailing lists and the evolving class and package libraries.
- Squeak is open source; there are no obstacles to the distribution of the BabyIDE laboratory to anybody who might want to experiment with it.
- The Squeak VM is also open source; the program is written in a subset of Smalltalk and automatically translated to C. This means that it is feasible to modify the BabyIDE VM if necessary.

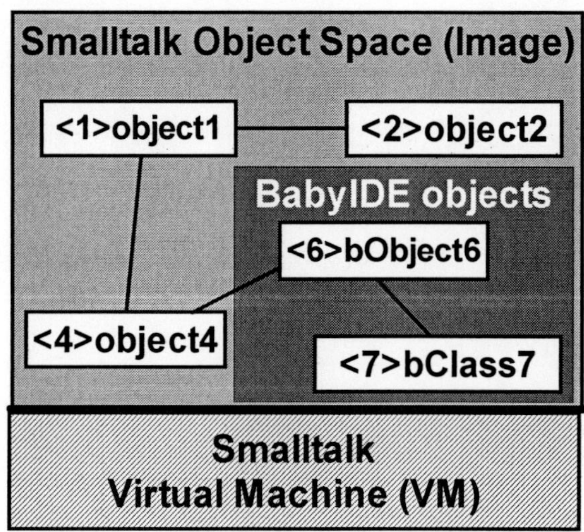

Figure 28. The BabyIDE laboratory is embedded in the Smalltalk object space.

Figure 28 illustrates the BabyIDE implementation. The baby objects have their own classes, metaclasses, and metametaclasses; but they can freely interoperate with regular Smalltalk objects because they all conform to the VM conventions.

6D.1. The BabyIDE Layered Architecture

Classes and metaclasses come in pairs in regular Smalltalk. The class object holds the properties of its instances. The corresponding metaclass is needed to hold the features of the class object itself such as static attributes and methods. Many Smalltalk novices find it hard to distinguish between regular and static attributes and methods. In BabyIDE, I initially remove the notion of static attributes and methods from the core classes. There is no loss of

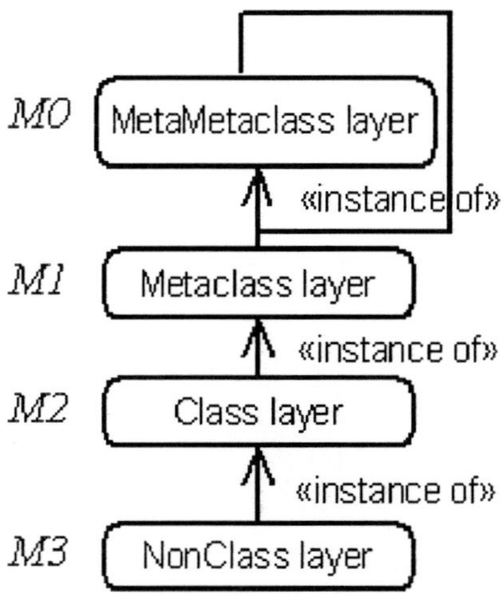

Figure 29. The BabyIDE Instantiation Architecture.

generality; I can always implement the notions of shared features at a higher abstraction level. The result is a set of clear core constructs that let me explore new languages and tools for my new discipline of programming.

Every object is an instance of a class. This is implemented by every object having a link to its class object. The class is represented by an object that has a link to *its* class object, the metaclass. Finally, the metaclass object has a link to the metametaclass which is an instance of itself. This idea of a layered architecture is fundamental to BabyIDE semantics, but the exact number of layers depends on circumstances. The core layers from the concrete to the abstract are shown in figure 29:

M3 - Non-class layer: Here are the non-class objects, typically domain and support objects.

M2 - Class layer: Here are the regular classes. Class objects create new instances, act as repositories for information common to these instances, and know how to translate code from a human form to executable binary.

M1 - Metaclass layer: Metaclass objects are class objects that have classes as their instances. They serve as repositories for the features that are common to their instances; i.e., a set of classes of the same kind. This ensures that BabyIDE is genuinely extendable because different sets of classes can have different compiles, inspectors, etc.

M0 - MetaMetaclass layer: There is a single object in this layer; it is called MetaMetaclass. Directly or indirectly, all BabyIDE objects are instances of this class. MetaMetaclass is an instance of itself so it had to be created by a somewhat tricky program.

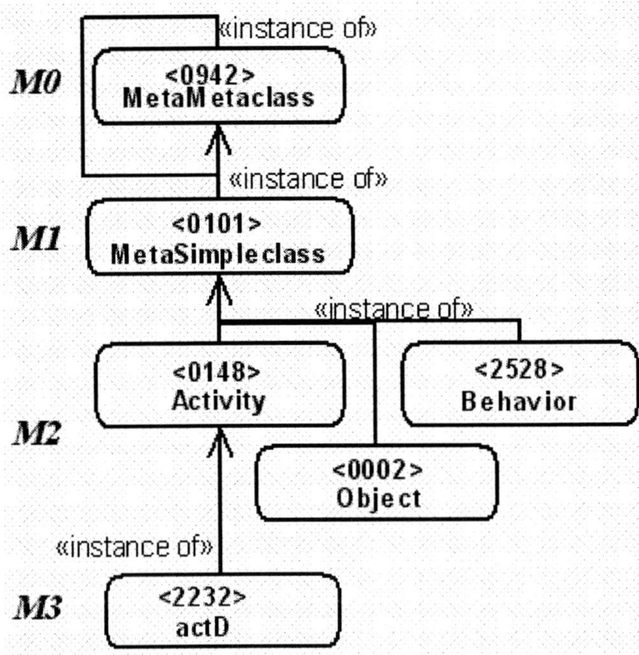

Figure 30. The example instantiation structure.

Note that the BabyIDE layered architecture is an *instantiation* hierarchy, the implementation of the <2232>actD object with its class and metaclasses is shown in figure 30.

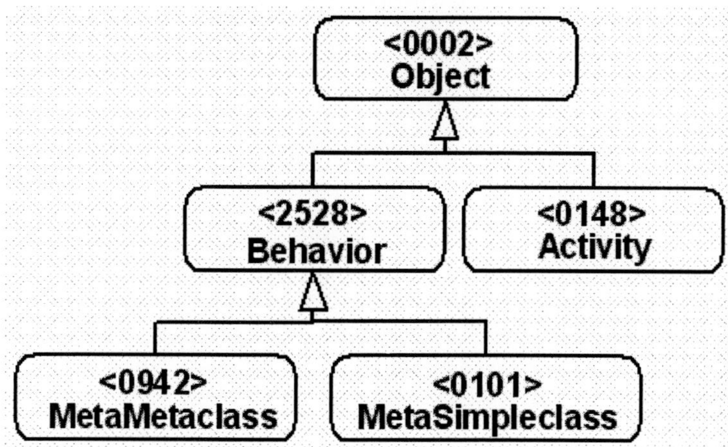

Figure 31. The example inheritance structure.

The orthogonal *class inheritance hierarchy* is a very powerful device for code reuse and code sharing. Figure 31 shows the inheritance hierarchy of the same network example. This particular solution is not very interesting because the inheritance hierarchy can be refactored without changing the system semantics. We particularly notice that it bears no relationship to the instantiation hierarchy of figure 30.

The human mind is well equipped for dealing with a hierarchy, but it finds it harder to handle two of them simultaneously. BabyIDE will gain its power and extensibility by exploiting both the instantiation and the inheritance hierarchies. But this should be isolated to the toolmaker's domain; application programmers should only see a single hierarchy that supports powerful concepts provided by the toolmakers.

6D.2. Example Implementation of the Class Layer

Figure 32 shows the actual objects that represent the <0148>Activity class. Note that I am using the conceptual object notation for the objects. A diagram showing all the objects would be a complete mess.

Note that the <0148>Activity class object responds to its own messages such as new and compile:. The corresponding methods are found in the methodDict of <2528>Behavior. Further note that <0101>MetaSimpleclass responds to its own versions of new and compile:. We have to look at the class of <0101>MetaSimpleclass to find the corresponding methods. They may or may not be identical to the <0148>Activity methods.

The theory is simple, but the actual realization gets rather complicated. It is a challenge to device concepts and tools that leverage the potential while hiding the complexity.

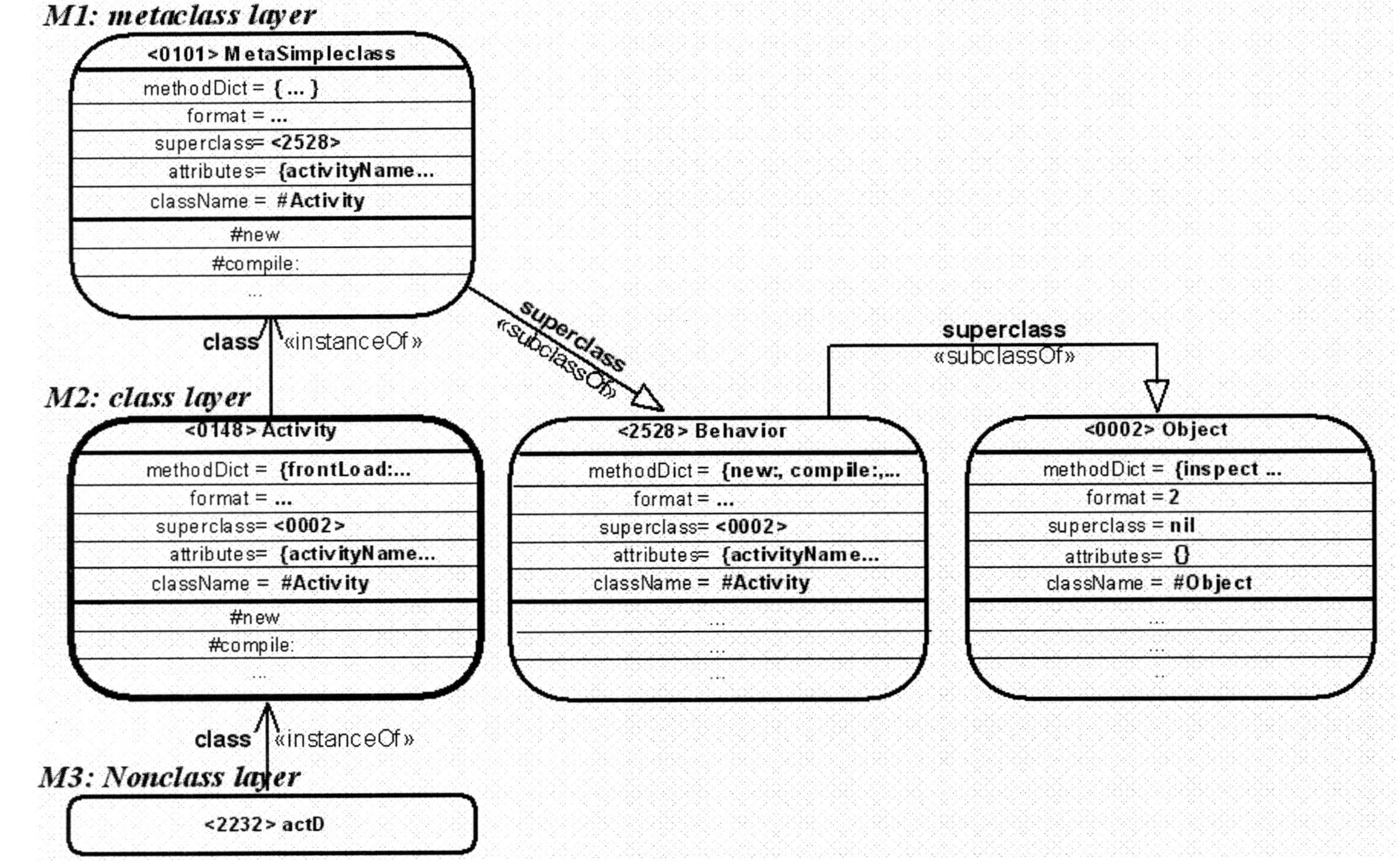

Figure 32. Implementation of the <0148>Activity class.

7. Conclusion

The BabyUML vision is that I shall regain the mastery of my programs by making them *"so simple that there are obviously no deficiencies"*. Early on, it became clear that a solution would have to focus on the inter-object space where we see the objects, the links between them and their interactions. Role modeling provides abstractions for explicitly describing those aspects of object systems, but modeling is not coding. The missing link was the bridge between the roles and the classes.

In a conversation with Kai Fredriksen[1], something he said gave me an aha! *The bridge is a query that finds the object(s) currently playing the role!* This lead to the unification between the role and class abstractions as depicted in figure 7.

I have done a quick Smalltalk implementation of the activity network example of section 2 and spent some time finding a neat way of storing and accessing collaborations with their roles and queries. This led to an interesting observation. An object belongs on the memory heap because it is meaningful until it is garbage collected. A collaboration with its role/object mappings appears to belong on the execution stack because it is only meaningful during an actual interaction. This observation could be the promising start of an interesting investigation.

An early idea was that a database-oriented architecture can be applied to the interior of a composite object. Figure 9 depicts the architecture of the Autokon CAD/CAM system that we deployed at the Norwegian *Stord Yard* in 1963. I believe this was the world's first software product with a database-oriented architecture, and it would be gratifying if the DCA paradigm will prove to be the world's first application of the same architecture in the context of an object.

The MVC has been well known since Jim Althoff and others implemented their own version in the Smalltalk-80 class library. In section 4, I have for the first time described my original MVC idea roughly as it was presented in the original technical notes at Xerox PARC. [10]

The end result of the BabyUML project shall be BabyIDE, a new interactive development environment with appropriate languages and tools for supporting the BabyUML high level abstractions. The role/class unification, the DCA architecture of complex objects, and the MVC as described here form a foundation for further experiments. What remains to be done is to specify, design, and implement BabyIDE. Its top level architecture is compactly expressed in figure 12, where the computer acts as an extension of the user's brain. Seen in this perspective, application programmers are the users of the tools that shall be created in the next experiment. The MVC and DCA paradigms will be the metamodels of the programmer's perception of a program and the corresponding program descriptions in the computer. This will give added leverage, improved program readability, and reduced program volume. MVC and DCA are but examples; BabyIDE shall be extensible so that it can support many different paradigms, making it an example of Coplien's *multi paradigm design.* [22]

A *first experiment* was to naïvely instantiate the UML metaclasses to get the run-time objects in my stored program object computer. This experiment failed as described in section 6C.

---

[1] See [21].

A *second experiment* was to implement my own versions of class and method objects in Smalltalk. This forced me to go deeply into the nature of objects and the fundamental difference between instantiation and generalization. The result was the *BabyIDE laboratory* as reported in section 6. This laboratory forms a powerful and conceptually simple foundation for further development.

I tried to continue the second experiment by populating the BabyIDE laboratory with high level programming tools, but quickly realized that I could not design and build the tools before I fully understood what they were to achieve, i.e., the interacting run-time objects.

The *third experiment* was done in order to create concrete examples of the desired results of the initial BabyIDEs. This *activity network* experiment was done in Java for two reasons. One was to decouple IDE issues from the structures themselves. The other was to communicate some of the BabyUML ideas to a broader community. The result was the MVC and DCA paradigms reported in sections 4 and 5. I believe these paradigms have a value in themselves in addition to being input to the next BabyIDE experiment.

The results of the *fourth experiment* will be decisive. In it, I will return to the BabyIDE laboratory and create high level tools for programming and documenting systems that follow paradigms such as DCA and MVC. I will clearly need to harness imperative, algorithmic programming as well as the declarative definition of data structures and queries. I will need class oriented programming to define the nature of the objects and I will need role model programming to define their interaction. I will also need new debuggers and inspectors to close the loop of figure 22. A great deal of work is needed, and it is probably far in excess of what can be achieved by a single programmer (me) working alone. So I hope that other people will be inspired to pick up the loose ends from my ideas and experiments to create new and interesting results. There might even be an adventurous person who will join me in realizing the BabyIDE vision.

Acknowledgements

The idea and implementation of the Smalltalk stored program object computer is due to Alan Kay, Dan Ingalls, Adele Goldberg and the Learning Research Group at Xerox PARC. UML is the combined result of a great number of people. Taken together, they have unified and documented a large number of powerful concepts for modeling large systems of interacting objects. I am grateful to Dan Ingalls for helping me create my own class, metaclass, metametaclass and method objects in Squeak. Many thanks to Ragnar Norman for sharing his deep understanding of database technology and for helping me force my brain to think in declarative terms without immediately translating to my usual imperative style. (I apologize for any misrepresentations of his advice). My sincere thanks to Johannes Brodwall for his intelligent support and advice on Java technology. I also thank Øystein Haugen for his thorough commenting of an earlier draft of this chapter.

References

[1] James S. Huggin. J. S. First Computer Bug. [web page] http://www.jamesshuggins.com/h/tek1/ first_computer_bug.htm

[2] Naur, P.; Randell, B. (Ed) Software Engineering. Report on a conference sponsored by the NATO Science Committee. Garmisch, October 1968. Scientific Affairs Division, NATO, Brussels 39, Belgium. p 16.

[3] Hoare, C. A. R.: The Emperor's Old Clothes. 1980 Turing Award lecture. *Comm.ACM* vol24-81, 2 (Feb. 1981)

[4] Dijkstra, E. D. 1930–2002. Structured programming. E. W. Dijkstra Archive, University of Texas, Document EWD268 [web page] http://www.cs.utexas.edu/users/ EWD/transcriptions/EWD02xx/ EWD268.html

[5] Dijkstra, E. D. The next fifty years. E. W. Dijkstra Archive, University of Texas, Document EWD1243a. [web page] http://www.cs.utexas.edu/users/EWD/ transcriptions/EWD12xx/EWD1243a.html

[6] Reenskaug, T.; Wold, P.; Lehne, O.A. *Working with objects. The OOram Software Engineering Method*; Manning; Greenwich, CT, 1996; Out of print. Early version at [web page] http:// heim.ifi.uio.no/~trygver/1996/book/WorkingWithObjects.pdf

[7] *UML Superstructure Specification, v2.0;* OMG, Needham, MA; 2005. [web page] http:// www.omg.org/cgi-bin/doc?formal/2005-07-04

[8] Reenskaug, T. *Applications and Technologies for Maritime and Offshore Industries.* In Bubenko, J. A. Jr.; Impagliazzo, J.; Sølvberg, A.; Eds.; *History of Nordic Computing*; ISBN 0-387-24167-1, ISSN 1571-5736 (Print), 1861-2288 (Online); Springer; Boston, MA, 2005; pp 369-390. [Weblink] http://dx.doi.org/10.1007/0-387-24168-X_34

[9] Goldberg, A,; Robson, D. *Smalltalk-80. The language and its implementation;* ISBN 0-201-11371-6; Addison-Wesley; Reading, MA, 1983

[10] Reenskaug, T. (1979) The original MVC reports. [web page] http://urn.nb.no/URN:NBN:no-14314

[11] Birtwistle, G. M.; Dahl, O.; Nygaard, K. *Simula begin.* ISBN 91-44-06211-7; Studentlitteratur; Lund, Sweden, 1973.

[12] Reenskaug, T. *Prokon/Plan. A Modelling Tool for Project Planning and Control.* In Gilchrist, B.; Ed.; *Information Processing 77, Proceedings of the IFIP Congress 77*; North-Holland; Amsterdam, Holland, 1977; pp 717-721

[13] Wirfs-Brock, R.; McKean, A. *Object Design. Roles, Responsibilities, and Collaborations*. ISBN 0-201-37943-0; Addison-Wesley; Boston, MA, 2003.

[14] Wirfs-Brock, R. J.; Johnson, R. E. Surveying Current Research in Object-Oriented Design. *Comm ACM.* 33 9 (Septeber 1990) 104-124.

[15] Reenskaug, T.; et.al. ORASS: seamless support for the creation and maintenance of object-oriented systems. *JOOP*, 5 6 (October 1992), 27-41.

[16] Andersen, E. P. *Conceptual Modeling of Objects. A Role Modeling Approach.* D.Scient thesis, November 1997, University of Oslo. [web page] http://heim.ifi.uio.no/ ~trygver/1997/EgilAndersen/ConceptualModelingOO.pdf]

[17] Gamma et.al. *Design Patterns;* ISBN 0-201-63361-; Addison-Wesley, Reading, MA. 1995.

[18] Krasner, G.; Pope, S.T. A Cookbook for Using the Model-View Controller User Interface in Smalltalk-80. *JOOP* 1 3(Aug./Sept. 1988), 26-49

[19] *IFIP-ICC Vocabulary of Information Processing;* North-Holland, Amsterdam, Holland. 1966.

[20] Sun Microsystems. *The Java tutorial, What is an object.* [web page] http://java.sun.com/docs/ books/tutorial/java/concepts/object.html

[21] Fredriksen, K. *UMLexe - UML virtual machine : a framework for model execution.* M.Sc. thesis, University of Oslo, 2005. [web page] http://urn.nb.no/URN:NBN:no-14309

[22] Coplien, J. *Multi Paradigm Design for C++*; ISBN: 0-201-82467-1; Addison-Wesley Professional, 1998,

[23] Kiczales, G.; Lamping, J.; Mendhekar, A.; Maeda, C.; Lopes, C., V.: Loingtier, J.; Irwin, J. (1997) *Aspect-Oriented Programming.* In Goos, G.; Hartmanis, J.; van Leeuwen, J. (Eds.) Proc. ECCOP 1977; Springer-Verlag 1997; ISSN 302-9743, DOI 10.1007/BFb0053371, ISBN 3-540-63089-9

[24] Hysing, T.; Reenskaug, T. *A System for Computer Plate Preparation.* Numerical Methods Applied to Shipbuilding. A NATO Advanced Study Institute. Oslo-Bergen, 1963.

[25] *Squeak.* [web page] http://www.squeak.org/

In: Computer Software Engineering Research
Editor: Ari D. Klein, pp. 89-110
ISBN 1-60021-774-5

Chapter 3

TOWARDS A REQUIREMENTS-DRIVEN COMPONENT BASED SOFTWARE DEVELOPMENT

Miguel A. Martinez, Ambrosio Toval (1) *
Manuel F. Bertoa and Antonio Vallecillo (2) †
(1) Computer and Systems Department. University of Murcia, Spain
(2) Languages and Computer Science Department. University of Malaga, Spain

Abstract

Requirements Engineering (RE) is a very active and decisive field of Software Engineering (SE). In this chapter our research aims to define a components selection method whose development is fast, agile and requirements driven. We try to ensure that an exact correspondence exists between the requirements and the architecture (components) and to raise the abstraction level in the development. In order to do so, it is necessary to us study the state-of-the-art of the main approaches of components selection that pay special attention to the system requirements. In addition, we present the preliminary ideas for a possible proposal for this aim within the framework of the RE SIREN method. The final aim of our proposal is to achieve a RE method that guides the selection, the development and the composition of a set of independent software components, and whose application is the simplest possible. This approach can be used in any Information System (IS) in general, and some simple examples related to the domain of the electronic mail applications are provided.

1. Introduction

Several experimental studies [1, 2, 3] have shown that the main problems in the development areas and software production are in the specification and the customer requirements and operation surroundings management.

There is also wide acceptance [4, 5] of the benefits that the reusability contributes and how these increase when the abstraction level is increased, and not only code but specifications and designs also are reused.

*E-mail address: mmart@um.es; atoval@um.es
†E-mail address: bertoa@lcc.uma.es; av@lcc.uma.es

Component-based Software Engineering (CBSE) also allows us to reuse pieces of previously elaborated code (software component) so that the system requirements are satisfied. The benefits of the CBSE, in addition to a reduction in the cost and the delivery times, are mainly:

1. A greater level of software reusability is attained.
2. It simplifies the tests. It allows the tests to be executed by first testing each one of the components before testing the complete set of assembled components.
3. It simplifies the maintenance of the system. When a weak link between components exists, the developer is free to update and/or to add components accordingly, without affecting other parts of the system.
4. Greater quality. Since a component can be built and then continuously improved by an expert or organization, the quality of an application based on components will improve with the passage of time.

In both disciplines, i.e. RE and CBSE, a common problem is the need to be able to select both requirements and components with different purposes, and one of the critical processes of the CBSE is the components selection which will comprise of the final product and which must fulfil the functional requirements defined by the user [6].

In the development process in CBSE [7] (identification, evaluation, selection, integration and update of the components), the requirements are the most important part for any effective COTS (Commercial Off-The-Shelf) components acquisition. Requirements will give the criteria to evaluate and select the component candidates, and even provide acceptance criteria that the client will use to verify if the given product satisfies his needs [8].

A crucial aspect, and that will be the center of attention of our research, is the importance of requirements when "rapid" software developments are carried out, since these are the key to success in this type of developments.

The aim of this chapter is, therefore, to identify the main proposals in the literature of components selection techniques that pay special attention, in one way or another, to the system requirements. To do so, we must make an exhaustive study of the literature on the main components selection approaches, which pay special attention to system requirements.

From the point of view of the state-of-the-art, in this chapter we have considered the most important proposals in the literature, but to obtain our final aim, we pursue a very simple direct process model, reducing the number of intermediate artifacts/activities to the minimum.

The final aim, although beyond the scope of this chapter, is to put forward a proposal for a selection method, and to identify the technology and mechanisms necessary to tackle the components selection problem for a system under construction from the corresponding requirements and considering all the links, interactions and possible contradictions with other system requirements.

In section 2. we show the main approaches identified as regards components selection techniques. Section 3. shows, as an example, a possible very basic selection method, within the SIREN framework, to illustrate the type of procedures sought and, finally, in section 4. we give the conclusions and further work.

2. Components Selection Techniques

In CBSE, the evaluation and early selection of the COTS candidates is one of the key aspects in the life cycle of the systems development. The success depends to a great extent on the correct understanding of the initial candidates components capacities and limitations. In addition, the requirements specification need to be much more flexible than in classic software development, which are less specific, and, in fact, with no guarantee that a COTS component can satisfy all the requirements, or even that some of COTS components include characteristics that originally are not required.

The use of the COTS, and therefore the CBSE, introduces new risks and problems for the software engineers, as for example a great difficulty in selecting the desired components (when the number of component candidates is reduced) and an insufficient analysis of the requirements (when new customer requirements are acquired) [7, 9].

Four dimensions are identified in [7] that should be considered during the selection phase:

1. Domain coverage. The components must provide all or part of the required capabilities necessary to satisfy core essential customer requirements. Among these requirements, nonfunctional requirements play a critical role during the evaluation process, improving the discrimination process between the COTS components that have already satisfied the core functional requirements.

2. Time restriction. Software companies usually operate within a very rigid development schedule, and the selection activity consumes a considerable amount of time to find and search all the potential COTS candidates.

3. Costs rating. The available budget is an important variable. The expenses when selecting COTS will be influenced by factors such as: cost of support, license acquisition, adaptation expenses, maintenance prices, etc.

4. Vendor guaranties. Some issues have to be taken into account, for example: vendor reputation and maturity, number and kind of applications that already use the COTS, characteristics related with the maintenance licenses, etc.

A successful selection and an effective integration of COTS components is problematic for, among others, the following reasons [7]:

- Lack of well defined process. The development team of a project, often does not have the time or the sufficient experience to plan the selection process in detail, so they do not use the most appropriate methods.

- Evaluation criteria. Sometimes evaluators include inappropriate attributes in the criteria and do not provide detailed specification discriminative attributes.

- Black-box nature of COTS components. Lack of access to component source code makes the understanding of components a hard task.

- Continuous COTS components updates. Rapid changes in the components marketplace and user needs makes COTS evaluation difficult.

- Lack of attention to the application requirements.

There are currently three strategies in COTS evaluation [7]:

1. Selection strategies. Products are evaluated against a key characteristic, such as vendor or type of technology.
2. Progressive filtering. Strategy whereby a COTS component is selected from a larger set of potential candidates, in which components that do not satisfy the evaluation criteria are progressively eliminated from the list.
3. Puzzle assembly model. A valid COTS solution will require fitting the various components of the system together.

The selection process initially decomposes the requirements for the selection of COTS components into a hierarchical criteria set. The criteria usually include functional requirements, non-functional requirements (reliability, portability, integrability, etc.), architecture constraints and other non-technical factors such as vendor guarantees and legal issues. During the selection activity, the properties of each COTS candidate are identified and evaluated according to this set of evaluation criteria [7].

Most of the processes and techniques of selection of existing components support the components selection, in an individual and independent way. Nevertheless, in real world applications, the decision to select a single component is not very habitual and usually depends on which other components are selected [10].

In most activities of components selection, it is difficult to determine sequences of low level processes to obtain high level objectives. For example, the information about customer requirements, components and suppliers, is often not available in the order in which it would be needed. Therefore, the sequence of acquisition, analysis and process of decision making cannot be ordered in advance. In addition, the information acquisition processes and components selection, are frequently interlaced, and the successful ending of one of them often depends on the successful ending of the other.

An additional problem in this type of activities, which seriously limits the use of these techniques in the industry, is that there are not so many components available on the market that are really useful, and those that are available the type of information provide by the vendor (especially non-functional) is insufficient and of little use for adequate selections.

2.1. Main Techniques of Components Selection

2.1.1. Off-The-Shelf Option (OTSO)

The OTSO method, was developed in 1996 by J. Kontio [11]. This method supports the search, evaluation and selection of reusable software, and provides specific techniques for defining the evaluation criteria, comparing the costs and benefits of the different alternatives, and consolidating the evaluation results for decision making.

The OTSO method was developed to facilitate a systematic, repeatable and requirements-driven COTS selection process. The main principles of this method are the following:

- Explicit definitions of tasks in the selection process, including entry and exit criteria.
- Definition of evaluation criteria in an incremental, hierarchical and detailed way.
- A model for comparing the costs and value associated with each alternative, making them comparable with each other.
- Use of appropriate decision making methods to analyze and summarize evaluation results.

The main phases of the OTSO method [12] are the following:

1. Search. The search in the selection process attempts to identify and find the potential candidates for reuse. The search is driven by the guidelines and criteria defined in the criteria definition process.
2. Screening. The aim of the screening process is to decide which alternatives should be selected for more detailed evaluation.
3. Evaluation. The aim of this process is to evaluate the alternatives selected by the evaluation criteria.
4. Analysis of Results. The aim of the analysis of results process is the decision making.
5. Deployment. Use of the alternative selected to develop the software product with COTS.
6. Assessment. To evaluate how good the COTS reuse decision was, with the aim of learning for future selections of COTS.

As regards the evaluation criteria definition process, basically what it does is decompose the requirements for the COTS into a hierarchical criteria set. Each branch in this hierarchy ends in an evaluation attribute. The criteria set is specific for each COTS selection case, but most of these can be classified into four great groups: functional requirements for the COTS; required quality characteristics (reliability, maintainability, portability); business concerns (cost, reliability of the vendor) and important aspects of the architecture (constraints presented by the operating system, specific communication mechanisms between modules).

In respect to the analysis of qualitative evaluation data, the OTSO method relies on the use of AHP (Analytic Hierarchy Process) method [13] for consolidating the evaluation data for decision making purposes.

These two aspects (evaluation criteria definition and analysis of evaluation data) are validated in [11] by means of a case study, related to the development of systems that integrate Earth environmental data from satellites, and to the fact that they must be available to scientists all over the world.

2.1.2. Procurement-Oriented Requirements Engineering (PORE)

The PORE method, was developed in 1999 by Cornelius Ncube and Neil Maiden [8] and it supports RE and the components evaluation/selection process in the CBSE development process.

The basic PORE life-cycle process model has six generic processes. These processes are defined at three levels: Universal Level, World Level and Atomic Level.

For example, the six generic Universal Level PORE processes (although not all the processes are performed during each product procurement) are the following:

- Management of System. The aims of this process are to plan and control the procurement process in order to fulfil the needs of the purchaser in time and at a reasonable cost. This process is developed during the whole life-cycle of the method, simultaneously with the rest of processes.
- Requirements Acquisition. This process acquires and validates customer quality requirements. Furthermore, it determines the system architecture so that new components can be integrated in it.
- Supplier Selection. Their aims are establish supplier selection criteria, evaluate suppliers, rank them according to the criteria and select the best-fit supplier.
- Software Packages/Components Selection. The aim of this process is to identify candidate packages (components), establish selection criteria using customer requirements, evaluate the identified components, rank them according to the criteria and to select one or more from those that best fulfil the core essential customer requirements.
- Contract Production. Its aim is to negotiate the legal contract with software components suppliers and resolve the legal issues related to purchasing and licensing.
- Package/Component Acceptance. The aim of this process is to check that the delivered package, component or market system fulfils the core essential customer requirements.

PORE, uses an iterative process of requirements acquisition and components selection/evaluation. The iterative process of components selection is based on the rejection, i.e. the components that do not satisfy the core essential customer requirements, will be selected for rejection and removal from the candidate list in the next iterations. At the same time as the components are selectively rejected, as a result of the decreasing number of candidate components, the number and detail of customer requirements will be increasing. The result is an iterative process whereby the requirements acquisition process enables components selection, and the components selection process informs of the requirements acquisition.

The PORE method integrates different methods, techniques and tools for requirements acquisition and components identification and selection/evaluation. Some of the techniques, methods and tools integrated within the PORE process are:

- Feature Analysis Techniques [14], to aid when scoring the compliance of each product feature to each customer requirement.

- Multi-Criteria Decision Making (MCDM) techniques such as Analytic Hierarchy Process (AHP) [13] and Out Ranking method [15] to aid in the decision making process during the product ranking and selection process.
- Argumentation techniques, to record and aid the decision-making process [16].
- Requirements engineering methods such as VOLERE [17], for aiding the analysis and management requirements process.
- Requirements acquisition techniques such as ACRE [18], for acquiring customer requirements.
- Component identification tools, such as the Internet or AGORA [19], for identifying products or components available in the market.

Another feature of this method is that it proposes four essential goals for selecting or rejecting components, which are integrated in a template to facilitate the evaluator's task. In this manner, PORE reject a component according to compliance or not with the following quality objectives:

- Essential atomic customer requirements (Goal 1).
- Non-essential atomic customer requirements (Goal 2).
- Complex non-atomic customer requirements (Goal 3).
- Customer user requirements (Goal 4).

In short, PORE is an approach to guiding the CBSE development process. In particular, it deals with the absence of process and method guidance for requirements acquisition and components evaluation/selection which must take place before system design.

The limitations of this proposal are:

- The iterative process of requirements acquisition and components evaluation/selection is very complex, where for example, stakeholders may define a large number of requirements, which can give rise to a large number of components, and so on, successively.
- The method needs a software tool (there is a prototype called PORE Process Advisor).
- It only focuses on the components evaluation process, but does not detail the concrete attributes that must be measured, or the metric to be used.
- It does not allow multiple components selection.

The PORE method was applied in [9] to select components in a system that that had to fulfil over 130 requirements. 11 learned lessons from the problems arising which would be useful to refine the PORE method, are displayed. For each of these lessons, a particular solution to avoid the problem in the future, is proposed. These lessons extend the state-of-the-art of the requirements acquisition techniques to the CBSE. Of these lessons, those most directly related to the requirements, are:

1. Acquire in more detail those requirements that enable effective discrimination between components.

2. Requirements must be as measurable as possible to enable effective components selection.

3. Weighting requirements for components selection can be problematic and very time consuming.

PORE also provides guidelines for the automatic generation of component evaluation test cases. The guidelines are provided using different templates (developed in [9]) for requirements acquisition and components selection. The process is structured into stages and the first three templates provided are:

- Template 1, to guide the requirements engineer when acquiring essential customer requirements and sufficient component information to select and reject components as a result of the information provided by the supplier.

- Template 2, to guide the requirements engineer when acquiring customer requirements and sufficient component information to select and reject components from a supplier-led demonstration using test cases for individual requirements.

- Template 3, to guide the requirements engineer to acquire customer requirements and sufficient component information to select and reject components as a result of customer-led component exploration.

Each template defines the types of components information (e.g. supplier, contract, architecture, etc.), types of requirements to acquire (e.g. functional, contractual, architectural, non-functional, etc.), requirements acquisition techniques to use and the best decision-making techniques to use.

At the beginning of the process, there will be few customer requirements but many candidate components. As components are rejected, customer requirements increase and candidate components decrease.

The iterative nature of the requirements acquisition and component selection means that each template may be used several times during the component selection process.

The PORE method has been validated in numerous case studies, giving good results, but according to the authors of the PORE method, has several clear limitations:

- It only supports the selection of one COTS component at a time.

- It does not scale to the types of systems which are commonplace in today's business and defence systems.

A new version of the PORE method is also proposed in [20]. It is extended with a modelling environment that will support trade-off analyses to enable COTS components selection.

The new PORE method, outlined in [20], has 2 extensions:

1. It will have a modelling environment which will act as a "test rig" to explore the impact of different components COTS on stakeholder and architectural requirements for a system.

2. The method will be extended with multi-criteria decision making techniques to enable software engineers to make trade-offs between the system performance and the cost and time to deliver this COTS components combination.

2.1.3. COTS-based Requirements Engineering (CRE)

The CRE method was developed in 2001 by Carina Alves and Jaelson Castro 2001 [7] and it facilitates a systematic, repeatable and requirements-driven components COTS selection process. A key issue supported by this method, is the definition and analysis of non-functional requirements during the COTS selection and evaluation phases. The COTS components selection is made by rejection. Components that do not fulfil the customer requirements, are rejected and removed from the candidate list. As the list decreases, the number and detail of the customer requirements increases. The result is an iterative process whereby the requirements acquisition process enables product selection, and this selection process also informs as to the requirements acquisition.

CRE is a goal-oriented method, i.e. each phase is oriented by predefined objectives. Each phase has a template that includes guidelines and techniques for the acquisition and requirements modelled and for the products evaluation. These templates describe the main goals as well as the final results of each phase. Each template can be used several times during the COTS selection process.

In CRE, 4 iteratives phases are proposed:

1. Identification. The first task of the identification process is the goals definition, based on a careful analysis of the influencing factors. CRE uses classification proposed by the OTSO method [12], which identifies 5 groups of factors that primarily influence the COTS selection.

   (a) User requirements.

   (b) Application architecture.

   (c) Project objectives and constraints.

   (d) Product availability.

   (e) Organization infrastructure.

2. Description.

3. Evaluation.

4. Acceptance.

CRE suggest that the RE process should drive the whole selection process in order to facilitate the discrimination of candidate products.

In [7], CRE method is validated in a real case study, related to the evaluation of clinical software packages available on the market for an oncology clinic, and in [21], the case study used is related to software packages for managing electronic mail.

As for the limitations of the method, the authors admit that in cases with a large number of COTS alternatives and evaluation criteria, the decision-making process can be very complex and a large number of possible situations can arise.

As further work, authors propose to detail the treatment of requirements prioritization and negotiation. Moreover, they need to address the issues related to multiple COTS selection.

2.1.4. Selecting Components Against Requirement (SCARLET)

The SCARLET method, developed by N. Maiden et al. [22] in 2003, proposes a tool-supported process (SCARLET Process Advisor), to guide the software component selection process. It integrates the use of scenarios, prototypes and measurable fit criteria into an iterative process of acquiring requirements and selection components using requirements as selection criteria. SCARLET is a PORE method extension.

Unlike other support tools for this purpose, SCARLET Process Advisor is not an add-in to the SCARLET process but an integral part of it, and it is not possible to implement of effective form the process without the support tool.

SCARLET provides process guidance for procurement team during a concurrent systems development process in which stakeholder requirements, the system architecture and the possible components are determined at the same time.

SCARLET proposes four essential goals for the component selection process. These goals will be useful to reject candidate components on the basis of non-fulfilment with different types of customer requirements. The goals are the following:

1. Simple customer requirements. For example, high-level services and functions, supplier requirements, basic features of the software component (cost, source, etc.), adherence to international standards.

2. Simple customer requirements that require access to the software component through test or use. For example, lower-level services and functions, demonstrable attributes of the software component (interface features), simple dependencies between customer requirements and component features.

3. Simple customer requirements that are demonstrable through short-term test use of the software component. For example, non-functional requirements such as performance, throughput, usability, training, etc.

4. More complex customer requirements with dependences on other already existing requirements and systems. For example, non-functional requirements that require more extensive test use (maintenance and reliability requirements), interdependences with other software components.

SCARLET gives four processes to achieve the four decision-making goals listed above:

1. Acquiring information about customer requirements, software components, contracts with the supplier.
2. Analyzing acquired information to ensure that this one is comprehensive and correct.
3. Using this information to make decisions about components-requirements compliance.
4. Rejecting one or more candidate components for non-fulfilment with customer requirements.

In [10] the method is validated in a simple case study on a COTS-based system for managing a meeting scheduler that will send notifications in advance to the participants and manage address books and distribution lists. It applied the i* approach [23] to model complex systems and their requirements, and in particular its Strategic Dependency (SD) between networks modeling dependence relationships among actors in a system.

Results in the research carried out within the framework of the BANKSEC project (project that investigated on component-based safe systems for the European banking sector, between 2000 and 2002) are presented in [24, 25]. Dependable systems such as Internet banking, generate new research challenges for CBSE, in particular how to select components when they are implemented in an architecture that must fulfil complex non-functional requirements such as security and reliability. SCARLET is presented as a light-weight method that must fulfil six meta-requirements identified to select components that must fulfil such non-functional requirements.

2.1.5. COTS-Aware Requirements Engineering and Software Architecting (CARE/SA)

The CARE/SA method was developed by L. Chung and K. Cooper in 2004. In [26] is presented the CARE/SA framework, which supports the iterative matching, ranking and selection of COTS components, using a representation of COTS components as an aggregate of their requirements (functional and non-functional) and their architecture.

CARE/SA can be viewed as an extension to previous methodologies with a systematic approach to match, rank, and select COTS components.

Five activities are identified in the CARE/SA process model:

1. Define goals. Once a collection of goals has been defined, the requirements engineer analyzes them to identify errors (conflicting, incorrect and redundant goals, missing goals). The requirements engineer will remove the redundant goals, will add those that are missing and will negotiate the conflicts among them. The need to create a new role, like the components engineer arises. This will be the person in charge of creating and maintaining the components repository, since the data available from a vendor may be incomplete.
2. Match components. In this activity, the requirements engineer begins the process by identifying goals that may be candidates to be implemented with one or more components.

3. Rank components. The COTS components that appear to be potential matches are grouped into sets that contain COTS components with varying degrees of system requirements fulfilment under construction.

4. Select set of COTS components.

5. Negotiate changes. For example, if a COTS component that provides the necessary functional capabilities has a high performance and high cost, then we can negotiate with the vendor to provide us a modified component with a moderate performance and moderate cost.

Matching of the system requirements under construction to COTS components can be done using keywords or case based reasoning.

CARE/SA approach has been validated in [26] in a case study based on a Digital Library System. The authors seek to research more heuristics for the matching, the meta-model creation for CARE/SA process and a Web support-tool to the process.

CARE/SA method uses techniques of cased based reasoning and multi-criteria decision-making techniques such as AHP, to carry out the classification tasks. AHP is useful to prioritize the significance of the components within each set of components, whereas case based reasoning is useful to group the different evaluation criteria and the similar measures collectively for each components set.

The authors conclude that the CBSE process should not be just unidirectional, i.e. from requirements to components retrieval. Instead, the searching and matching process should also support the reciprocal refinements of the stakeholders requirements.

A technique to elicit the stakeholders requirements, using on the one hand software components models and on the other hand, models of components evaluation is presented in [27]. These techniques are illustrated in a case study related to a home appliance control system.

This work on requirements elicitation through model-driven evaluation of software components is based on ideas from previous works in the area of components research. The most important are: Knowledge Based Automated Component Ensemble Evaluation' (KBACEE), which is an expert system for component selection which uses keywords search [28]; Evolutionary Process for Integrated COTS-Based Systems (EPIC), which is a framework that redefines acquisition, management, and engineering practices to more effectively leverage the COTS marketplace and other sources of preexisting components [29]; and also in methods such as PORE [8], SCARLET [22] and OTSO [12], already described.

2.2. Comparative Study

In this section, we compare the various previously studied components selection methods, according to decisive features that we identified as desirable in a components selection method. In table 1 we see this comparative analysis, where those methods that have a specific feature have the value "YES", otherwise they will have the value "NO", and in case that they have it partially they will have the value "PART".

If we observe the features in Table 1 from the different methods, we can say that the only method studied that has no well defined requirements acquisition process, is OTSO. With

Table 1. Summary-Table of the main components selection methods

Feature / Selection Method	OTSO	PORE	CRE	SCARLET	CARE/SA
Year of publication	1995	1999	2001	2002	2004
Requirements acquisition	NO	YES	YES	YES	YES
Non-Functional requirements	PART	PART	YES	YES	YES
Components evaluation	YES	YES	YES	YES	YES
Analysis decision	YES	YES	YES	YES	YES
Based on rejection	NO	YES	YES	YES	NO
Multiple selection	NO	NO	NO	YES	NO
Components identification	YES	YES	YES	YES	YES
Ease of use	YES	PART	PART	NO	NO
CARE Tool[1]	NO	NO[2]	NO	YES	NO
Component acceptation	YES	YES	YES	YES	PART
Feature analysis technique	NO	YES	NO	YES	NO
Defines metrics to use	NO	NO	NO	NO	NO
Requirements Negotiation	NO	NO	NO	NO	PART

respect to the treatment that the different methods make of the non-functional requirements, they all contemplate them in their processes, except OTSO and PORE, which deal with them partially. Finally, if we consider that methods have a support-tool to their process, and simultaneously deal with the problem the multiple components selection, the only method that would be a good candidate is SCARLET.

According to these results, we could conclude that SCARLET would be a good components selection method that pays explicit attention to the requirements to be used in the industry. Nevertheless, we think that the creation of a new method is necessary, since two of the most important features that should be present in this type of methods do not appear in SCARLET. Features like the ease of use and a requirements negotiation activity as part of the process are essential from our point of view.

These methods generally, have deficiencies in their treatment of the requirements. Thus for example, PORE and OTSO do not deal totally with the non-functional requirements. In addition OTSO has no requirements acquisition explicit process. In the same way, all methods except CARE/SA, which do it partially, do not incorporate requirements negotiation techniques in their processes.

This research is therefore motivated by the absence of a components selection method driven explicitly by requirements and in which these are explicitly identified and negotiated. At the same time it should be, as agile as possible and eliminate the rigidness of current processes, which require several phases to arrive at the selected component.

[1]Computer-Aided Requirements Engineering

[2]There is a tool prototype (PORE Process Advisor)

3. SIREN and DSBC

SIREN (SImple REuse of software requiremeNts) method [30, 31], proposed by the Software Engineering Research Group from University of Murcia, is a practical approach to select and specify the requirements of a software system based on SE standards and above all in reuse.

SIREN encompasses a spiral process model, requirements document templates, a reusable requirements repository and a tool (SirenTool) that supports the method. The requirements templates proposed are hierarchical and based on IEEE standards. The repository has requirements organized by catalogs in different application domains or profiles.

Catalogs and PRD (Product Requirements Document) in use can share a sub-document common hierarchy or use different structures. Initially, a hierarchy of empty specification templates is established. Those templates fill up with generic requirements (easier to reuse), proceeding in the general case from different domains of application or fixed profiles. For example, at the moment we have defined the following profiles in SIREN:

- *Personal Data Protection (PDP) Profile* [31, 32].
- *Security in Information Systems Profile* [30].
- *Electronic Medical Record Catalog*, which is already in development.

Catalog requirements, in addition to the text itself, contain associate meta-information (attributes with information on each requirement) that enrich the requirement. At the moment there are 18 attributes defined, among which the following are emphasized: source, security level, rationale, priority, fulfilment.

An important question to consider is how SIREN manages traceability, since generally in a PRD there appear many requirements related to each other. At the moment, in SIREN only traceability relations between requirements (inclusive, parent-child and exclusive) are defined. The aim of this work includes the definition of new traceability relations, in this case between requirements and components.

As we said in the introduction to this chapter, in the CBSE development process, requirements are the most important part for any effective COTS acquisition. The requirements inform about the criteria to evaluate and to select the component candidates, and even provide acceptance criteria that the client will use to verify if the given product satisfies his needs. Another essential factor is the components documentation, where it is necessary to count on precise and complete specifications to be able to make a suitable selection. This source of information about the component (datasheet) usually comes from the vendor component, although according to a study presented in [33], this information is usually little and insufficient to be able to evaluate the component quality.

3.1. Requirements-Components Selection Procedure

In order to provide the development team with the components search and design that verify the requirements established in the requirements specification document, we initially propose the following "agile" approach, in which the requirements of the catalog, will have an attribute that indicates the source where one software component (or several) can be found which, when incorporated into the system that is being developed, cause the requisite to be validated. The values introduced in this attribute will depend on where the components are (url, components repository, etc.).

When a requirement is incorporated into the final requirements specification document, it may happen that it contains references to components that validate it or it may not contain such references.

If it has not registered any component, the development team has only one option, to begin to develop the project considering that one of the developed components will have to validate that requirement.

On the other hand, it may also happen that the requirement does not correspond exactly with the necessities of the project and it is necessary to adapt it so that such thing happens. In this case the components that validated it possibly no longer do so, or do so partially and therefore it is also necessary to redesign such components.

Therefore, the range of possibilities that can be found is that shown in Table 2, which leads us to three different situations.

Table 2. Incorporation of a requirement into PRD.

SITUATION	SOLUTION
References are not registered to components that validate requirements	The development team starts from scratch and must complete all the component development process.
There are references to components that validate the requirement. The requirement is incorporated as it stands.	Selecting the most appropriate component is enough, and the development team only needs to must assemble it in the application.
There are references to components that validate the requirement partially.	Requirement is adapted so that a component exists that fulfils it, or the development team must adapt some of the components according to the requirement.

For example, if we are in situation two, where we find one or several software components that fulfil each one of the requirements (or at least the most critical) included in the PRD and extracted from the templates of the generic requirements PDP catalog. Each one of these requirements has an initial list of links to components, which does not imply that they are all valid for the current project, since we only can affirm that with these initial components associated to the requirement the functionality of this onc, can bc implemented.

In order to select the most suitable component, we must take into account the rest of related requirements, especially, those non-functional requirements that impose some type of restriction in the final application (programming language, operating system, memory, etc.).

In order to help in this task, we make a selection matrix (Table 3) for each requirement, which will contain a column for each one of the related requirements to it, and a row with each of the identified components. The criterion to decide which requirements to consider and which not, it is left to choice of the analyst, although we could apply more sophisticated techniques such as applied metric to the requirements attributes [34] or automatic generation of test cases for the product evaluation [9].

This selection matrix is equipped with greater functionality, to take into account the following considerations:

- A requirement can be fulfilled by a component to a certain degree. Depending on the requirement and the component features, it is possible to score the fulfilment between requirement and component. In this case, the entries of the selection matrix will have a score instead of a simple binary value. This score can be calculated using the Feature Analysis Technique proposed by DESMET[3] [14], or any other similar technique.
- Weights using some multi-criteria decision making techniques [35] can be assigned to a requirement, so we can know how a particular requirement affects the final score of a component.

To help us in the selection, we will apply the technique called Weighted Scoring Method (WSM): let s_1, s_2,..., s_n be the scores for the requirements r_1, r_2,..., r_n obtained using Feature Analysis Technique for the component c_1; let w_1, w_2, ..., w_n be the weights for each requirement obtained using, for example, the multi-criteria decision making technique called Analytical Hierarchical Process (AHP) [13]. The final score for c_1 would be:

$$score(c_1) = w_1 s_1 + w_2 s_2 + \ldots + w_n s_n$$

The result of the selection process will be either a single component or a set of finalist components, which are in the same conditions with respect to the requirements included in the PRD. In this case, the final decision will depend on the analyst's or designer's preferences.

Another aspect to consider in a components selection process based on requirements is that other requirements in the final PRD, not only the technical requirements, can impose more limitations (in cost, available licenses, development team qualities) until even the selection procedure finishes in an empty list of components. In order to make a quality selection, it is helpful to have for each component a precise specification of its features (datasheet).

3.2. Illustrative Example

In this section we present simple example of ours first approach to the selection method proposed, using the electronic mail applications as domain.

Let us suppose that a developer team is beginning a project in which the application to develop must have the capabilities of sending a receiving electronic mails. We also suppose, that we are in the second of the possible situations displayed in Table 2.

Requirement A has the following textual description:

The application, will use protocols SMTP, POP3 and MIME to send and receive electronic mails.

[3]DESMET is a method for the evaluation of tools and SE methods

It is obvious that many components[4] can exist that give us capabilities of sending and receiving electronic mails, which is why Requirement A, will have in its "component" attribute a list with all those components that validate this requirement. In particular, in the commercial components repository we found 77 components that fulfilled this requirement. This set will be the one that constitutes our initial set of candidate components, which we will be leaking progressively when considering the rest of the requirements.

We also want our electronic mail application, to allow the creation of digital signatures, thus fulfilling Requirement B:

The electronic mail application must provide the creation of digital signatures.

As well as fulfilling these functional requirements, the developer team also must fulfil several (non-functional) requirements related to the technology used, the programming language, operating system, etc. Thus, we have a Requirement C, with the following textual description:

The application will have to be implemented using the paradigm C++Builder or Microsoft Visual C++.

On the other hand, Requirement D is defined in the following way:

The application must be able to execute under the Windows XP Operating System.

These requirements limit rather the components technology that we can use to cover the needs of sending and receiving electronic mails of our application. In this case the list of components that fulfil the required functionality in Requirement A is reduced to two candidates, as we can see in Table 3.

Table 3. Example of Selection Matrix for the requirements A.

Component	Requirement B	Requirement C	Requirement D
EasyMail Objects v6.5		X	
EasyMail .Net v3.0			X
PowerTCP Mail .NET v2.1.4		X	X
PowerTCP Mail Tool v2.9.2		X	
eMail Wizard Toolpack v3.0	X	X	X
Catalyst Internet Mail v4.5	X	X	X
Rebex Mail .NET v.1.0.2537.0		X	X
Active Mail Professional v1.9			X

Once we have made the first pre-selection of those candidates which have the mandatory features (simple features) that we wished our application to have, we must elaborate another decision matrix to determine how it is the most adequate selection, in respect to other desirable features (compound features) that we considered important. These characteristics, a value have assigned corresponding to the importance that these have in the final appearance of the application. This value will be fixed by the development team and the customer at the beginning of the selection process. The values that can be given, are: *highly desirable* (3), *desirable* (2) and *optional* (1). We can see in Table 4 the importance that the

[4]Components used for the elaboration of this example have been taken from http://www.componentsource.com

different parameters of quality used have.

As regards fulfilment, a scale of 3 possible values is established: *not fulfilled* (-1), *favourable fulfillment* (1) and *highly favourable fulfillment* (2). In Table 5 we see the decision matrix with the fulfilment degree for both preselected component.

Table 4. Importance assigned to the quality parameters.

Quality Parameters	IMPORTANCE
Component cost	3
Confidence in the vendor	2
Component usability	3
Documentation quality	2

Table 5. Degree of fulfilment of the different components.

FULFILMENT	eMail Wizard Toolpack v3.0	Catalyst Internet Mail v4.5
Component cost	1	2
Confidence in the vendor	2	1
Component usability	2	2
Documentation quality	1	2

Once we have made both matrices, we calculate the score for each one of the preselected components, applying the formula from section 3.. The calculations are shown below:

$$score(eMail\ Wizard\ Toolpack\ v3.0) = 1 * 3 + 2 * 2 + 2 * 3 + 1 * 2 = 15$$

$$score(Catalyst\ Internet\ Mail\ v4.5) = 2 * 3 + 1 * 2 + 2 * 3 + 2 * 2 = 18$$

We thus obtain the component that we will use to add the functionality to send and to receive electronic mails to the application which we are developing, in this case *Catalyst Internet Mail Control v4.5* is selected, since it has obtained a slightly superior score.

4. Conclusion

The most important conclusions of this research are:

1. There are several proposals in the Literature for components selection methods based on rejection, according to the requirements identified for the system.

2. Selection and negotiation requirements techniques are not directly contemplated in any of the proposals found.

3. Our initial proposal, based on a RE method such as SIREN, would allow us to solve the components selection problem based on requirements more efficiently, since from the first moment the existence of quality requirements documents is guaranteed, and

in theory, is devoid of inconsistencies or conflicts between the requirements of the PRD.

In this chapter, we have centred on the study of the most important proposals as regards components selection methods. In order to achieve our final aim of developing a components selection method driven by the requirements, we followed a process model that is as simple and direct as possible, reducing to the number of artifacts and intermediate activities to the minimum. As future work, we will analyze the different methods studied from the point of view of the "agile" development methodologies, thus extending the work presented in [36]. Our aim with this research, is to know if the current agile methodologies (XP, Scrum, etc.) can be applied to the context of the CBSE.

Our first research in this matter, led us to affirm that these methodologies tend to be centred only on taylormade developed software systems by a programmer team where the reusability is limited to a software components repository, handled mainly by the team itself which is way why a great portion of the software on the market is not considered where the development of systems is based on the acquisition and integration of COTS components.

Currently, and to complement the state-of-the-art of this type of techniques, we are identifying the main proposals that deal with the requirements negotiation problem. This is a well known problem in RE, and must be discovered, negotiated and solved before the software development process, be this based on components or not.

There are several unresolved issues with respect to the use of this type of methods and when these methods give benefits for the customer and for the developer. Some of these open questions are the following:

1. If many components are needed to deliver a requirements set, then at what point is it still an advantage to use the COTS component instead of developing the system from scratch?

2. If the COTS components are considered when developing the architecture of the system, then what are the impacts on the system? For example, an architecture that is well suited for the use of COTS components may not have an adequate performance.

3. What is the smallest granularity for a COTS component that provides a benefit (i.e., overall reduced effort) when used in a system?

We are researching to be able to give an answer to the second of the above questions exhaustively studying the different techniques of definition of architectures and construction of components, with focus on the problem of passing of the system requirements to the components that will fulfil them.

With respect to the third question, the context in which we move in this paper is medium size COTS components, since these are related to the domain of the electronic mail applications.

Acknowledgements

This work has been partially financed by the Spanish Ministry of Science and Technology, project DEDALO (Desarrollo de sistEmas De calidad bAsado en modeLos y requisitOs),

TIN2006-15175-C05-03, and by the CALIPSO network (TIN2005-24055-E) supported by the Spanish Ministry of Education and Science.

References

[1] Glass, R.: *Software Runaways: Monumental Disasters.* (1998)

[2] Smith, J.: *Troubled IT Projects prevention and turnaround.* (2001)

[3] Glass, R.: *Software Engineering: Facts and Fallacies.* (2002)

[4] Cybulski, J.L., Reed, K.: Requirements Classification and Reuse: Crossing Domain Boundaries. In Frakes, W.B., ed.: ICSR. Volume 1844 of *Lecture Notes in Computer Science.* (2000) 190–210

[5] Glass, R.: *Software Engineering* (6th edition). (2001)

[6] Bertoa, M.F., Troya, J.M., Vallecillo, A.: Measuring the usability of software components. *Journal of Systems and Software* 79 (2006) 427–439

[7] Alves, C., Castro, J.: CRE: A systematic method for COTS components selection. In: *Proceeding of the XV Brazilian Symposium of Software Engineering (SBES)* Rio de Janeiro, Brazil. (2001)

[8] Ncube, C., Maiden, N.: PORE: Procurement-Oriented Requirements Engineering Method for the Component-Based Systems Engineering Development Paradigm. In: *Proceedings of the 2nd International Workshop on Component Based Software Engineering (CBSE)* (in conjunction with ICSE'99), Los Angeles, USA. (1999)

[9] Maiden, N.A., Ncube, C.: Acquiring COTS Software Selection Requirements. *IEEE Software* 15 (1998) 46–56

[10] Franch, X., Maiden, N.A.: Modelling component dependencies to inform their selection. In: *ICCBSS '03: Proceedings of the Second International Conference on COTS-Based Software Systems*, London, UK, Springer-Verlag (2003) 81–91

[11] Kontio, J.: A Case Study in Applying a Systematic Method for COTS Selection. In: *18th International Conference on Software Engineering, Springer* (1996) 201–209

[12] Kontio, J., Chen, S., Limperos, K., Tesoreiro, R., Caldeira, G., Deutsch, M.: A COTS Selection Method and Experience of Its Use. In: *Proceeding of the 20th annual Software Engineering Workshop. NASA*. Greenbelt, Maryland. (1995)

[13] Vargas, L.G., Saaty, T.L.: Models, Methods, Concepts and Applications of the Analytic Hierarchy Process. (2001)

[14] Kitchenham, B.A., Jones, L.: *Evaluating Software Engineering Methods and Tools; Part 5 The Influence of Human Factors. ACM SIGSOFT Software Engineering Notes* 22 (1997) 13–15

[15] Fenton, N.: *Out ranking method for multi-criteria decision aid: with emphasis on its role in systems dependability assessment.* Technical report, Centre for Software Reliability, City University, London, UK. (1994)

[16] Shum, S.B., Hammond, N.: Argumentation-based design rationale: what use at what cost? *Int. J. Hum.-Comput. Stud.* 40 (1994) 603–652

[17] Robertson, S.: Volere: Requirements Specification Templates. 6th Edition. (1998)

[18] Maiden, N.A., Rugg, G.: ACRE: Selection methods for requirements acquisition. *Software Engineering Journal* 11 (1996) 183–192

[19] Robert C. Seacord, Scott A. Hissam, K.C.W.: Agora: A search engine for software components. *IEEE Internet Computing* 02 (1998) 62–70

[20] Ncube, C., Maiden, N.: COTS Software Selection: The need to make tradeoffs between system requirements. In: *COTS Workshop. Continuing Collaborations for Successful COTS Development*. (2000)

[21] Alves, C., Castro, J.: Um Método Baseado em Requisitos para Seleçao de COTS. In: *Proceeding of the 4th Iberoamerican Workshop on Software Engineering and Software Environment (IDEAS'01)* San Jose, Costa Rica. (2001)

[22] Maiden, N.A.M., Croce, V., Kim, H., Sajeva, G., Topuzidou, S.: SCARLET: Integrated Process and Tool Support for Selecting Software Components. In Cechich, A., Piattini, M., Vallecillo, A., eds.: *Component-Based Software Quality - Methods and Techniques.* Volume 2693 of LNCS. (2003) 85–98

[23] Yu, E.S.K.: Towards modelling and reasoning support for early-phase requirements engineering. In: *Proceedings of the 3rd IEEE Int. Symp. on Requirements Engineering (RE'97)*, Washington D.C., USA. (1997) 226–235

[24] Maiden, N.A., Kim, H.: SCARLET: Light-weight component selection in BANKSEC. *Business Computer-based Software Engineering* 705 (2002)

[25] Maiden, N.A., Kim, H., Ncube, C.: Rethinking process guidance for software component selection. In: *Proceedings 1st International Conference on COTS-Based Software Systems. LNCS* 2255, Springer-Verlag. (2002) 151–164

[26] Chung, L., Cooper, K.: COTS-Aware Requirements Engineering and Software Architecting. In: *Software Engineering Research and Practice.* (2004) 57–63

[27] Chung, L., Ma, W., Cooper, K.: Requirements elicitation through model-driven evaluation of software components. In: Proc., *IEEE International Conference on COTS-Based Systems (ICCBSS'06)*. (2006) 187–196

[28] Seacord, R.C., Mundie, D.A., Boonsiri, S.: K-BACEE: Knowledge-based automated component ensemble evaluation. In: EUROMICRO. (2001) 56–63

[29] Albert, C., Browmswood, L.: *Evolutionary process for integrating COTS-based systems (EPIC): An overview.* Technical report, CMU/SEI-2002-TR-009, Software Engineering Institute, Carnegie-Mellon University, Pittsburgh (2002)

[30] Toval, A., Nicolás, J., Moros, B., Garcia, F.: *Requirements Reuse for Improving Information Systems Security: A Practitioner's Approach. RE J.* 6 (2002) 205–219

[31] Toval, A., Olmos, A., Piattini, M.: Legal Requirements Reuse: A Critical Success Factor for Requirements Quality and Personal Data Protection. In: RE, *IEEE Computer Society* (2002) 95–103

[32] Martínez, M.A., Lasheras, J., Toval, A., Piattini, M.: An Audit Method of Personal Data Based on Requirements Engineering. In: *Proceedings of the 4th International Workshop on Security in Information Systems* , (WOSIS'06), In conjunction with ICEIS'06, Paphos, Cyprus. (2006) 217–231

[33] Bertoa, M.F., Troya, J.M., Vallecillo, A.: A survey on the quality information provided by software component vendors. In: P*roceedings of the 7th ECOOP Workshop on Quantitative Approaches in Object-Oriented Software Engineering* (QAOOSE'03. Darmstadt, Germany. (2003) 25–30

[34] Piattini, M., Cechich, A., Vallecillo, A., eds.: *Component-Based Software Quality - Methods and Techniques.* Volume 2693 of LNCS., Springer (2003)

[35] Triantaphyllou, E.: *Multi-Criteria Decision Making Methods.* (2000)

[36] Navarrete, F., Botella, P., Franch, X.: *How agile cots selection methods are (and can be)?* In: EUROMICRO-SEAA. (2005) 160–167

In: Computer Software Engineering Research
Editor: Ari D. Klein, pp. 111-141
ISBN 1-60021-774-5

Chapter 4

TOWARDS THE USE OF PLANNING TECHNIQUES TO ASSEMBLE COMPONENT-BASED SYSTEM

PauloSalemdaSilva*, AnaC.V.deMelo† and Leliane Nunes de Barros^

University of São Paulo
Department of Computer Science
São Paulo – Brazil

Abstract

Systems modularisation is one of the requirements for software development today due to applications complexity. One cannot build systems as a single piece of software. Moreover, reuse is one of the development principles highly required. Object-oriented programming, for example, is an initiative of programs modularisation and reuse in the sense that classes are abstraction units, from which objects inherit behaviour, and a set of objects work together to build a system. Component-based systems have also become popular because systems are built from a set of object-components and the reuse principle is mainly applied, making systems costly effective and in the time to market.

Despite highly required, reusing components and making them work together to accomplish the desired system behaviour is still a challenging task. This requires finding the appropriate components to generate the required behaviour and assembling instances of components (object-components) to result in the whole system. This chapter presents a study on the use of planning techniques to assembling software components to build systems. In this study, a tool, based on goal-driven planning techniques, has been developed together with a software components library and an analysis on the effectiveness of building systems using such techniques is conducted.

1. Introduction

The concept of modularization is frequently present in the several existing programming paradigms. That is, the idea that programs should be divided in distinct parts is broadly accepted. In the last decade, for instance, the Object Orientation paradigm, in which the

*E-mail address: salem@ime.usp.br
†E-mail address: acvm@ime.usp.br
^ E-mail address: lleliane@ime.usp.br

class abstraction is one of the fundamental modularization units, has dominated the market for software development tools. More recently we have also seen the advance Component Orientation [17], which, in a way, constitutes a refinement of Object Orientation.

Software modularization brings the possibility of its reuse. From the moment that it is possible to isolate and generalize program fragments, multiple projects may employ them. Moreover, the decomposition of the system allows the division of work among programmers.

Thus, we are led to think about how can such characteristics be employed in order to simplify software development. A natural idea is to create a repository with reusable modules, where programmers may search manually what they need. However, as these repositories grow, it becomes harder for programmers to be efficient.

In this chapter, we define a specific kind of repository and propose an automated approach to Object Oriented software construction. We consider a repository as a set of classes, interfaces and their dependency relations. Automatic construction is obtained by exploring the several dependency relations, through Automated Planning [1] technology. Such a technology allows the automatic generation of a *plan*, which, in our case, consists of a sequence of steps that should be carried out in order to have an implementation out of repository elements.

Even though Object Orientation is a paradigm that covers several languages, each one of them has its own idiosyncrasies. Therefore, we have chosen to deal with the paradigm according to one particular language implementation, Java.

At last, although we have succeeded in modeling the problem in a way that can be handled by Planning technology, performance issues have shown to be a major problem with its actual use. It is not clear, therefore, if our approach can be further developed toward success.

Summarizing, this chapter describes a new code generation method, based on Software Reuse and Automated Planning. Our approach consists of defining a repository of classes, interfaces and dependency relations in order to later reuse them to generate new software. Such reuse is automated through the application of Planning technology. To this end, we provide a formalization of the problem in a suitable language. Moreover, we present the results of some case studies. While, in principle, the proposed approach works, it turns out that performance issues prevent it from being used in non-trivial cases. Hence, we conclude by discussing the merits and possibilities of advancement regarding our method. Section 2. surveys the related works. Section 3. provides an overview of fundamental concepts in Automated Planning. Section 4. presents a formal model of the problem, while Section 5. describes a process through which such a model can be used to automatically generate a program. Section 6. comments on the implementation. Section 7. shows two experiments that we have performed. Finally, Section 8. considers the advantages, disadvantage and lines of future research regarding our work. We also include two appendixes. Appendix A. provides the source code of our implementations and Appendix B. collects the UML diagrams for the second experiment.

[1]By 'Automated Planning' we mean the Artificial Intelligence field originated specially by the STRIPS system. See [13].

2. Related Works

Reusability cannot be classified as an independent area in computer science, it is in a way an approach of looking at the software development problem [7]. It is basically a principle that requires certain techniques to be embedded in software/hardware development methods.

The idea of reusing existing designs has been practised since the very beginning of engineering products as much as software development. In the software field, operating systems, software packages such as editors, and spreadsheets, or even mathematical libraries, are forms of software reuse. Besides these end products, certain methodologies, such as some management and training encouraging reuse and some design techniques focusing reuse concepts, carry characteristics that enhance reusability. But, in most cases reusability has been practised in a very informal way; the current methods of developing software/hardware have been shown to be inefficient for reuse. The waste of people and resources has grown at such an uncontrollable rate, that the development of techniques for enhancing reusability is urged to develop software.

In a very simplistic view of systems information, it can be classified as: knowledge–based and description–based information. The knowledge–based information comprises all the designer's experience, usage of tools and methods involved in systems development, widespread knowledge of application domains, how existing systems are used in practice, and other information which involves acquiring knowledge from the environment of development or usage of existing products design. Apart from very few application domains, such as compilers, there are no established methods for developing systems, even for those widely spread systems like accounting or bank–transaction systems [12].

The description–based information concentrates upon structural and behavioural description of components. This involves information such as subsystems that are elements of the entire system, the specification of communications among these subsystems and behavioural descriptions of all parts. This descriptive information actually gives the specification of systems from high levels of descriptions down to implementation.

Many solutions have been given to drive reuse of code and design. These solutions might concentrate on languages that emphasize abstraction on specifications of systems, or on recognition of patterns that, in a transformational approach, ends up with final implementations, or on patterns that represent distinct features of systems and are plugged together to make the entire system [8, 3, 2, 16]. The evolution of ideas by McIlroy [14], who advocated the creation of components repositories to build software, came up with the more recent concept of *Component-Based Software Engineering* (CBSE) in which software systems are to be assembled from existing components. Despite being very promising, this approach still carries out problems [5, 1, 10, 18], such as how to assemble components and guarantee they provide the desired behaviour.

We are unaware of other works that employ Automated Planning techniques to solve automatic program generation problems. However, code generators that rely on other approaches have existed for a long time. Among the modern ones, we may emphasize the *Model Driven Architecture (MDA)* [15]. References for several other techniques and tools can be found at [4].

Both theory and applications concerning Automated Planning can be found in [13].

3. Automated Planning

Before moving on, we present here some fundamental ideas concerning Automated Planning that will be employed later. If the reader is already familiar with this area, he may skip this section.

Automated Planning is concerned with *planning problems*. Roughly, a planning problem consists of a set of *actions* that are available and a *goal state* that one wishes to achieve. Each action has some *preconditions* and some *effects*. Preconditions are what must hold in the *current state* in order to the action be applicable in that state. The effects are the changes that are produced in the state after the action is applied. An *initial state* must be provided in order to inform what propositions are valid in the beginning. The objective is to find a sequence of actions that transform the initial state into the specified goal state.

A *planner* is a software that perform such a search. A sequence that describes which actions to take is called a *plan*. It is usual to divide a planning problem into a *domain* and a more restricted *problem*. The domain contains elements that are applicable to a wide range of problems of a certain type. Domains define the "language" that is used to write problems and, thus, are reusable assets.

In our work, the domain contains the actions and other elements that are necessary every time our approach is employed. The actual problems are left for the user to write, though we present two examples in Section 7..

4. Domain Specification

Programs written in Object Oriented languages can be seen as sets of related objects, which communicate through messages. By definition, each object is an instance of some class, which, in turn, determines the kinds of messages it can send and receive. Assuming that one may know *a priori* what are these kinds of messages for each class in a system, one may establish dependency relations among them and, therefore, among the several objects that compose a program. That is, we can find out which classes are necessary for the operation of others. For example, a system that manages a company's customer information might be built out of some standard parts such as database connectors (e.g., to access customer data), graphical user interfaces (e.g., to visualize data) and network components (e.g., to send email to customers). Each of these parts, however, depend on the others. For instance, in order to visualize a specific kind of data, a specific kind of data source must be available.

This topological dependency structure can be used both in the analysis of existing programs and in the development of new ones. It is in the later that we are interested. The method that we propose here assumes the existence of a *repository* containing classes and interfaces, and aims at generating a *plan* that shows how to implement a *target program*.

More precisely[2], we have the following definitions.

Definition 1 (Repository) *A* repository *is a tuple* $(C, I, Q, R_{of}, R_{dep}, R_q)$, *where:*

- $C = \{c_1, c_2, \ldots, c_l\}$, *a set of classes;*

[2]This formalization merely defines the problem in a theoretical manner to the reader. The implementation that we provide is based in another formalism, the PDDL.

- $I = \{i_1, i_2, \ldots, i_m\}$, *a set of interfaces;*

- $Q = \{q_1, q_2, \ldots, q_n\}$, *a set of quality of classes. A quality is some non-structural characteristic that can be attributed to classes. For example, we may define the quality 'secure' in order to attribute it to classes whose implementations are trustworthy;*

- $R_{of} = \{(c, i) | c \in C \land i \in I\}$, *a relation that establishes the interfaces provided by each class;*

- $R_{dep} = \{(c, i) | c \in C \land i \in I\}$, *a relation that establishes the interfaces required by each class;*

- $R_{cq} = \{(c, q) | c \in C \land q \in Q\}$, *a relation that establishes the qualities of each class.*

Definition 2 (Target program) *A* target program *is a tuple* $(Rep, I_{target}, R_{iq})$, *where:*

- *Rep, a repository;*

- $I_{target} \subseteq I$, *a set of interfaces that should be implemented and made available by the system;*

- $R_{iq} = \{(i, q) | i \in I \land q \in Q\}$, *a relation that establishes quality restrictions over interfaces. The classes employed to implement such interfaces should have the respective qualities.*

The automatic generation of a target program can be achieved recursively starting at I_{target}. It suffices to determine which classes offer the desired interfaces respecting the imposed restrictions. Each class found will have its own dependencies, which should be solved in an analogous manner, and so on, until all dependencies have been satisfied. Finally, classes should be instantiated at the steps that they are necessary, resulting, thus, in an implementation.

Besides the dependency restrictions, we can define other more sophisticated structural ones. In our current implementation, we allow the use of the *Singleton* design pattern [9] and the *Layers* architectural pattern. The first allow us to define that specific classes have only one instance. The second make it possible to define layered architectures and restrict the use of certain classes to certain layers.

We have adopted technologies from Automated Planning to implement the system. Note that the proposed problem ca be easily seen as a planning problem, where the main action is the instantiation of classes and the goal is the provision of a certain set of interfaces. We have implemented a planning domain using the Planning Domain Definition Language (PDDL) [11] with these ideas.

In the next subsection we shall describe precisely how this was done (Section 4.1. and Section 4.2.). We then show how we employed this domain in order to solve the problem of automatic program generation (Section 5.). All PDDL implementations are given in Appendix A..

4.1. Domain Architecture

The elements in our planning domain are divided in *types*, *constants*, *propositions* and *actions*. Among actions, the ones related to instantiation are specially troublesome, as we shall see.

Constants define the existing resources. Each constant is associated to one of the following types:

- Interfaces ($interface$);
- Classes ($class$);
- Instances ($instance$);
- Layers ($layer$).

Propositions aim at representing properties attributed to the constants. Such properties can be organized in the following manner:

- *Static structural properties*. Define the static structure of the system. That is, the structure that always hold, for all target programs. For instance, the class hierarchy available in the repository is a static structure.
- *Dynamic structural properties*. Define the dynamic structure of the system. For example, the relation among the several objects that should be instantiated constitutes a dynamic relation.
- *Qualitative properties*. Define non-structural qualities regarding classes, interfaces an instances. In our approach, arbitrary qualities can be attributed to classes, as we shall see shortly.

At last, actions represent the following:

- *Class instantiation.* The production and use of instances.
- *Structural properties realization.* Owing to the limitations of PDDL, it is necessary to include a special set of actions to represent static structural properties. In Section 6. we shall analyze this problem.
- *Qualitative class validation.* Some actions are responsible for checking if classes satisfy certain qualitative criteria (i.e., if they have certain qualities attributed to them).

That said, we can describe our instantiation strategy. In general, planning systems demand that the quantity of constants in the planning problem do not change. That is, all constants must be defined *a priori*. This restriction causes problems in the instantiation process, since the most straightforward method of implementing it is through the dynamic creation of new constants that represent the instances.

The solution that we have adopted, therefore, does not create new constants. Rather, we first define a set of 'non-initialized' instances. As instantiations are needed during the execution of the planning system, instances are removed from this set and associated with corresponding classes.

4.2. Domain Elements

In this section we analyze in detail each of the elements in our domain. We shall refer to each one using the name employed in the PDDL implementation.

4.2.1. Types and Constants

As we outlined previously, the following types are available:

- $interface$. Class interfaces;
- $class$. Class implementations;
- $instance$. Class instances;
- $layer$. System layers. Classes can belong to layers, which restrict the instantiations that can be performed. Classes in a layer can only be associated to instances whose classes belong to a superior or inferior layer, or to no layer at all;
- $quality$. Non-structural qualities that can be attributed to classes.

Constants vary according to the application. However, in any application it is necessary to have a set of constants to account for instances of classes.

A family of applications may share constants among each other. As we shall see in Section 7., it is convenient to define, *a priori*, several interfaces, classes and relations. This collection of constants and the predefined relations constitute a repository.

4.2.2. Propositions

Propositions create properties to be manipulated during the planning process. Our domain is composed by three kinds of properties. In what follows we examine each one of them.

Static Structural Properties

- $subclass(c_1, c_2)$. Defines that the class c_1 is subclass of c_2;
- $subinterface(i_1, i_2)$. Defines that the interface i_1 is subinterface of i_2;
- $class - provides(c, i)$. Defines that the class c implements the interface i;
- $class - requires(c, i)$. Defines that the class c requires an instance of another class that implements the interface i;
- $singleton(c)$. Defines that the class c can have only one instance and that such an instance is shared. That is, a unique instance of c shall resolve the dependencies related to c;
- $on - layer(l_1, l_2)$. Defines that the layer l_1 is over the layer l_2;
- $class - in - layer(c, l)$. Defines that class c belongs to layer l. That is, that instances of c can only instantiate and associate to instances either of classes in adjacent layers or of classes that do not belong to a layer.

Dynamic Structural Properties

- $instance - provides(o, i)$. Defines that instance o implements the interface i;
- $instance - requires(o, i)$. Defines that the instance o requires another instance that implements the interface i;
- $in - instance - pool(o)$. Defines that the instance o has not been initialized. That is, that it is not associated with any classes;
- $instance - of(o, c)$. Defines that o is an instance of the class c;
- $is - instantiated(c)$. Defines that class c has at least one instance;
- $attached(o_1, o_2)$. Defines that the instance o_1 belongs to the instance o_2;
- $instance - in - layer(o, l)$. Defines that the instance o is in layer l.

Qualitative Properties

- $class - provides - quality(c, q)$. Defines that the class c has the quality q;
- $instance - provides - quality(o, q)$. Defines that the instance o has the quality q;
- $interface - requires - quality(i, q)$. Defines that any implementation of the interface i must have the quality q;
- $is - validated(o)$. Defines that the instance o fulfills the specified qualitative criteria.

4.2.3. Actions

Class Instantiation

- $attach - instance(o_1, o_2)$. Attaches the instance o_1 to the instance o_2. That is, defines that o_2 should create an association to o_1. Once this has been made, no other instance may have a reference to o_1. It is an exclusive relationship.
- $attach - singleton - instance(o_1, o_2)$.

  Attaches the instance o_1 of a singleton class to the instance o_2. o_1 is the unique instance of some class and should be shared by all other instances that need such a class;
- $instantiate(c, o)$. Instantiates the class c using the non-initialized instance o;
- $instantiate - singleton(c, o)$. Instantiates the singleton class c using the non-initialized instance o. If the class already has an instance, then it will not be possible to instantiate it again.

Structural Properties Realization

- $find-superclass-interfaces(c_1, c_2, i)$. If c_1 is subclass of c_2 and c_2 implements the interface i, then this action defines that c_1 also implements i;
- $find-superinterface-interfaces(i_1, i_2, c)$. If i_1 is a subinterface of i_2 and class c implements i_1, then this action defines that c also implements i_2.

Qualitative Class Validation

- $validate - instance(o)$. Checks if the instance o satisfies the necessary quality criteria.

5. Automatic Generation Process

The process of automatic code generation has as its main component the planning domain described above. However, the process is not restricted to it. To be complete, all of the following steps should be carried out:

1. *Classes and interfaces collection.* The first step is the collecting of classes and interfaces that shall be available in the repository. That is, it is necessary to describe, for each class and interface, the properties that hold, using the propositions defined in the planning domain. This step should be done manually. For example, a programmer might create such information for each class and interface that he writes.

2. *Target program definition.* After collecting the repository elements, it becomes possible to reuse them. To this end, it is necessary to define a problem to be solved. That can be done through the creation of two classes, $start$ and $system$, with the following characteristics:

   - $start$ provides interfaces that are known to be implemented by other systems. That is, $start$ is merely a way to reuse what is known to exist outside the repository or that we wish to build manually, without the help of the generator. Moreover, $start$ is a singleton. In the initial state of the planner, the proposition $class - provides(start, i)$ should be present for each interface i that $start$ provides;
   - $system$ has as dependencies all interfaces that the generated program is supposed to provide. $system$ must also provide a special interface i. This way, the automatic generation can be achieved through a planning problem that defines as a goal the implementation of i.

   Again, this step should be carried out manually. Usually, this will be done when a programmer already has a large repository available, out of which many target programs may be generated.

3. *Planning problem resolution.* With the previous step, a planning problem is created. A planner, then, must solve it in order to generate a plan, which is, essentially, a sequence of class instantiations. This step, of course, can be accomplished automatically.

4. *Program generation from plan.* Once the plan is available, it can be converted in Java code. This step can also be accomplished automatically.

The first two steps are simple and we shall not deal with them here, although they appear in the example of Section 7.. The third step is, essentially, the resolution of the planning problem we defined earlier. Thus, we are left with the fourth step, which bears important technical details.

Once we have a plan, it is necessary to have a way of converting it in executable code. That can be done employing some conventions for each class and defining some simple rules of conversion for each action in executable code to be inserted inside the classes' constructors.

The conventions are:

- All classes should have public constructors;
- Such constructors must be designed foreseeing that code will be automatically inserted in them;
- Singleton class must provide a method called $instance()$ that returns its unique instance.

Now let us see the adopted rules:

- $attach - instance(o_1, o_2)$: Translated to something like $setX(o_1)$ inside the constructor of o_2, where X is the name of the variable to which o_1 is to be attributed;
- $attach - singleton - instance(o_1, o_2)$: Translated in the same manner that $attach - instance(o_1, o_2)$;
- $instantiate(c, o)$: Translated to something similar to $co = new\ c()$ inside the constructor of the class that depends of c;
- $instantiate - singleton(c, o)$: Translated to something like $co = c.instance()$ inside the constructor of the class that depends of c;
- $find - superclass - interfaces(c_1, c_2, i)$: Nothing to be done. The language compiler guarantees the effect of this action;
- $find - superinterface - interfaces(i_1, i_2, c)$: Nothing to be done. The language compiler guarantees the effect of this action;
- $validate - instance(o)$: Nothing to be done. This action is only useful in the planing phase.

Notice that once the implementation is generated, programmers might refine it manually as needed.

In this work, we have implemented and studied only the planning domain. Naturally, a working system needs other components. In the present state, collecting and conversions to code must be done manually.

6. Implementation

As we have already stated, in this work we have only implemented the planning domain necessary for the proposed system. We have chosen PDDL 1.2 [11] as the description language for the domain and the problems. We believe that for being the official language of planning competitions and for the 1.2 version being somewhat old [3], the quantity of available planners that support it should be great and increase over time. Among the available planners, we have chosen the Fast-Forward (FF) system [6] to accomplish our tests and experiments.

All PDDL implementation produced is available in the Appendix A.. It is divided in the proposed domain and in the examples that shall be given in Section 7.. Having in mind what we have already described in the previous sections, it should be easy to ready the actual PDDL specification. Thus, we do not describe it in this section. Here, we aim at emphasizing a few points.

PDDL provides rich elements that we would like to have used (e.g., domain axioms). However, many of these elements are optional and few planners implement them. That has forced us to adopt solutions not very elegant in our model. For example, the fact that a subclass inherits the interfaces of its superclass could have been captured with a domain axiom. But, as they are not available in actual planners, we had o create actions to implement the inheritance system.

Even mandatory PDDL elements are sometimes not present in planners. We have found out, for instance, that FF do not recognize the *situation* command, which allows the definition of a initial state common to several problems. That would have helped us greatly, since we could have defined what is common to all our problems (e.g., non-initialized instances).

That said, it is worth noting that we used several interesting language features, such as universal and existential quantifiers. In fact, without such quantifiers, the domain modeling would have been severely restricted, since we would not be able to make assertions about, for example, *all* class dependencies.

7. Case Studies

In this section we present the framework that we developed, using two fictitious examples. The first is very simple and merely shows that the system works for small problems. It does not model a realistic system and, hence, we have not assigned any special semantics to its elements. The second, on the other hand, tries to model a more realistic problem, a set of components in a layered architecture.

[3]October 1998.

As we shall see, the planner could not solve interesting problems in the second case study. Since the problems are not so hard and, in fact, can be solved manually, we believe that this shows that the planning technology employed is not suitable for our intentions. Nevertheless, the case study is presented in order to allow the reader both to understand how an actual problem might be modeled with our approach and to experiment himself with the domain (e.g., modifying it in order to analyze how it can be improved). Section 8. speculates about ways of improving the efficiency of the approach.

Let us now present the examples.

7.1. Case Study 1: A Simple Problem

Here we present a very simple problem, aiming at showing that the domain works. It does not model a realistic system. Appendix A.3. contains its PDDL description. Fig. 1 shows its main components.

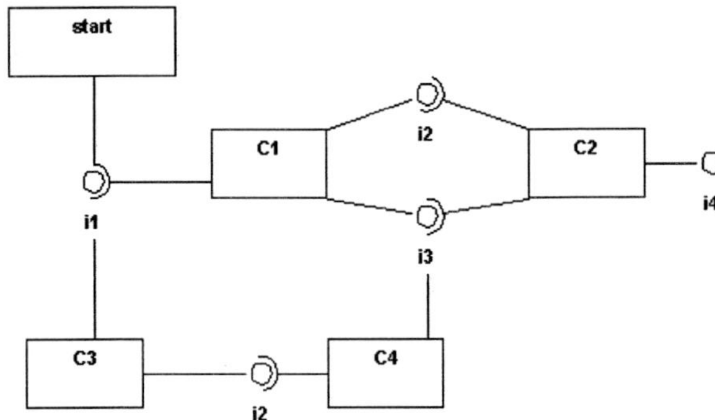

Figure 1. A simple repository. The figure shows the dependencies and capabilities of each class. The goal is to provide the interface i_4.

The FF planner quickly provides the following answer:

```
ff: found legal plan as follows

step    0: INSTANTIATE START O1
        1: VALIDATE-INSTANCE START O1
        2: ATTACH-INSTANCE O1 O2
        3: INSTANTIATE C1 O2
        4: VALIDATE-INSTANCE C1 O2
        5: ATTACH-INSTANCE O2 O10
        6: INSTANTIATE C2 O10
        7: REACH-GOAL
```

Let us interpret this answer backwards. In step 6, the class c_2 is instantiated as the o_{10} instance, which satisfies the goal. But class c_2 has dependencies that must be fulfilled. From step 4 to step 5, class c_1 is instantiated in order to this end. c_1, in turn, has its own dependencies, which are satisfied by the class $start$.

7.2. Case Study 2: A Consumer Notification System

Consider the following hypothetical situation. A company produces customized software for online commerce. In such a well defined domain, we may use the idea of keeping a component repository from which new systems can be built.

The company, thus, has a large collection of classes and interfaces, which can be seen in Appendix B.. These classes are divided in a layered architecture, as follows:

1. *Presentation layer*. Provides classes that implement user interaction;
2. *Business layer*. Provide classes that implement use cases in the context of online commerce;
3. *System layer*. Provide classes that implement the basic functionalities of the system, such as database access and email service.

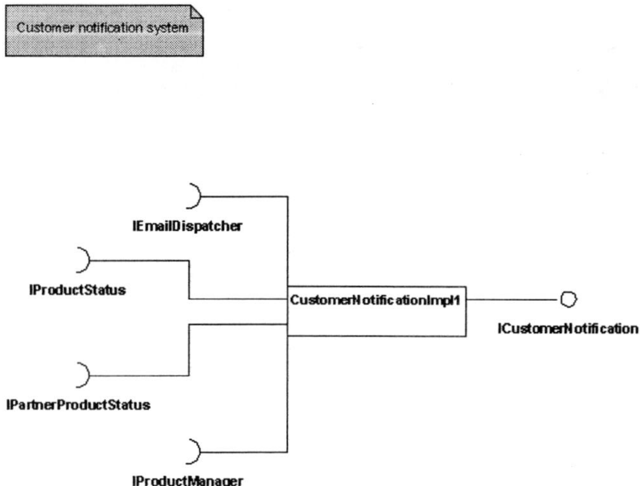

Figure 2. The final class that we wish to generate automatically.

Assume that the company aims at developing a system that notifies the customers of a store regarding the availability of some ordered goods. This could be implemented using our generator in the following manner. It would suffice to create a goal class that has as its dependencies the interfaces that we wish to provide (see Fig. 2) and that provides a new interface, $ICustomerNotification$. With that, the planner would be capable of assembling a system using the classes available in the repository.

planner would, for instance, be able to take advantage of layer information in order to restrict search (i.e., examining classes only if they are in an appropriate layer). In fact, if other architectural and design patterns are incorporated in the domain, there would be even more restrictions to employ and, hence, performance could improve. This, we believe, is the most promising line of research that can follow the present work.

A. PDDL Code

A.1. Domain

```
;;;;;;;;;;;;;;;;;;;;;;;;;;;;;;;;;;;;;;;;;;;;;;;;;;;;;;;;;;;;;;;;;;;;;;;;;;;;;;;;
;; Automatic software construction domain
;;;;;;;;;;;;;;;;;;;;;;;;;;;;;;;;;;;;;;;;;;;;;;;;;;;;;;;;;;;;;;;;;;;;;;;;;;;;;;;;


(define (domain software-construction)
  (:requirements :strips :typing :universal-preconditions
                 :existential-preconditions
                 :disjunctive-preconditions
                 :conditional-effects)

  (:types interface class instance layer quality)
  (:constants i - interface c - class o - instance l - layer
              safety unsafe cheap expensive - quality
              start - class

  )
  (:predicates
               ;;;;;;;;;;;;;;;;;;;;;;;;;;;;;;;;;;;;;;;
               ;;; Fundamental structural properties
               ;;;;;;;;;;;;;;;;;;;;;;;;;;;;;;;;;;;;;;;

               (subclass ?c1 - class ?c2 - class)
               (subinterface ?i1 - interface ?i2 - interface)
               (class-provides ?c - class ?i - interface)
               (class-requires ?c - class ?i - interface)

               (instance-provides ?id - instance ?i - interface)
               (instance-requires ?id - instance ?i - interface)

               (in-instance-pool ?id - instance)
               (instance-of ?id - instance ?c - class)
               (is-instantiated ?c)
               (attached ?ic1 - instance ?ic2 - instance)

               (class-provides-quality ?c - class ?p - quality)
               (instance-provides-quality ?id - instance ?p - quality)
               (interface-requires-quality ?i - interface ?p - quality)
               (is-validated ?id - instance)



               ;;;;;;;;;;;;;;;;;;;;;;;;;;;;;;;;;
               ;;; Structural design patterns
               ;;;;;;;;;;;;;;;;;;;;;;;;;;;;;;;;;

               (singleton ?c - class)

               (on-layer ?l1 - layer ?l2 - layer)
```

```
              (class-in-layer ?c - class ?l - layer)
              (instance-in-layer ?id - instance ?l - layer)


  )

;;;;;;;;;;;;;;;;;;;;;;;;;;;;;;;;;;;;;;;;;;;;;;;;;;;;;;;;;;;;;;;;;;;;;;;;;;;;;;;;;;;;;;;;;
;;
;;  Actions
;;
;;
;;;;;;;;;;;;;;;;;;;;;;;;;;;;;;;;;;;;;;;;;;;;;;;;;;;;;;;;;;;;;;;;;;;;;;;;;;;;;;;;;;;;;;;;;


  ;;;;;;;;;;;;;;;;;;;;;;;;;;;;;;;;;;;;;;;;;;;;;;;;;;;;;;;;;;;;;;;;;;;;;;;;;;;;;;;;;;;;;;;
  ;; Attatches a class instance to another class instance
  ;;;;;;;;;;;;;;;;;;;;;;;;;;;;;;;;;;;;;;;;;;;;;;;;;;;;;;;;;;;;;;;;;;;;;;;;;;;;;;;;;;;;;;;
  (:action attach-instance
     :parameters (?ic1 - instance  ?ic2 - instance)

      :precondition (and

                     ;; Validation
                     (is-validated ?ic1)

                      ;; Must not be already attached to instance 2
                      (not (attached ?ic1 ?ic2))

                      ;; The instance is not already attached to
                      ;; some other instance
                        (not(exists
                               (?o - instance)
                               (attached ?ic1 ?o)
                            )
                         )

                      ;; Layer restrictions. If the instance
                      ;; being attached is in a layer,
                      ;; then the other instance must respect
                      ;; layering constraints
                      (forall
                        (?l1 - layer)
                        (imply
                          (instance-in-layer ?ic1 ?l1)

                            ;; If the other instance is in a layer too,
                            ;; then the layer must be adjacent
                           (forall
                             (?l2 - layer)
                             (imply
                               (instance-in-layer ?ic2 ?l2)
                               (or
                                   (on-layer ?l1 ?l2)
                                   (on-layer ?l2 ?l1)
                                )

                             )
                          )

                      )
                 )
         )

           :effect (attached ?ic1 ?ic2)
```

```
 )


;;;;;;;;;;;;;;;;;;;;;;;;;;;;;;;;;;;;;;;;;;;;;;;;;;;;;;;;;;;;;;;;;;;;;;;;;;;;;;;;;
;; Attatches a class instance to another class instance
;;;;;;;;;;;;;;;;;;;;;;;;;;;;;;;;;;;;;;;;;;;;;;;;;;;;;;;;;;;;;;;;;;;;;;;;;;;;;;;;;
(:action attach-singleton-instance
   :parameters (?ic1 - instance  ?ic2 - instance)

        :precondition (and
              ;; Must not be already attached to this instance
             (not (attached ?ic1 ?ic2))

                   ;; Validation
                  (is-validated ?ic1)

                   ;; The instance must be of a singleton class
                  (exists
                      (?c - class)
                      (and
                         (singleton c?)
                         (instance-of ?ic1 ?c)
                       )
                   )


                   ;; Layer restrictions. If the instance being
                   ;; attached is in a layer,
                   ;; then the other instance must
                   ;; respect layering constraints
                  (forall
                     (?l1 - layer)
                     (imply
                         (instance-in-layer ?ic1 ?l1)

                          ;; If the other instance is in a layer too,
                          ;;then the layer must be adjacent
                         (forall
                            (?l2 - layer)
                            (imply
                                (instance-in-layer ?ic2 ?l2)
                                (or
                                  (on-layer ?l1 ?l2)
                                  (on-layer ?l2 ?l1)
                                 )
                             )
                         )

                      )
                   )
              )

           :effect (attached ?ic1 ?ic2)
)


;;;;;;;;;;;;;;;;;;;;;;;;;;;;;;;;;;;;;;;;;;;;;;;;;;;;;;;;;;;;;;;;;;;;;;;;;;;;;;;;;
;; Instantiates a class
;;;;;;;;;;;;;;;;;;;;;;;;;;;;;;;;;;;;;;;;;;;;;;;;;;;;;;;;;;;;;;;;;;;;;;;;;;;;;;;;;
(:action instantiate
   :parameters (?c - class ?id - instance)
         :precondition (and
```

```
                ;; Singleton restriction
                (not(singleton ?c))

                ;; There must be a free instance in the pool
                (in-instance-pool ?id)

                ;; Class dependencies
                (forall (?i - interface)
                        (imply
                            (class-requires ?c ?i)
                            (exists (?o - instance)
                                    (and
                                       (instance-provides ?o ?i)
                                       (attached ?o ?id)
                                    )
                            )
                        )
                   )

        )

        :effect (and
                     (not(in-instance-pool ?id))
                     (instance-of ?id ?c)
                     (is-instantiated ?c)

                     ;; Instance layer
                     (forall
                             (?l - layer)
                             (when
                                   (class-in-layer ?c ?l)
                                   (instance-in-layer ?id ?l)
                             )
                     )

                      ;; Class interface instantiation
                      (forall
                              (?i - interface)
                              (when
                                    (class-provides ?c ?i)
                                    (instance-provides ?id ?i)
                              )
                      )

                )
)


;;;;;;;;;;;;;;;;;;;;;;;;;;;;;;;;;;;;;;;;;;;;;;;;;;;;;;;;;;;;;;;;;;;;;;;;;;;;;;;;
;; Instantiates a singleton class
;;;;;;;;;;;;;;;;;;;;;;;;;;;;;;;;;;;;;;;;;;;;;;;;;;;;;;;;;;;;;;;;;;;;;;;;;;;;;;;;
(:action instantiate-singleton
   :parameters (?c - class ?id - instance)
        :precondition (and

                ;; Must be a singleton
               (singleton ?c)

               ;; There must be a free instance in the
               ;; pool if the singleton has to be instantiated
               (imply (not(is-instantiated ?c))
                      (in-instance-pool ?id)
               )
```

```
                ;; Enforce class dependencies if the
                ;; singleton has to be instantiated
                (forall (?i - interface)
                        (imply
                              (and
                                 (not(is-instantiated ?c))
                                 (class-requires ?c ?i)
                              )
                              (exists (?o - instance)
                                      (and
                                        (instance-provides ?o ?i)
                                        (attached ?o ?id)
                                      )
                              )
                        )
                )
            )

            :effect (and
                        (not(in-instance-pool ?id))
                        (instance-of ?id ?c)
                        (is-instantiated ?c)

                        ;; Instance layer
                        (forall
                                (?l - layer)
                                (when
                                      (class-in-layer ?c ?l)
                                      (instance-in-layer ?id ?l)
                                )
                        )


                        ;; Instantiate interfaces if the singleton
                        ;; has to be instantiated
                        (forall (?i - interface)
                                (when
                                      (and
                                          (not(is-instantiated ?c))
                                          (class-provides ?c ?i)
                                      )
                                      (instance-provides ?id ?i)

                                )
                        )

                    )
)


;;;;;;;;;;;;;;;;;;;;;;;;;;;;;;;;;;;;;;;;;;;;;;;;;;;;;;;;;;;;;;;;;;;;;;;;;;;;;;;;
;; Finds the inherited interfaces of a class
;;;;;;;;;;;;;;;;;;;;;;;;;;;;;;;;;;;;;;;;;;;;;;;;;;;;;;;;;;;;;;;;;;;;;;;;;;;;;;;;
(:action find-superclass-interfaces
   :parameters (?c - class ?s - class ?i - interface)
           :precondition (and
                              (subclass ?c ?s)
                              (class-provides ?s ?i)
                              (not (class-provides ?c ?i))

                        )
```

```
            :effect (class-provides ?c ?i)
)


;;;;;;;;;;;;;;;;;;;;;;;;;;;;;;;;;;;;;;;;;;;;;;;;;;;;;;;;;;;;;;;;;;;;;;;;;;;;
;; Finds the inherited interfaces of an interface
;;;;;;;;;;;;;;;;;;;;;;;;;;;;;;;;;;;;;;;;;;;;;;;;;;;;;;;;;;;;;;;;;;;;;;;;;;;;
(:action find-superinterface-interfaces
   :parameters (?i1 - interface ?i2 - interface ?c - class)
           :precondition (and
                              (subinterface ?i1 ?i2)
                              (class-provides ?c ?i2)
                              (not (class-provides ?c ?i1))
                         )
           :effect (class-provides ?c ?i1)
)


;;;;;;;;;;;;;;;;;;;;;;;;;;;;;;;;;;;;;;;;;;;;;;;;;;;;;;;;;;;;;;;;;;;;;;;;;;;;
;; Checks whether the specified instance fulfills all non-structural
;; requirements
;;;;;;;;;;;;;;;;;;;;;;;;;;;;;;;;;;;;;;;;;;;;;;;;;;;;;;;;;;;;;;;;;;;;;;;;;;;;
(:action validate-instance
   :parameters (?c - class ?id - instance)

       :precondition (and

                      (not(is-validated ?id))

                       (instance-of ?id ?c)



                       ;; If an interface of the instance
                       ;; requires a quality, then
                       ;; the instance must provide it
                       (forall
                           (?i - interface)
                           (forall
                              (?p - quality)
                              (imply
                                  (and
                                    (interface-requires-quality ?i ?p)
                                    (instance-provides ?id ?i)
                                  )
                                 (instance-provides-quality ?id ?p)
                              )
                       )

                      )

         )

            :effect (is-validated ?id)

 )

)
```

A.2. Consumer Notification System Problem

```
;;;;;;;;;;;;;;;;;;;;;;;;;;;;;;;;;;;;;;;;;;;;;;;;;;;;;;;;;;;;;;;;;;;;;;;;;;;;;;
;; Customer Notification System Example
;;;;;;;;;;;;;;;;;;;;;;;;;;;;;;;;;;;;;;;;;;;;;;;;;;;;;;;;;;;;;;;;;;;;;;;;;;;;;;

(define (problem software1)
  (:domain software-construction)
  (:objects
          IMessageDispatcher IEmailDispatcher ISMSDispatcher      - interface
          ICustomerEditor IProductEditor IPartnerEditor           - interface
          IChartViewer IChartEnabled                              - interface
          ICustomerManager IProductManager IPartnerManager        - interface
          ICustomerMarketing ICustomerNotification                - interface
          ICustomerScore IProductStatus IPartnerProductStatus     - interface
          ICustomerDAO IProductDAO IPartnerDAO                    - interface

          SystemLayer BusinessLayer PresentationLayer  - Layer

          o1 o2 o3 o4 o5 o6 o7 o8 o9 o10  - instance

          MessageDispatcherImpl1 EmailDispatcherImpl1 SMSDispatcherImpl1   - class
          CustomerEditorImpl1 ProductEditorImpl1 PartnerEditorImpl1        - class
          CustomerPurchaseViewerImpl1 PartnerViewerImpl1                   - class
          CustomerManagerImpl1 ProductManagerImpl1 PartnerManagerImpl1     - class
          CustomerScoreImpl1 CustomerScoreImpl2                            - class
          ProductStatusImpl1 PartnerProductStatusImpl1                     - class
          DAOImpl1 CustomerDAOImpl1 ProductDAOImpl1 PartnerDAOImpl1        - class

          CustomerNotificationImpl1                                        - class
  )

  (:init

       ;;;;;;;;;;;;;;;;;;;;;;;;;;;;;;;;
       ;; Initialize instance pool
       ;;;;;;;;;;;;;;;;;;;;;;;;;;;;;;;;

       (in-instance-pool o1)
       (in-instance-pool o2)
       (in-instance-pool o3)
       (in-instance-pool o4)
       (in-instance-pool o5)
       (in-instance-pool o6)
       (in-instance-pool o7)
       (in-instance-pool o8)
       (in-instance-pool o9)
       (in-instance-pool o10)

       ;;;;;;;;;;;;;;;;;;;;;;;;;;;;;;;;;;;;;;;;;;;;;;;;;;;;;
       ;; Define class and interface inheritance structure
       ;;;;;;;;;;;;;;;;;;;;;;;;;;;;;;;;;;;;;;;;;;;;;;;;;;;;;
       (subclass EmailDispatcherImpl1 MessageDispatcherImpl1)
       (subclass SMSDispatcherImpl1 MessageDispatcherImpl1)

       (subinterface IEmailDispatcher IMessageDispatcher)
       (subinterface ISMSDispatcher IMessageDispatcher)


       ;;;;;;;;;;;;;;;;;;;;;;;;;;;;;;;;;;;;;;;;;;;;;;
       ;; Define class requirements and capabilities
       ;;;;;;;;;;;;;;;;;;;;;;;;;;;;;;;;;;;;;;;;;;;;;;

       (class-provides MessageDispatcherImpl1 IMessageDispatcher)
```

```
(class-provides EmailDispatcherImpl1 IEmailDispatcher)

(class-provides SMSDispatcherImpl1 ISMSDispatcher)

(class-provides CustomerEditorImpl1 ICustomerEditor)
(class-requires CustomerEditorImpl1 ICustomerManager )

(class-provides ProductEditorImpl1 IProductEditor)
(class-requires ProductEditorImpl1 IPartnerManager)

(class-provides PartnerEditorImpl1 IPartnerEditor)
(class-requires PartnerEditorImpl1 IPartnerManager)


(class-provides CustomerPurchaseViewerImpl1 IChartViewer)
(class-requires CustomerPurchaseViewerImpl1 ICustomerManager)
(class-requires CustomerPurchaseViewerImpl1 IProductManager)

(class-provides PartnerViewerImpl1 IChartViewer)
(class-requires PartnerViewerImpl1 IChartEnabled)


(class-provides CustomerManagerImpl1 ICustomerManager)
(class-requires CustomerManagerImpl1 ICustomerDAO)

(class-provides ProductManagerImpl1 IProductManager)
(class-requires ProductManagerImpl1 IProductDAO)

(class-provides PartnerManagerImpl1 IPartnerManager)
(class-provides PartnerManagerImpl1 IChartEnabled)
(class-requires PartnerManagerImpl1 IPartnerDAO)

(class-provides CustomerScoreImpl1 ICustomerScore)
(class-requires CustomerScoreImpl1 ICustomerDAO)

(class-provides CustomerScoreImpl2 ICustomerScore)
(class-requires CustomerScoreImpl2 ICustomerDAO)
(class-requires CustomerScoreImpl2 IProductDAO)

(class-provides ProductStatusImpl1 IProductStatus)
(class-requires ProductStatusImpl1 IProductDAO)

(class-provides PartnerProductStatusImpl1 IPartnerProductStatus)
(class-requires PartnerProductStatusImpl1 IProductDAO)
(class-requires PartnerProductStatusImpl1 IPartnerDAO)

(class-provides DAOImpl1 ICustomerDAO)
(class-provides DAOImpl1 IProductDAO)
(class-provides DAOImpl1 IPartnerDAO)

(class-provides CustomerDAOImpl1 ICustomerDAO)

(class-provides ProductDAOImpl1 IProductDAO)

(class-provides PartnerDAOImpl1 IPartnerDAO)

;; The target class
(class-provides CustomerNotificationImpl1 ICustomerNotification)
(class-requires CustomerNotificationImpl1 IEmailDispatcher)
(class-requires CustomerNotificationImpl1 IProductStatus)
(class-requires CustomerNotificationImpl1 IPartnerProductStatus)
(class-requires CustomerNotificationImpl1 IProductManager)
```

```
        ;;;;;;;;;;;;;;;;;;;;;;;;;;;
        ;; Add layer constraints
        ;;;;;;;;;;;;;;;;;;;;;;;;;;;

         ;; Presentation layer
        (class-in-layer CustomerEditorImpl1 PresentationLayer)
        (class-in-layer ProductEditorImpl1 PresentationLayer)
        (class-in-layer PartnerEditorImpl1 PresentationLayer)
        (class-in-layer CustomerPurchaseViewerImpl1 PresentationLayer)
        (class-in-layer PartnerViewerImpl1 PresentationLayer)

         ;; Business layer
        (class-in-layer CustomerNotificationImpl1 BusinessLayer)
        (class-in-layer CustomerManagerImpl1 BusinessLayer)
        (class-in-layer ProductManagerImpl1 BusinessLayer)
        (class-in-layer PartnerManagerImpl1 BusinessLayer)
        (class-in-layer CustomerScoreImpl1 BusinessLayer)
        (class-in-layer CustomerScoreImpl2 BusinessLayer)
        (class-in-layer ProductStatusImpl1 BusinessLayer)
        (class-in-layer PartnerProductStatusImpl1 BusinessLayer)

        ;; System layer
        (class-in-layer DAOImpl1 SystemLayer)
        (class-in-layer CustomerDAOImpl1 SystemLayer)
        (class-in-layer ProductDAOImpl1 SystemLayer)
        (class-in-layer PartnerDAOImpl1 SystemLayer)
        (class-in-layer MessageDispatcherImpl1 SystemLayer)
        (class-in-layer EmailDispatcherImpl1 SystemLayer)
        (class-in-layer SMSDispatcherImpl1 SystemLayer)


        ;; Layering relationships
        (on-layer PresentationLayer BusinessLayer)
        (on-layer BusinessLayer SystemLayer)


        ;;;;;;;;;;;;;;;;;;;;;;;;;;;;;;;
        ;; Add singleton constraints
        ;;;;;;;;;;;;;;;;;;;;;;;;;;;;;;;

       (singleton DAOImpl1)
       (singleton CustomerDAOImpl1)
       (singleton ProductDAOImpl1)
       (singleton PartnerDAOImpl1)

  )

  (:goal

        ;; Our aim is the provision of ICustomerNotification
        (exists
               (?o - instance)
               (instance-provides ?o ICustomerNotification)
        )
  )
)
```

A.3. Simple Problem

```
;;;;;;;;;;;;;;;;;;;;;;;;;;;;;;;;;;;;;;;;;;;;;;;;;;;;;;;;;;;;;;;;;;;;;;;;;;;;;;
;; Simple problem
;;;;;;;;;;;;;;;;;;;;;;;;;;;;;;;;;;;;;;;;;;;;;;;;;;;;;;;;;;;;;;;;;;;;;;;;;;;;;;

(define (problem software1)
  (:domain software-construction)
  (:objects
          i1 i2 i3 i4 - interface
          c1 c2 c3 c4 - class
          o1 o2 o3 o4 o5 o6 o7 o8 o9 o10  - instance
  )

  (:init

        ;; Initialize instance pool
        (in-instance-pool o1)
        (in-instance-pool o2)
        (in-instance-pool o3)
        (in-instance-pool o4)
        (in-instance-pool o5)
        (in-instance-pool o6)
        (in-instance-pool o7)
        (in-instance-pool o8)
        (in-instance-pool o9)
        (in-instance-pool o10)

        ;; Declare classes requirements and capabilities
        (class-provides c1 i2)
        (class-provides c1 i3)
        (class-requires c1 i1)

        (class-provides c2 i4)
        (class-requires c2 i2)
        (class-requires c2 i3)

        (class-provides c3 i2)
        (class-requires c3 i1)

        (class-provides c4 i3)
        (class-requires c4 i2)

        ;; Declare the capabilities of the base instance
        (class-provides start i1)

  )

  (:goal
        (exists
              (?o - instance)
              (instance-provides ?o i4)
        )
  )

)
```

B. UML Diagrams of the Case Study

In this appendix we provide the UML diagrams that detail the domain used in the case study described in Section 7..

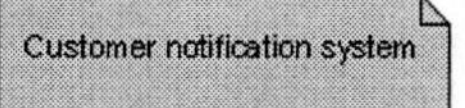

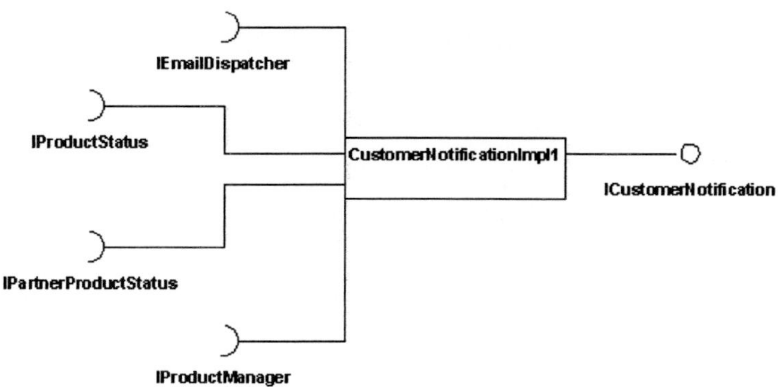

Figure 3. Final class that we wish to obtain through automatic generation.

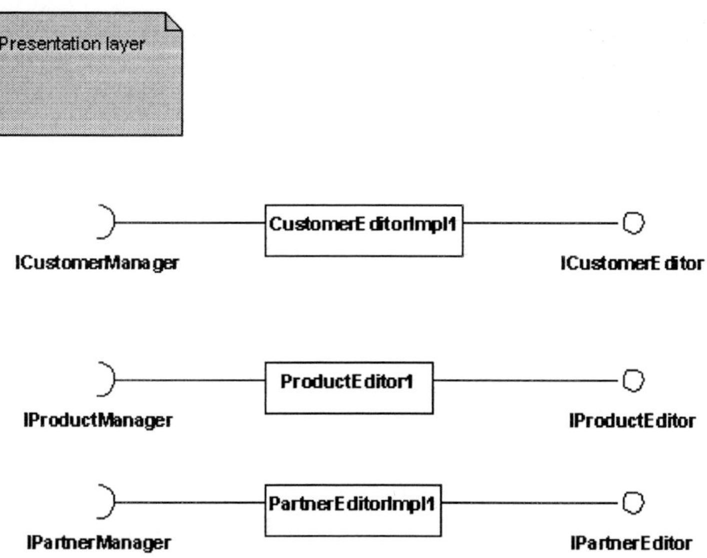

Figure 4. Presentation layer classes.

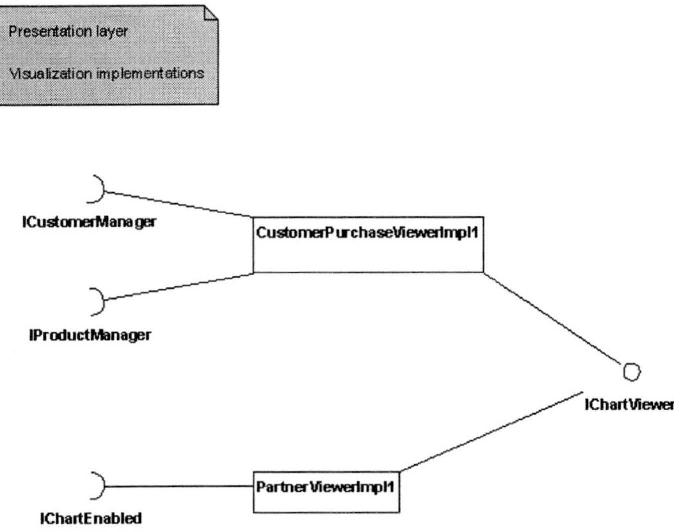

Figure 5. Presentation layer classes.

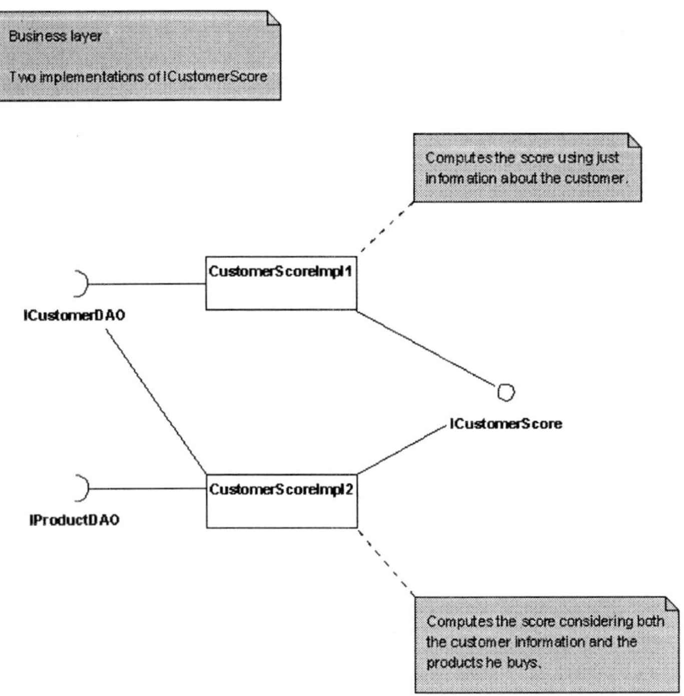

Figure 6. Business layer classes.

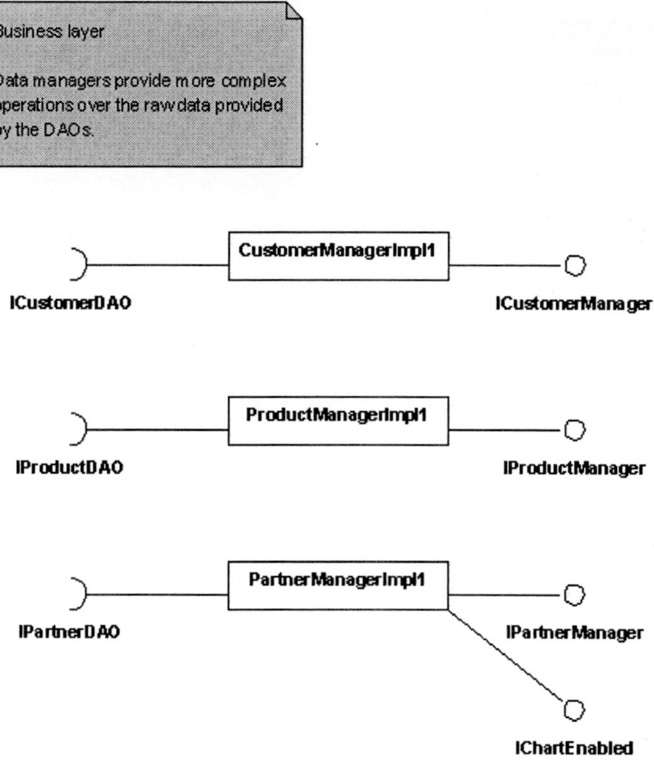

Figure 7. Business layer classes.

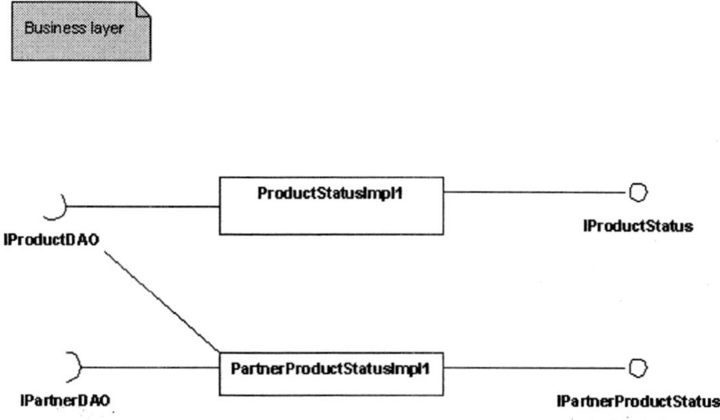

Figure 8. Business layer classes.

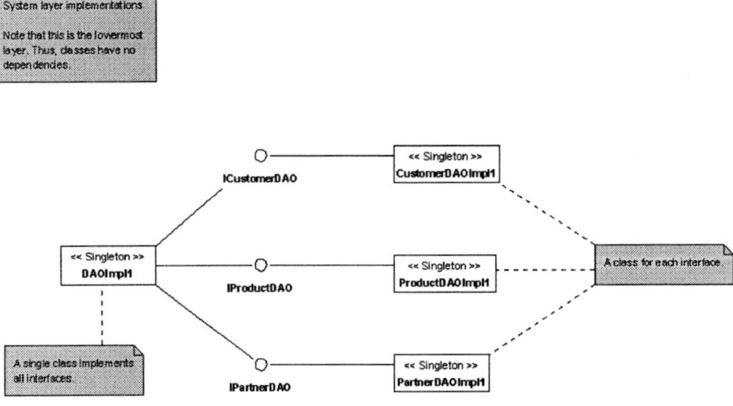

Figure 9. System layer classes.

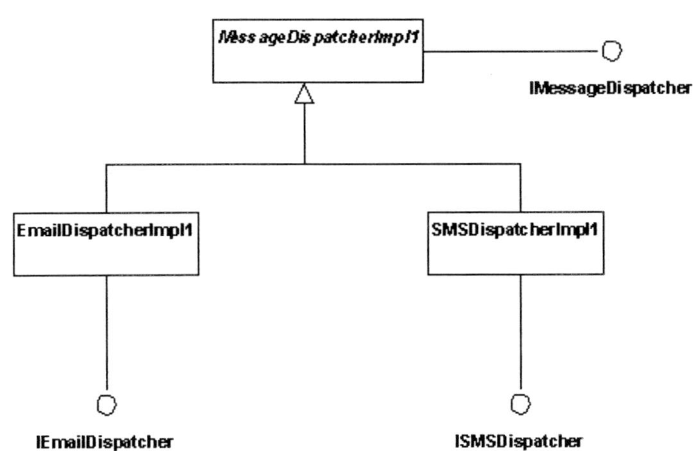

Figure 10. System layer classes.

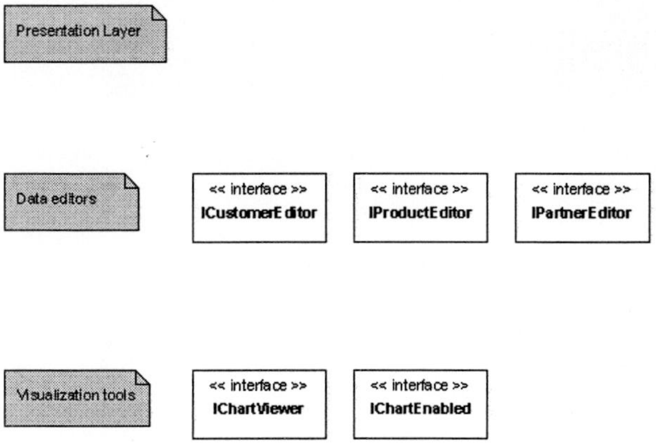

Figure 11. Presentation layer interfaces.

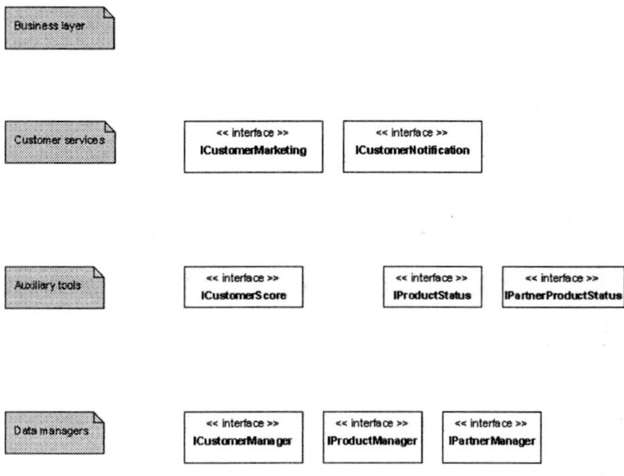

Figure 12. Business layer interfaces.

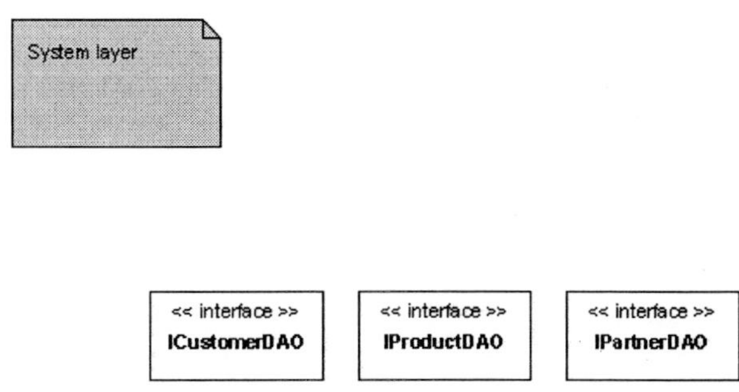

Figure 13. System layer interfaces.

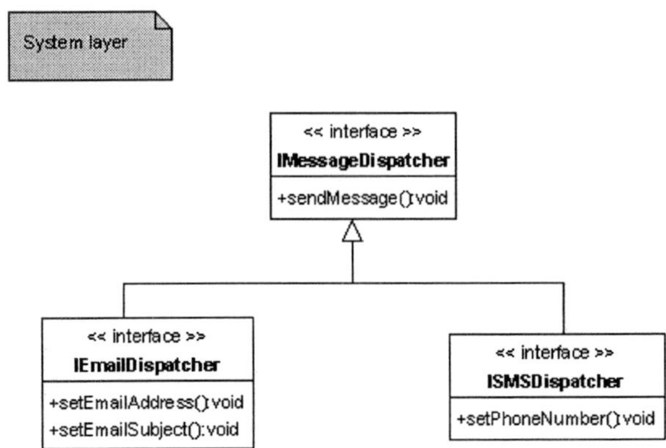

Figure 14. System layer interfaces. The interfaces' operations are not taken in account by the planner.

References

[1] L. Bass, C. Buhman, S. Comella-Dorda, F. Long, J. Robert, R. Seacord, and K. Wallnau. Market assessment of component based software engineering. *Internal Research and Development*, 2001.

[2] T. J. Biggerstaff and A. J. Perlis. *Software Reusability – Applications and Experience*, volume 2. Addison–Wesley Publishing Company, first edition, 1989.

[3] T. J. Biggerstaff and A. J. Perlis. *Software Reusability – Concepts and Models*, volume 1. Addison–Wesley Publishing Company, first edition, 1989.

[4] Code generation network. http://www.codegeneration.net/.

[5] Ivica Crnkovic and Magnus Larsson. *Building Reliable Component-based Software Systems*. Artech House, 2002.

[6] Homepage of fast-forward. http://www.mpi-sb.mpg.de/ hoffmann/ff.html.

[7] P. Freeman. A perspective on reusability. In P. Freeman, editor, *Tutorial: Software Reusability. IEEE* – The Computer Society Press, 1987.

[8] P. Freeman. *Tutorial: Software Reusability*. *IEEE* – The Computer Society Press, 1987.

[9] Erich Gamma, Richard Helm, Ralph Johnson, and John Vlissides. *Design Patterns: Elements of Reusable Object-Oriented Software*. Addison-Wesley, 1995.

[10] David Garlan, Robert Allen, and John Ockerbloom. Architectural mismatch, or, why it's hard to build systems out of existing parts. In *Proceedings of the 17th International Conference on Software Engineering*, pages 179–185, Seattle, Washington, Abril 1995.

[11] Malik Ghallab, Adele Howe, Craig Knoblock, Drew McDermott, Ashwin Ram, Manuela Veloso, Daniel Weld, and David Wilkins. Pddl – the planning definition language. 1998.

[12] E. Horowitz and J. B. Munson. An expansive view of reusable software. In T. J. Biggerstaff and A. J. Perlis, editors, *Software Reusability*. Addison–Wesley Publishing Company, 1989.

[13] Dana Nau Malik Ghallab and Paolo Traverso. *Automated Planning : Theory and Practice*. Morgan Kaufmann, 2004.

[14] M. D. McIlroy. Mass produced software components. In P. Naur and B. Randell, editors, *Software Engineering*, pages 138–155, Brussels, 1969. Scientific Affairs Division, NATO. Report of a conference sponsored by the NATO Science Committee, Garmisch, Germany, 7th to 11th October 1968.

[15] Omg model driven arthitecture. http://www.omg.org/mda/.

[16] W. Schäfer, R. Prieto-Díaz, and M. Matsumoto. *Software Reusability*. Ellis Horwood, 1994.

[17] Clemens Szyperski. *Component Software*. Addison-Wesley, 2002.

[18] Jeffrey M. Voas. The challenges of using cots software in component-based development. *Computer*, **31**(6):44–45, 1998.

In: Computer Software Engineering Research
Editor: Ari D. Klein, pp. 143-159

ISBN: 1-60021-774-5

Chapter 5

Impact of a Value-Based Approach to Training Software Inspectors: Empirical Results of a Controlled Software Inspection Experiment

Lesley P.W. Land and Shieh Nee Cheah
University of New South Wales, School of Information Systems, Technology and Management, Sydney, NSW 2052, Australia

Abstract

Software inspection is a manual software quality technique for ensuring that software defects are identified early in the software development lifecycle, and therefore prevents these defects from propagating to the later stages of development where rework would be a lot more expensive. There is abundant evidence in the literature that if properly applied, it improves the overall productivity of developers by reducing unnecessary effort and time [10]. Most empirical investigations test relative effectiveness of different defect detection methods. Given the complexity of software, and the lack of proper training of software engineers in institutions, more empirical investigations is warranted to understand how to better train inspectors. Constraints in the real-world (limited time and effort resources) and the size/complexity of software also mean that not all software artefacts can be inspected; and any time consuming activity such as inspector training should be as optimal as possible. Defects left undetected in artefacts are deemed as risks to the final quality of the software product.

In recent years, a series of experiments compare methods of training software inspectors [7, 8]. This study builds on these experiments, by proposing that a value-based approach is consistent with existing support for the overall discipline of value-based software engineering [5], and therefore should be built in as a strategy for training software inspectors. We report on a laboratory experiment testing the impact of a value-based approach to training software inspectors, and compared the performance of these inspectors to a control group with no specific defect detection training. We derived the value-based training approach by modifying the taxonomy of software development risk proposed by SEI to suit the inspection task [5]. This taxonomy ensures that the breadth of all software development risks is dealt with in a systematic way. For comparisons with previous results, these were also compared with a treatment group where inspectors were trained using work examples. An initial pilot was conducted to validate the instruments and experimental procedure, and a main experiment was conducted following the pilot. Our results showed significant improvement in the number of defects identified using the value-based approach, over the other treatment groups. This study has implications for how inspectors should be trained for both students and practitioners.

Keywords: Software quality, inspection, review, value-based software engineering, inspector training.

1. Introduction

Software inspection is a well established technique for improving software quality via defect detection [10]. It is typically applied manually, although there has been some effort to try to automate the process. In broad terms, most research in the area of software inspection has as its major objective – to improve the software inspection/review process, through a number of factors such as different review designs and defect detection methods [2, 24, 25]. In particular, most of the research has been focused on comparing the relative effectiveness of defect detection methods. Despite some positive results in methods such as perspective-based reading techniques, we do not see them being widely adopted in practice. Defect detection methods focus on the use of specific inspection aids (e.g. perspectives) during defect detection.

It is indisputable that the inspection task is complex, as it requires technical skills and experience [29], and perhaps even non-technical inspector characteristics [20], as the latter theory suggests. Sauer et. al.'s work [29] (Figure 2) suggests that task training could indirectly improve inspection training by improving the individual's task expertise. However their proposition has not been validated.

Not much work has been focused on training inspectors. Given the labour intensive nature of this technique, it seems rationale to find ways to better train inspectors so that they can learn to apply the technique more effectively. The literature on program comprehension attempts to understand how programmers study and understand program code, which will benefit programmers in programming and related activities. Storey summarizes the theories used in program comprehension [30]. Unfortunately, these cannot be applied to other types of software artifact (e.g. requirements, designs) which are vastly different to code artifacts.

The central target of training is the inspector/reviewer, and training can address both qualitative (e.g. education and service professionalism) and quantitative aspects of inspection performance (Kim, Sauer et al. 1995). Earlier empirical studies on training inspectors were very positive in terms of improving inspection performance. However, only a few approaches have been tested [7, 8, 19] : process training (representing the conventional training received by inspectors) with/without practice, and worked examples. In the light of recent emphasis on value-based software engineering approaches, our main motivation for the current study is to test the value of value-based approaches within the context of inspector training. To our knowledge this has not been studied before.

Our key research questions are therefore:

Is a value-based approach to inspector training beneficial for improving inspection performance?

What is the relative effectiveness of software inspector's training methods – using value-based, worked examples and perspective-based approaches?

2. Literature Review

The main objective of defect detection methods is to maximize defect finding and the two stage defect detection model (Figure 1) is commonly adopted. These are the two stages which directly affect the detection of defects – individual preparation followed by group meeting. Therefore inspector training can refer to both stages. We feel effort should focus on gaining a good understanding of training individuals for Stage 1, before dealing with training for Stage 2. There is evidence that individual preparation is essential and greatly influences final performance, in fact nominal group performance (calculated by merging unique defects from Stage 1) has been shown to exceed interacting group performance [18]. Stage 2 training involves dealing with group dynamics, and the process and outcome of training for Stage 2 would also depend on how well individuals have been trained for Stage 1. Therefore, it is essential to focus on Stage 1 training first.

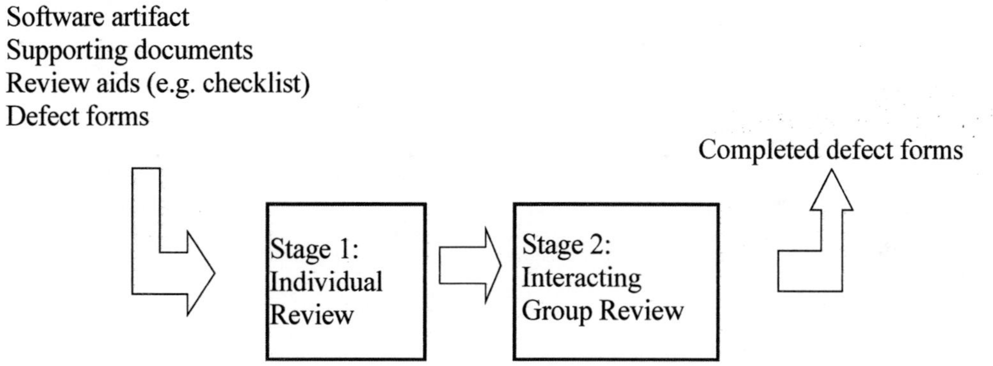

Software artifact
Supporting documents
Review aids (e.g. checklist)
Defect forms

Completed defect forms

Stage 1:
Individual
Review

Stage 2:
Interacting
Group Review

Figure 1. The two-staged defect detection model (Land, Tan et al. 2005).

A recent review of the empirical research in software defect detection methods concluded that because studies on defect detection techniques, inspections and testing have been conducted in isolation, we understand little about the relationship between inspection and testing, and the effects of combining them; and our collective knowledge of testing is still very limited [28]. We argue that rather than continuing along this line of research, i.e. determining which technique(s) to choose and how best to combine them, our view is that software developers are generally quite able to choose technique(s) during the software development process. Besides, the artifact type already partially forces the choice of techniques. For example, inspections can be applied to all software artifacts, but execution testing can only be applied to code. Furthermore, there is empirical evidence to suggest that the choice of techniques depends on context dependent factors such as developer characteristics (e.g. responsibility), communication between developers, management and customers, project/organizational resources, and culture [14]. Therefore generic guidelines for quality technique use would be hard to construct because usage decisions are intertwined with contextual factors.

On the other hand, there is ample evidence (both empirical and practical) on the potential benefits of applying software inspections/reviews to improve software quality [10, 12, 13]. However, anecdotal and informal discussions with researchers and practitioners reveal that few organizations widely practice inspections, if at all. Given the complexity of the inspection task, it is quite surprising that not many empirical studies address this area.

There are only a few theoretical frameworks underlying this work. Models are important as it enables research to be more focused and more scientifically driven. Sauer and colleagues [29] provided a framework based on the behavioural literature to investigate the factors which might affect software inspection performance [29] (see Figure 2). This framework clearly informs us that task training impacts the expertise of inspectors which in turn directly impacts his/her inspection performance. The relationship between inspector expertise and performance is at the heart of Sauer et al's framework. To our knowledge, it has not been proven incorrect. However, software artifacts are so diverse in multiple attributes such as domain of application, size, complexity, notations/programming language, etc, it would be very difficult and impractical to provide guidelines for the expertise requirement of inspectors. A more practical and fruitful approach to research is to investigate alternative ways to improve inspector's performance.

In the software inspection literature, inspection training is highly recommended. Strauss and Ebenau [31] claimed that '*Training is an important part of inspection implementation*' (p.99). At AT&T, Fowler (1986) found that inspection training could improve the performance of software inspection. Rifkin and Deimel [27] also reduced the customers reported errors by 90% through a software reading training.

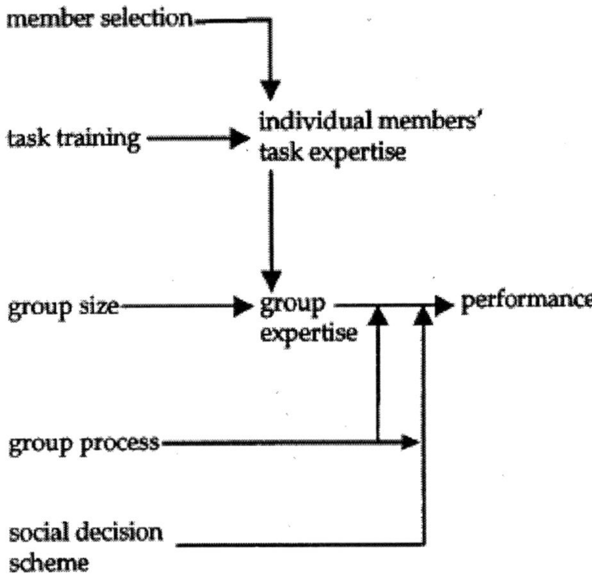

Figure 2. Schematic summary of the behavioral theory of group performance [29].

Training has been targeted for all project members as well as management. Inspection training for management aims at '*providing an understanding of the inspection process, benefits, cost, and the need for management commitment*' [31] (p.99). Inspection training for the staff aims at '*teaching the staff inspection procedures and how to perform them*' [31] (p.99). The inspection training in this paper refers to the training for (non-management) staff as well as for any other stakeholders who are not part of the technical development team (such as customers), and also specifically focused at Stage 1 of the 2-stage defect detection model mentioned. Managers usually do not participate in inspection processes [12], therefore management training is not within the scope of this paper.

It is generally agreed that inspection training is essential for the success of the software inspection, however training requirements differ with different review types such as walkthroughs [35], technical reviews [12] and Fagan's [10] inspections; this is mainly because these review types vary in formality. Strauss and Ebenau [31] suggest having a maximum of 25 trainees in order to maintain training efficiency. However, there are few experiential reports or controlled experiments on training inspectors. Experiential reports like that of Tyran's [33] are however uncontrolled and thus introduces many extraneous variables which makes performance prediction almost impossible. They are however useful for exploring and piloting training methods.

Chowdhury and Land [7, 8] conducted two experiments (the second was a replication) and quite conclusively showed that training had positive effects on inspection performance. However, their work was based on only one type of training method – training by using worked examples, and was tested on the inspection of requirements documents. They were motivated by the literature from the Education area. Worked examples significantly increase the students' understanding about the knowledge taught during class [32]. Worked examples were examples of different types of defect introduced during the training session [7]. The contents of process training with worked examples include [19]:

- All of the contents of process training (see below).
- Worked examples consisting of a variety[1] of different defect instances, including parts of the software artifact where the defects occurred and explanations of why those were considered to be defects and what their defect classifications were. Worked examples are used to enhance the trainees' understanding about the taught knowledge. For instance, instructor can use worked examples to illustrate the differences among the different defects types; also they can use worked examples to teach the inspectors about the most likely defect locations.

In a following study [19], Land and colleagues extended upon Chowdhury and Land's earlier work to include other training methods. Specifically, they separated the 'classic' training documented in the literature and added special features to them. They were also interested to discover if earlier results translate to other types of documents identified in the early lifecycle of software development, such as Entity-Relationship Diagrams. O'Neill [23] introduced "**process training**". Each participant was educated on the structured review process and its components, including the defined roles of participants, product checklists, and defect forms and reports. In a nutshell, inspectors were told "what to do" and "how to do" in process training. Inspectors were also told the reasons for inspection ("why"), in order to motivate the task. The contents of inspection **process training** [19] include:

[1] The exact number of worked examples required to make a difference to performance effectiveness is still a point of contention.

- Benefits for conducting software inspection.
- Description of defects types, including tips for categorizing.
- The structured review process: described in stages.
- The different roles and responsibilities of inspectors.
- Descriptions of defect forms and any other materials required.

Another training variation introduced was process training with **practice**. In the practice phase, subjects engage in real experience with the inspection task, in addition, feedback is given to inspectors in order to enhance their understanding about how to handle the inspection task. Therefore, the practice phase was an interactive session between the instructor and the inspectors. They found that simply knowing the details about the "what" and the "why" of the inspection process does not assist with improving performance. Furthermore, process training with practice and process training with worked examples both show to be promising in improving performance, compared with no training at all, and practice alone, significantly improved defect detection of true defects [19].

Inspector training may also take on a value-based approach. The notion of **Value-Based Software Engineering** has been discussed [5], and software engineering researchers are increasingly aware of the need to make value perspectives explicit to all stakeholders of software projects. Current software engineering practices are commonly conducted in value-neutral settings: user requirements are treated with equal importance; design methodologies merely involve logical mappings and transformation (e.g. object-oriented development); end systems track project costs and schedule, rather than stakeholder/business values; software engineers are only responsible in turning the software requirements into verified codes [5]. Incorrect software decisions negatively influence system's cost, schedule, value and the business itself. Moreover, it is also claimed that most software project failures are caused by value-neutral oriented shortfalls such as lack of user input, incomplete requirements, changing of requirements, and lack of resources, unrealistic expectations, unclear objectives, and unrealistic time frames. [5]

An important element to the value-based approach is **risk analysis and management.** In the context of the software inspection, we argue that it is a unique quality technique that permits artifacts produced in any stage of the software lifecycle to be inspected by diverse stakeholders. Consequently, it offers a good opportunity to address and manage risk issues. While value-based testing has been raised as being important for software quality in order to maximize business value contribution [26], finding problematic issues (according to the values defined by key stakeholders) of artefacts produced earlier in the software lifecycle using software inspection, would be even more critical, and this approach could potentially save further rework.

To fully support stakeholder value proposition in "value-based" testing, it is crucial to consider arising opportunities and perceived risks [3]. A risk may lead to a positive or negative consequence, and the concept of risk reflects the variation in outcomes [1]. Thus, a risky alternative is one for which the variance is large [34]. Using a value-based, risk-driven approach to inspector training has these advantages. Firstly, it reinforces the importance of delivering stakeholder values to inspectors. This is a reminder that real world constraints (e.g. limited resources) cannot be ignored in ensuring software quality, and that a value-based approach directs defect detection to locations which contravenes value propositions.

Secondly, it defines value from a risk management framework and therefore ensures all aspects of risks are covered. We therefore propose that using a value-based approach derived using a 'generic' risk framework, would be useful for training inspectors. This ensures a good coverage of risk categories that have been derived from accumulation of previous research in software project risks.

While value-based, risk-driven approach to inspector training is novel, the notion of using risk to derive perspectives in perspective based reading, is not new. [21] empirically tested a new form of perspective-based reading called value-based reading vs. value-neutral checklist-based reading. Reviewers using value-based reading, negotiated with stakeholders to define the priority of each system capability. The experimental subjects focused on the system capabilities in decreasing priorities. The results showed that value-based reviews were roughly twice as cost-effective as value-neutral techniques [21]. Prior to their work, the derivation of perspectives in different studies was not explained. This blackbox approach to the construction of perspectives is problematic for both practice and further research, as different perspectives were needed for reading different software artifacts, therefore without explanation, construction of perspectives was not possible. The use of value-based inspector training has overlaps with value-based perspective reading approach in that both promote the use of value perspectives to drive defect detection. The former however incorporates "training" elements by using an instructor to facilitate the training, and provide interactive feedback to the inspectors. This way any issues or misunderstanding faced by the inspectors can be immediately clarified by the instructor. This is tantamount to a facilitated "practice" with feedback component.

2.1. Research Questions

Our main research questions are therefore:

Question 1:
Do software inspectors trained using a value-based risk-driven approach outperform those who were trained using worked examples?

Question 2:
Do software inspectors trained using a value-based, risk-driven approach outperform those who use the perspective-based defect detection?

Question 1 tests the viability of a value-based risk-driven approach, compared with inspectors trained using worked examples. This question builds on previous research questions that showed that inspectors trained using worked examples outperformed those who were not trained [7, 8]. Question 2 tests whether this value-based training is more effective than the perspective-based reading technique? The key difference between the two is the use of instructor or facilitator for face to face feedback in value-based training, whereas perspective-based training uses the questions to guide inspectors in their reading of the artefact concerned. If affirmative, question 2 shows that the value-based training intervention is the preferred option mainly due to facilitator feedback and interaction.

3. Research Hypotheses

Based on the research questions in Section 2.1, we formulated the following research hypotheses:

H1: Training with value-based, risk-driven approach (T_{VB}) yields better defect detection performance than training using worked examples (T_{EG}).

H2: Training with value-based, risk driven approach (T_{VB}) yields better defect detection performance than perspective-based reading (T_P) derived in the same way as those used by T_{VB}.

T_{VB} defines the training with value-based, risk driven approach which is interactive and with feedback, between the instructor and inspectors. T_{EG} defines training using worked examples as in previous studies [7, 8]. T_P defines perspective-based reading approach, using the same perspective as in T_{VB}, except has no instructor involvement in the inspectors' defect detection task. In other words, T_P is the same as T_{VB} except minus the facilitator involvement that occurs in T_{VB}.

H1 tests whether T_{VB} improves over T_{EG}. Since T_{EG}.was already shown to improve over no training in previous work [7, 8], this comparison focuses on just T_{VB} and T_{EG}. It proposes that T_{VB} as better than T_{EG}. If proven to be true, T_{VB} will be shown to be a promising new training approach, over approaches tested so far. H2 proposes that T_{VB} will be better than the widely mentioned T_P. If shown to be true, it will highlight the importance of the role of the instructor/facilitator in the training process.

4. The Experiments

Two controlled experiments (1 and 2) were conducted. Experiment 1 tests H1. Experiment 2 tests H1-H3.

We view Experiment 1 as a pilot to Experiment 2. Conversely, Experiment 2 also served as a replication of Experiment 1, and therefore strengthens the conclusions if their results are the same. Both experiments used exactly the same software artifact – an entity-relationship design diagram, and only included Stage 1 of the defect detection task (Figure 1), that is, Stage 2 was not included in the experiments.

Experiment 1 manipulated one independent variable (inspector training). The control group is given training with worked examples similar to those used by [7, 8] and the treatment group with the value-based, risk driven approach. The purpose of Experiment 1 is twofold:

1) It acts as a pilot for validating the experimental instruments.
2) It explores the value of a new type of training we propose, which adopts the value-based software engineering paradigm, using a software risk framework defined by SEI. We call this training value-based training (T_{VB}).

Experiment 1 enables us to test H1. Table 1 summarizes how the independent variable is exposed to the treatment and control groups.

Table 1. Experimental Manipulation for Experiment 1

Control Group	Treatment Group
Training with worked examples (T_{EG})	Training with value-based risk-driven approach (T_{VB})

Experiment 2 manipulated only one independent variable (inspector training). A new control group is introduced - T_P, which enables comparison with value-based perspective based reading. In T_P, there is no instructor intervention, inspectors receive no training from the instructor, beyond basic process training (see Section 2) (as with all other treatment groups). The treatment groups are T_{VB} and T_{EG}, as previously defined. The purpose of Experiment 2 is twofold:

1. To validate the findings and outcome of Experiment 1.
2. It explores the relative effects of T_{VB} and T_P, and therefore enables us to test H2. Since T_P has been shown to be more effective than say checklist or ad-hoc defect detection methods, it would be interesting to see if instructor training makes any difference. Inclusion of T_{EG} enables replication of Experiment 1.

Table 2. Experimental Manipulation for Experiment 2

Control Group	Treatment Groups
Training with value-based perspective (T_P)	Training with value-based (T_{VB})
	Training with worked examples (T_{EG})

The same set of questionnaire regarding subjects' programming expertise and experience precedes both experiments. This will be used to discover subjects' background and inspection experience before each experiment and it will also serve as a baseline for identifying training effects. Subjects were randomly assigned to the treatment and control groups in each experiment. This ensured that confounding factors were ruled out.

4.1. Dependent Variables

The experiments use these dependent variables:

1) Total number of defects (D_T). These include both major and minor defects, these are issues which need rework and if left undetected will decrease the quality of the design.
2) Number of major defects (D_{MJ}). These are defects that affect the functionality and production of the software.
3) Number of minor defects (D_{MN}). These are defects that will affect the overall quality of the technical document but will not affect functionality.

4.2. Experimental Procedure

The procedure for the two experiments was similar. For each experiment, the inspection task was designed and integrated into an undergraduate introductory data management course. The experiments were undertaken towards the end of two consecutive teaching sessions, so that students would have gained familiarity over the design concepts and notations used in the experiments' software artefact – an entity-relationship diagram. As part of software quality assurance, all subjects were lectured on the basics of the software inspection process, ensuring the same process training[2] was undertaken for all subjects. The study was approved by the University's Ethics Committee. Student consent and confidentiality agreement were obtained prior to the experiments as required by the Ethics Committee of The University of New South Wales. Just before the inspection task began, each subject completed the questionnaire previously discussed.

27 undergraduate students undertaking the introductory data management course (about 30% response rate) participated in Experiment 1. AUD 10 was offered to each subject for completion of the task. We were not certain that the incentive was effective since not all subjects collected the money token even if they had completed the task. Therefore in Experiment 2, the offer of money as an incentive for participation was withdrawn. In Experiment 1, subjects were allowed between 40 minutes to complete the task, after 40 minutes of inspector training (either T_{EG} or T_{VB}).

61 undergraduate students undertaking the same introductory data management course participated in Experiment 2. There was a mixture of undergraduate and postgraduate students in this sample. However, background data from the questionnaire showed no significant difference in the work and inspection experience of both the undergraduates and postgraduates. All subjects had very little or no work and inspection experience. In Experiment 2, subjects were also allowed 40 minutes to complete the task, however the inspector training which precedes it was slightly shorter (30 minutes) due to a longer duration to organise bigger class size.

The experiments were randomized (within the logistics and timetabling constraints of the courses) to allow direct manipulation and control of the hypothesized independent variables (both treatments and control). The need to randomize subjects stems from the importance of eliminating the influence of extraneous variable [4]. This is a suitable method as it is a practical and effective way to test the relationship between the treatment and the control in a limited time frame. It has also been discovered that controlled experiments '*enable strong casual explanations between the variable of interest due to the controlled setting, and generate stronger statistical confidence in conclusion*' [2].

4.3. Experimental Materials

These are the main materials used for both experiments:

1. General instructions for completing the task. These instructions are tailored to each treatment.

[2] This covers the "what", "how" and "why" of the inspection process, but excludes practical component.

2. Software inspection artifact – an entity relationship diagram (ERD) (using the Chen notation which was taught to students in the course) accompanied with business requirements. The database describes a tour company setting up a database for recording employee details and tours. The diagram is one A4 page in size. It was validated by two database designers prior to the experiment to check for obvious errors. Then, 35 (major and minor) defects were seeded in the diagram.
3. Defect form - which was completed by each subject to record the location, defect type and defect descriptions.
4. Value-based, risk driven perspective. The same perspective was used for all subjects in the T_{VB} and T_P treatment groups. The perspective contains descriptions, explanations, hints and/or questions addressing the context of specific defects. It is generated based on the important values deemed important by the stakeholders. In the experiments, the stakeholders were identified to be the lecturers for database courses. Therefore the values of the main stakeholders were conveyed by represented by a number of lecturers experienced in the database areas. In particular, the characteristics of good entity relationship designs and common mistakes made by students were elicited from three experienced lecturers. Then, using these responses and SEI's software project risk identification taxonomy [6], we generated the perspective. The use of the taxonomy ensured that all risks were systematically addressed. The taxonomy consisted of questions with cues and follow-up probe questions. Due to its comprehensive nature, it contains questions that are not relevant for our task. The perspectives were carefully generated after several iterations with authors, to ensure they reflect the values expressed by the lecturers (from analysis of our interview transcripts), as well as cover the relevant risk areas defined in the taxonomy.

   During experimental execution, the T_{VB} treatment groups were facilitated by an instructor in a face-to-face teaching mode, students were encouraged to interact and ask questions to make sure they fully understood how to execute the task. However, subjects subjected to T_P undertook the inspection task independently without any instructor intervention. They only used the given perspective as a guide to the task execution.
5. Worked examples of defects. These worked examples were based on an entity relationship diagram and the requirements of a hospital's patient billing system, these were specially designed for training the T_{EG} treatment group. Thus the ERD on which the worked examples were based was different to that used in the actual inspection task undertook after the training. The same 5 worked examples were discussed with all the subjects in the T_{EG} treatment group. Subjects subjected to T_{EG} were not given the perspective. The instructor used these worked examples to explain each defect shown in the worked example, and indicated the location of defect in the artefact, as well as a description of the defect concerned.
6. Pre/Post Experimental Questionnaire – All subjects completed a series of questions before and after the task. The pre-questionnaire is a pre-test to discover subjects' experience in programming and in software inspections, as well as their technical capabilities. The post-questionnaire is completed at the end of the task, mainly as a feedback to the authors as to their satisfaction level of the task undertaken, difficulties faced, they can also offer suggestions for future improvement. This is a useful source of information for experimental replications.

4.4. Data Collection and Data Analysis

We collected and coded 88 defect forms from the experiments using the variables defined in Section 4.1. We applied normality and homogeneity tests to the data before the choice of either parametric or non-parametric tests. The significant criterion is set at 0.05 as recommended by [22]. Incorrect classification of defects was not penalized, we focused on defect identification during data coding. Data from the questionnaire was also coded. The research hypotheses were tested using all three dependent variables. Data was first analyzed separately for each experiment then combined since the results were no different for each experiment.

4.5. Experimental Validity

Internal validity describes the extent to which the research design permits us to reach causal conclusions about the effect of the independent variable on the dependent variable [16]. We consider the following internal validity threats below.

Selection refers to any pre-existing differences between subjects in the different sessions of the experimental conditions that can influence the dependent variable. We minimised the differences between individuals in the different treatment groups (i.e. the selection threat) by randomly assigning individual subjects to the treatment groups. Subjects were not aware about the experimental manipulation.

Maturation refers to those naturally occurring process within subjects that could cause a change in performance [9, 17]. Variation in the time of the day may have caused maturation effect. For example, experiment conduct later in the day may suffer more than an experiment conducted earlier in the day when subjects were less tired. We did however ensure through piloting, that sufficient time was allowed to complete the task. The only possible maturation threat was the use of the same trainer across both experiments. It was possible that training for Experiment 2 had improved over time. However, we controlled this by using the same scripts (training materials in Powerpoint slides and notes) for the same treatment groups across the experiments to ensure that experiment 2 subjects did not have undue advantages due to learning effect on the part of the trainer. Subjects were only exposed to the review code during the experiment and not before; this was again to prevent them from discussing the code before the experiment. The overall maturation threat is hence negligible.

Instrumentation refers changes in the measuring instrument [11]. Instruments were not changed in the same treatment groups across the 2 experiments unless to reflect a different treatment. Therefore we did not anticipate any instrumentation threat.

Threats to External Validity

External validity threats limit our ability to generalise our research results to the general software engineering population and settings. We identify the possible external validity threats below.

Representativeness of subjects – The subjects participating in the experiments were undergraduates from various disciplines and at different levels of study. This would mean difficulties in our ability to generalize our experimental results to the population of software professionals. However, a study on estimation task showed that there was no significant difference between student and professional subjects [15].

Artificiality of artifacts – The business requirements and the ERDs used may not be a true representation of what is currently being used in the industry today. It is much simpler and less complex than those used in the real contexts. In addition, the defects in the ERDs were artificially seeded (i.e. not naturally occurring). We attempted to insert defects across different defect categories and diagram locations. Defects were carefully validated by software inspection professionals/database designers/IT professionals. There was no indication from our observation during the experiment that the task set for the subjects were unmanageable, too simplistic, or could not be completed in the given time. This is important so that we know the reviewers were provided with sufficient time for the task and hence lack of performance was not due to time factor. Hence the issue of the representativeness of the materials is mitigated. In addition, we were more interested in measuring the relative performance of subjects across treatment groups rather than their absolute performance values. We believe that a well controlled experimental setting would help us achieve this objective, and that the problems associated with artificiality of artifacts were less important comparatively.

5. Results

The results presented in this section is that from the data combined from both experiments.

Results for H1 (T_{VB} vs. T_{EG})

H1 was supported for D_T, D_{MJ}, and D_{MN} (see Table 3). Subjects trained with value-based, risk-driven approach found significantly more defects ($p<0.05$), by about 24%, 18% and 42.5%, for D_T, D_{MJ} and D_{MN} respectively. Note that the value-based approach appeared to have least impact on major defects.

Table 3. H1 Results: Means for treatment groups T_{VB} vs T_{VB}

	T_{EG}	T_{VB}	p value
Total number of true defect (both major and minor) (D_T)	9.12	12.06	p= 0.005*
Total number of major defect (D_{MJ})	7.36	9.00	p= 0.028*
Total number of minor defect (D_{MN})	1.76	3.06	p= 0.004*

* $p<0.05$

Results for H2 (T_{VB} vs. T_P)

H2 is also supported (see Table 4). Subjects trained with value-based, risk-driven approach outperformed subjects using perspective-based reading, each by a percentage of 31.7%, 27.5% and 44% for D_T, D_{MJ} and D_{MN}, respectively. Note that the value-based approach also appeared to have least impact on major defects.

Table 4. H2 Results: Means for treatment groups T_{VB} vs. T_P

	T_P	T_{VB}	p value
Total number of true defect(both major and minor) (D_T)	8.24	12.06	p= 0.005*
Total number of major defect (D_{MJ})	6.52	9.00	p= 0.028*
Total number of minor defect (D_{MN})	1.71	3.06	p= 0.004*

* $p<0.05$

5.1. Further Analysis

Results of the two main hypotheses show that inspectors trained with the value-based, risk driven approach outperform inspectors trained using worked examples as well as those who used perspective based approach (where the perspective taken is value-based and risk driven). In the inspection literature, experiments comparing perspective-based defect detection with other methods often showed the former method outperforming other methods [1]. Perspective-based defect detection is not a training method in the sense that it does not involve an instructor or facilitator in the more conventional sense of normal training. It does however utilise an aid (i.e. perspective) to assist each inspector accomplish the inspection task, therefore it can thought of as a self-training method. We were curious as to how this self-training method compares with other training approaches which used instructor interventions (such as those used in T_{EG} treatment group). Further statistical analysis showed that the T_{EG} treatment group outperforms T_P treatment group in terms of D_T and D_{MJ} but not D_{MN}. This may reflect the choice of the examples used during the training for the T_{EG} treatment group, where more serious (major) defects were selected for training purposes. The value-based risk driven perspective used in the T_P treatment group however placed no emphasis on the severity of defects, instead the emphasis was more on improving risk coverage.

Results for Hypothesis 3 (T_P vs. T_{EG})

Table 5. Means T_P vs T_{EG}

	T_P	T_{EG}	p value
Total number of true defect(both major and minor) (D_T)	8.24	9.12	p=0.005*
Total number of major defect (D_{MJ})	6.52	7.36	p=0.028*
Total number of minor defect (D_{MN})	1.71	1.76	n.s.

* $p<0.05$, n.s. no significance

6. Conclusion

Two controlled experiments were conducted to test whether value-based risk-driven approach to training software inspectors outperform training via worked examples and perspective-based defect detection. The results were positive. The results showed that a value-based risk-driven approach is preferred over other methods previously tested – namely training using worked examples and perspective-based defect detection. A value-based approach help focus inspectors' attention to a particular value proposition deemed important from the project perspective. In our study, we found that a risk driven perspective was quite useful since risks are inherent in all software projects. A risk driven perspective in software inspection enables human effort to be channelled towards risk identification. Moreover, our risk perspective is driven by a popular risk framework which ensures good coverage of risk areas. Other value(s) perspective (including a hybrid of values) may also be chosen depending on the project setting and/or value(s) deemed most important to the project stakeholders.

The key difference between training using worked examples and perspective-based defect detection is the use of a facilitator in the former. This study suggests the value of a facilitator / instructor present during training process. The presence of a facilitator allows inspectors opportunities to pose questions about the task or artefact. Moreover feedback is obtained immediately and the discussion and learning is shared with all other trainees as well. It is not clear if individual (as opposed to group) inspector training may yield the same benefit. That is an avenue for further study. While training using worked examples yield better results than perspective-based defect detection in most instances (total number of true defects and major defects), the results showed no significant difference in performance in terms of minor defects. This was most likely due to the choice of worked examples used and/or inspectors not paying attention to minor defects. Given that previous empirical results showed the benefits of perspective-based defect detection methods over other methods. This current study suggest that extra intervention in the form of facilitator mediated training may be useful.

This study was limited to one particular value-based perspective – risks. We believe that appropriate value(s) (in the eyes of the stakeholders) is a prerequisite to formulation of inspectors' training strategy. For example, if stakeholders consider quality to be of utmost importance, then value-based training for inspectors will be based on selected quality attributes (instead of risks) considered important for stakeholders. These may be determined after stakeholder deliberations and debates.

References

[1] Arrow, K., *Essays in the theory of risk-bearing*. 1970, Amsterdam: North Holland.

[2] Basili, V.R., et al., *The Empirical Investigation of Perspective-Based Reading*. Empirical Software Engineering,, 1996. 1(2): p. 133-164.

[3] Biffl, S., et al., eds. *Value-Based Software Engineering* 2006, Springer-Verlag: Berlin Heidelberg.

[4] Black, T.R., *Evaluating Social Science Research: An Introduction*. 1993: SAGE Publications.

[5] Boehm, B., *Value-Based Software Engineering*. ACM Software Engineering Notes, 2003. 28 March(2).

[6] Carr, M.J., et al., *Taxonomy-Based Risk Identification*. 1993, Software Engineering Institute, Carnegie Mellon University.

[7] Chowdhury, A. and L.P.W. Land. *An Empirical Investigation on the Impact of Training-by-Examples on Inspection Performance*. in *5th International Conference for Product-Focused Software Process Improvement (PROFES 2004)*. 2004a. Japan.

[8] Chowdhury, A. and L.P.W. Land. *The Impact of Training-by-Examples on Inspection Performance Using Two Laboratory Experiments,*. in *Australian Software Engineering Conference (ASWEC 2004)*. 2004b. Melbourne, Australia.

[9] Dooley, D., *Social Research Methods*. 2001: Prentice Hall.

[10] Fagan, M.E., *Design and Code Inspections to Reduce Errors in Program Development.* IBM Systems Journal, 1976. 15(3): p. (182-211).

[11] Frankfort-Nachmias, C.a.D.N., *Research methods in the social sciences* 1996, New York: St. Martin's Press.

[12] Freedman, D.P. and G.M. Weinberg, *Handbook of Walkthroughs, Inspections, and Technical Reviews: Evaluating Programs, Projects, and Products,*. Third Edition ed. 1990: Dorset House Publishing.

[13] Gilb, T. and D. Graham, *Software Inspection,*. 1993: Addison Wesley.

[14] Higgs, J., *A framework for software quality process improvement: Evidence from an Australian software company.* 2006, School of Information Systems, Technology and Management, The University of New South Wales. p. 169.

[15] Höst, M., B. , B. Regnell, and C. Wohlin, *Using students as subjects: A comparative study of students and professionals in lead-time impact assessment* Empirical Software Engineering 2000. 5: p. 201-214.

[16] Judd , C.M., E.R. Smith, and L.H. Kidder, *Research Methods in Social Relations*. Sixth Edition ed. 1991: Harcourt Bruce Jovanovich College Publishers.

[17] Kamsties, E. and C. Lott. *An empirical evaluation of three defect detection techniques.* in *Proceedings of 5th European Software Engineering Conference.* 1995.

[18] Land, L.P.W., R. Jeffery, and C. Sauer. *Validating the defect de-tection performance advantage of group designs for software reviews: Report of a replicated experiment.* in *Proceedings of 1997 Australian Software Engineering Conference.* 1997. Sydney, Australia.

[19] Land, L.P.W., B. Tan, and B. Li. *Investigating Training Effects on Software Reviews: A Controlled Experiment.* in *2005 International Symposium on Empirical Software Engineering Proceedings*. 2005.

[20] Land, L.P.W., B. Wong, and R. Jeffery. *An Extension of the Behavioral Theory of Group Performance in Software Development Technical Reviews,*. in *Tenth Asia-Pacific Software Engineering Conference (APSEC)*. 2003. Thailand.

[21] Lee, K. and B. Boehm, *Empirical results from an experiment on value-based review (VBR) processes.* International Symposium on Empirical Software Engineering, 2005.

[22] Miller, J., et al., *Statistical Power and its Subcomponents - Missing and Misunderstood Concepts in Empirical Software Engineering Research.* Information and Software Technology, 1997. 39: p. 285-295.

[23] O'Neill, D., *Software Inspections Course and Lab.* , in *O'Neill, Don. Software Inspections Course and Lab.* 1989, Software Engineering Institute, Carnegie Mellon University: Pittsburgh, PA.

[24] Parnas, D.L. and D.M. Weiss, *Active design reviews: Principles and Practices.* The Journal of Systems and Software, 1987. 7: p. (259-265).

[25] Porter, A.A., L.G. Votta, and V.R. Basili, Comparing detection methods for software requirements inspections: A replicated experiment. *IEEE Transactions on Software Engineering*, 1995. 21(6): p. 563-575.

[26] Ramler, R., S. Biffl, and P. Grunbacher, *Value-based management of software testing*, in *Value-Based Software Engineering* 2006, Springer-Verlag: Berlin Heidelberg. p. 225-244.

[27] Rifkin, S. and L. Deimel. Applying program comprehension techniques to improve software inspections. in *19th Annual NASA Software Laboratory Workshop*. 1994.

[28] Runeson, P.C., et al., *What do we know about defect detection methods?* IEEE Software, 2006. May/June: p. 82-90.

[29] Sauer, C., et al., The Effectiveness of Software Development Technical Reviews: A Behaviorally Motivated Program of Research. *IEEE Transactions on Software Engineering,* 2000. 26(1): p. (1-14).

[30] Storey, M.-A., Theories, tools and research methods in program comprehension: past, present and future. 2006. *Software Quality Journal*(14): p. 187-208.

[31] Strauss, S.H. and R.G. Ebenau, *Software Inspection Process*. 1994: McGraw-Hill.

[32] Sweller, J. and G.A. Cooper, *The use of worked examples as a substitute for problem solving in learning algebra. Cognition and Instruction*, 1985. 2: p. 59-89.

[33] Tyran, C.K., A software inspection exercise for the systems analysis and design course. *Journal of Information Systems Education*, 2006. 17(3): p. 341-351.

[34] Wallace, L., M. Keil, and A. Rai, How Software Project Risk Affects Project Performance: An Investigation of the Dimensions of Risk and an Exploratory Model. *Decision Sciences*, 2004. 35(2 (March)): p. 289-321.

[35] Yourdon, E., *Structured walkthroughs*. Fourth Edition ed. 1989: Prentice Hall.

In: Computer Software Engineering Research
Editor: Ari D. Klein, pp. 161-177
ISBN 1-60021-774-5

Chapter 6

UML2B vs B2UML Bridging the Gap between Formal and Graphical Software Modeling Paradigms

Akram Idani*
University of Technology, Compiègne – France
CNRS/Heudiasyc Laboratory

Abstract

In this chapter we give an overview and a comparison of the existing coupling approaches of B and UML for circumventing the shortcomings of these two specification languages with respect to their practical applicability. We also deal with our contribution to documenting B specifications with graphical UML notations more intuitive and readable.

1. Introduction

The complex requirements of software systems justify the use of the best existing techniques to ensure high quality specifications and then preserve this quality during the programming phase of a software life-cycle. Formal methods, such as B, make it possible to reach such a level of quality. Their main characteristics are:

(*i*) They allow to precisely check the correction of a program against its specification.

(*ii*) They need a great knowledge of logic.

The first point, which represents the major advantage of these methods, raises from the fact that mathematics allow to rigorously reason about the coherence of a software system. The second point, which is the primary "brake" to the adoption of formal methods, is

*E-mail address: Akram.Idani@imag.fr

strongly related to formal languages notations which are often complex. These two characteristics made formal methods used especially to model critical systems, for which safety and perfection are essential. One of the solutions developed by several research teams is to specify the whole system using a semi-formal language (*e.g.* UML) and then translate the semi-formal model into a formal one (*e.g.* B). The resulting formal specifications can then be used in order to achieve a rigorous reasoning of the same system.

Although such an approach is widely developed, several companies which have a great expertise on formal languages notations, don't adopt a development process which initially builds a semi-formal model. For example, Siemens Transport [5], Clearsy [29], Gemplus [4] and KeesDA [11], have an established software development process which is uniquely based on the B method. This formal development process is known to lead to high quality developments: for exemaple, in [1], P. Behm reports that the Meteor subway development reached the "zero-fault" objective. But one of the remaining difficulties is to make sure that the various stakeholders of a critical project (developers, customers, certification authorities) agree on the meaning of the formal specification. Several research works are then intended to contribute to a better comprehension of B specifications by producing UML views from the formal developments.

Bridging the gap between formal and graphical notations has been a challenge since several years [9]. Its main goal is to overcome the shortcomings of the ones by contributions of the others. In this chapter, we particularly deal with B and UML languages, and we distinguish the three following categories of integration:

1. Derivation from UML to B,
2. Multi-view development using conjointly B and UML,
3. Derivation from B to UML.

2. Linking B and UML Paradigms: a Brief Overview

2.1. About B

The B method was successfully used during the last years in several projects: for example, the automatic control system of the subway METEOR (Paris/France) [1] was entirely developed using B; the Gemplus company uses it for the development of pilot applications in the smart card field and applications which use smart cards; Peugeot have done studies with B for the validation of some critical embedded systems on board of its cars... Furthermore, many studies showed that the use of formal methods such as B improves significantly applications quality without generating a significant over-cost. However, one of the principal barriers to the use of these techniques is related to the required training on mathematic concepts and formalisms, which justify the difficulty of their integration, especially during the validation and the certification steps of an industrial software development process. In fact, these two steps don't necessarily imply persons who have a great knowledge of mathematics.

2.2. About UML

UML is an industrial standard developed by the OMG[1] which is a group gathering great actors in the software development field such as Oracle, SUN, Nokia, Siemens, Rational, ... UML proposes a unified framework based on a pallet of graphic notations to specify and develop software systems. Since its introduction in industry, it becomes widely used and many tools were developed to assist the edition of UML diagrams and use them for automatic code generation. Nowadays, UML is considered as a part of software engineers culture. However, the UML semantics are often described as fuzzy owing to the fact that they miss mathematical bases. Consequently, UML diagrams can lead, sometimes, to ambiguous models and cause misunderstandings as well as difficulties of interpretation [7,32].

2.3. Why Linking B and UML?

Several research teams worked on the links between UML and the B method. We can cite in France works of the CEDRIC/CNAM (university of Evry) [17,22,26], or those done in the LORIA laboratory (Nancy) [19,25], or at the University of Versailles [24], and also in the United Kingdom at the University of Southampton [34] or in the Imperial College of London [18]. These teams privileged the translation from UML to B, and the UML extension by annotations written in B language. Their objectives are: to formally specify UML semantics, to complete this language with the aim to increase its expression capacity, and to translate semi-formal specifications into B in order to be able to use B tools (prover, model-checker, ...).

Thus, the first category of derivation (from UML to B) is widely studied today. In fact, we can notice the existence of several tools supporting this translation: *e.g.* **UML2B** [13], **UML2SQL** [16,21], **U2B** [33], **ArgoUML+B** [20]. Nevertheless, there are few works which address the two other categories of integration. Indeed, in these categories we distinguish, on the one hand, works of D.-D. Okalas Ossami [27,28] for a multi-view development in UML and B, and on the other hand, works of H. Fekih [8], those of J.-C. Voisinet [35], and the ours for a derivation from B to UML.

These works are indeed complementary because they treat all coupling directions of these two formalisms. A comparative study done by M. Satpathy and his co-authors [30] shows the importance of such a coupling basing on B and UML specifications of the same system, and attests that: "*a combination of both is needed in order to achieve good visibility as well as precision*". In this study, two agents X and Y start by producing a first part of specifications respectively in UML (called UML_X) and in B (called B_Y), and after few months of development they interchange their specifications so that X continues the development in B (B_{X+Y}) and Y continues the development in UML (UML_{X+Y}). We present below the principal "lessons" consigned by this study [30]:

- the global model structure is more intuitive when specified in UML thanks to the use of diagrams,
- to lead precise and detailed specifications, UML is insufficient and must be increased by formal notations,

[1]Object Management Group.

- ambiguities of requirements documents are better identified during the B development than when using UML,
- X finds that B_Y is not sufficiently documented, whereas Y finds that UML_X is very abstract and has a lack of details.

These observations which result from experiments confirm the complementarity between UML and B integration techniques. In the following, we address the conceptual bases and a comparison of these techniques.

3. From UML to B

3.1. Survey and Objectives

Terms "*shallow embedding*" and "*deep embedding*" [2, 36] are often used to point out a transformation or an integration of formalisms. The first term indicates a direct translation of a source model into an equivalent one but expressed in a different language, whereas the second term describes a translation of formalisms leading to constructions which represent data types. Works which studied the derivation from UML to B can be classified following a similar reasoning.

Shallow embedding. This approach consists in giving rules to translate a UML model into an equivalent B specification. We cite, for example, the following translation rule, taken from [6], which addresses the inheritance notion. Let us consider entities "Secretary" and "Engineer" as specializations of entity "Person":

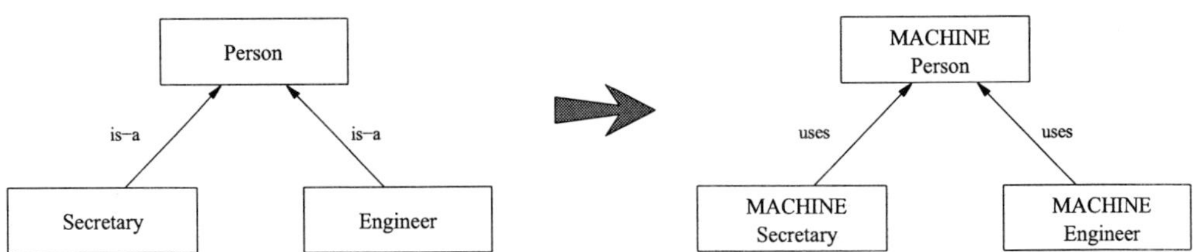

Translation rule : Create a B machine for every class of the hierarchy with a "use" dependency from each sub-class machine to the super-class machine. Then, add an other B machine which includes all the other machines and which represents the interface of the hierarchy.

Figure 1. Translation of the inheritance notion following a shallow embedding approach [6].

Note that a great majority of works dealing with the derivation from UML to B adopt such a principle [17, 22, 25, 34]. The interest of this technique is that it is carried out by a direct translation of a semi-formal model into a formal one. However, its disadvantage is that the semantics of the mappings between B and UML are not explicitly formalized since they are hidden in the translation rules.

Deep embedding. Few works applied this type of approaches for the derivation of B specifications from UML models. This is based on a mixture of formal specifications issued from elements of the meta-model and those of the semi-formal model prone of the translation. Works which follow such an approach propose, in a first step, a meta-model formalization, and in a second step they inject specific parts of a system in this formalization. For example, to treat the inheritance UML notion, a class is not translated into an abstract machine. We won't obtain as much machines as classes like shallow embedding, but only one machine (fig. 2) which includes: (*i*) the set of all objects of the system, (*ii*) a function which associates to each class name the set all instances of the classe, (*iii*) a function which associates to each association name an equivalent relation between sets of objects, and (*iv*) a function which associates to each object and attribute a corresponding value.

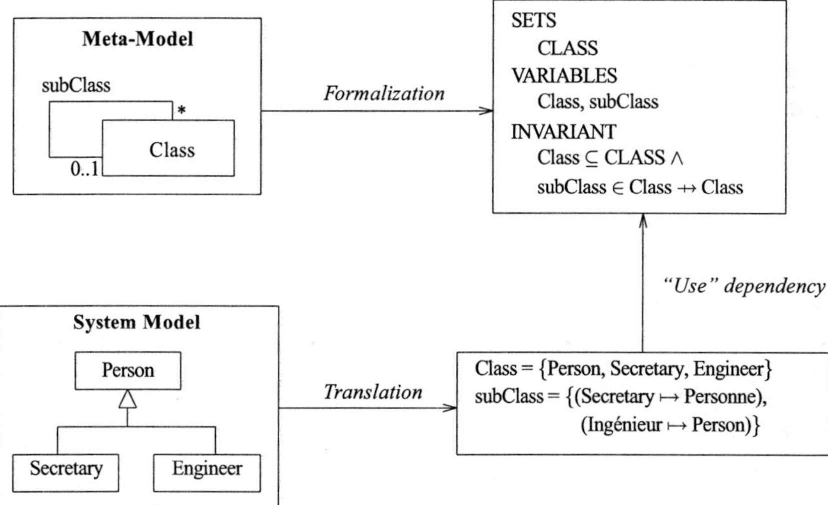

Figure 2. Translation of the inheritance notion following a deep embedding approach [17].

Contrary to deep embedding, the shallow embedding technique is more direct because the formal specifications which result from this approach reflect in a natural way the traduced model. However, for semantic reasons, the deep embedding approach is useful because it makes it possible to explicitly specify and clarify constructions of meta-models.

3.2. Translation of Structural Features

3.2.1. Classes

The translation of a UML class C into B data implies the formalization of the set of possible objects (which we note *Possible_Objects*) of the class. This consensus of the various translation approaches results in an abstract set in the formal specification (Fig. 3) from which the set of existing objects (which we note *Existing_objects*) is defined. *Existing_objects* is declared as a state variable in the B machine issued from class C as the following:

$$Existing\_objects \subseteq Possible\_Objects$$

Note that an equivalent translation is considered by [34], which is:

$$Existing\_objects \in \mathbb{P}(Possible\_Objects)$$

In addition, [25] adds a layer to distinguish the set of all possible objects (noted *OBJECTS*) and defines *Possible_Objects* by a constant such that:

$$Possible\_Objects \subseteq OBJECTS$$

When several classes are considered, two sights can be distinguished to translate the UML class diagram: (*i*) unique machine, or (*ii*) set of machines bounded by clauses *USES*, *SEES* or *INCLUDES*. Nevertheless, the second point of view is privileged by the most techniques because it allows modularity and structuring of resulting B specifications. Moreover, the single machine sight can be obtained by application of a flattening technique.

3.2.2. Attributes

A class attribute translation is done by considering the set of existing objects. Suppose that t is an attribute of a class C whose type is *TypeAttribut*. Then t will be formalized by a relational function which distinguishes values of t for each instance of C:

$$t \in Existing\_Objects \leftrightarrow TypeAttribut$$

In [17, 22, 26], whether t is mono-valued or set-valued, and according to its optional or mandatory character, its formalization implies specializations of the derived relation as a total or a partial function. This distinction between mono-valued and set-valued attributes is not considered by the other approaches. In fact, [25] considers only relations "$\leftrightarrow$", and [34] produces only total functions "$\rightarrow$".

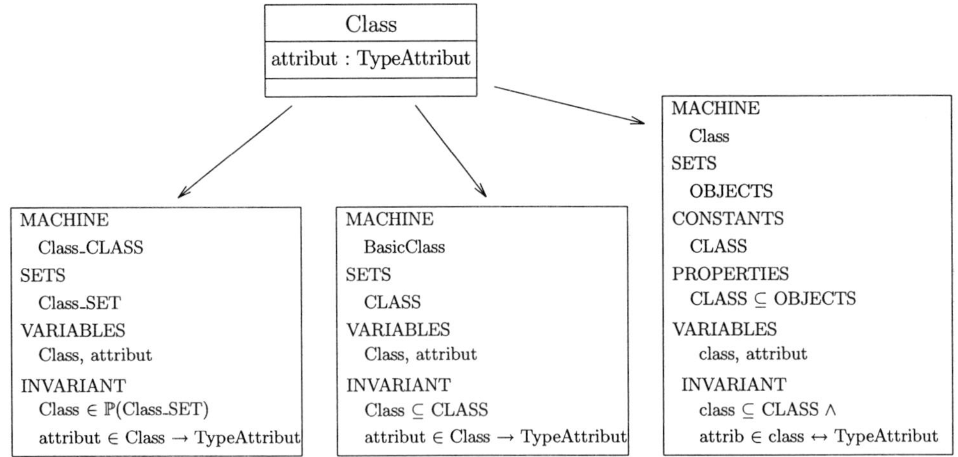

Figure 3. Translation of class and attribute constructs into B.

3.2.3. Associations

Intuitively, translation of associations should take into account: (*i*) association name, (*ii*) multiplicities, (*iii*) B data derived from the two extremities of the association, and (*iv*) the direction of navigation. Consider $Class_1$ and $Class_2$ two state variables issued from two UML classes with an association *Assoc* defined from $Class_1$ to $Class_2$, then a natural translation of *Assoc* into B is to define relation *Assoc* between sets of existing objects:

$$Assoc \in Class_1 \leftrightarrow Class_2$$

Specializations of *Assoc* could be defined depending from its multiplicities. For example, if *Assoc* is qualified by a multiplicity "$*$" in side of $Class_1$ and a multiplicity "1" in side of $Class_2$ then the created relation from $Class_1$ to $Class_2$ is a total function. In order to structure resulting B specifications, [25] proposes to produce for every association an abstract B machine which defines a variable *Assoc*, and which uses (clause *USES*) the two B machines produced from $Class_1$ and $Class_2$. Nevertheless, [34] doesn't define an additional B machine to traduce the association, but imposes the use of roles to qualify its extremities. These roles will then be translated into variables of machines produced for $Class_1$ and $Class_2$.

3.2.4. Synthesis

In this sub-section we presented translations of some basic UML constructs: classes, attributes and associations. The following table gives an overview of common points and specificities of existing derivation approaches from UML to B with respect to most useful UML structural features:

Table 1. Common points and differences between approaches which derive B specifications from UML structural features.

	[26] [22] [17]	[25] [19]	[34]
Classes (unspecified instances)	+	+	+
Classes (known instances)	-	-	+
Class attributes	+	+	+
Distinction between mono/set-valued attributes	+	-	-
Inheritance mechanism	+	+	+
Association multiplicities	+	+	+
Navigation direction of associations	-	+	+
Role name	+	-	+
Constraints between associations	+	+	-
Distinction between fixed and non-fixed associations	+	-	-
Associative classes	+	+	-
Associative classes linked to associations or to a specialization/generalization	+	-	-
Template classes	-	-	+

Legend : "+" (criterion token into account) ; "-" (not considered criterion)

3.3. Translation of Behavioural Features

As we deal with basic UML constructs, in this section we only consider states and transitions. One of the first works for the combination of state/transition diagrams and B had as a finality to conceive, in a graphical way, reactive systems [31]. In this approach, reactive systems design is initially carried out by a state-chart [12] which is translated, thereafter, in a B machine. This translation allows to allot a formal B semantic to the Harel's diagrams, generally used for their expressive form. Various aspects of this work appear interesting to highlight such as the translation of hierarchical and concurrent states, and also communicating states. Although the rules suggested by [31] are rather precise and cover the most specificities of state/transition diagrams, they do not take into account static aspects. Works of H.P. Nguyen [26] and E. Meyer [25] present some attempts to formalize UML state/transition diagrams while taking into account bonds with class diagrams. In fact, these works consider that states describe possible situations in the life of objects.

3.3.1. States

Sekerinski [31] represents states by (*i*) an enumerated set $States = \{State_1, \ldots, State_n\}$ and (*ii*) an abstract variable *state* defined by $state \in States$. The transitions between states are then ensured by a value change of this variable. To translate states of a class *Class*, [25] takes also this formalization by an enumerated set and defines the variable *state* by a total function as follows: $state \in Class \rightarrow States$. Note that this variable is declared in the B machine which is derived for class *Class*:

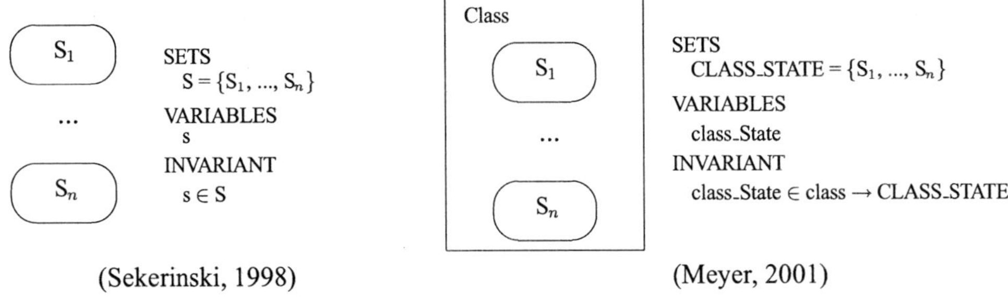

Figure 4. Translation of states into B.

3.3.2. Transitions

The translations of transitions consider several cases: simple events, conditioned events, conditioned events with actions, events activating several transitions, etc. We present in Fig. 5 the proposals made by [31] to treat these various cases. H.P. Nguyen in [26] distinguishes these cases in terms of scenarios mono-entity[2]. The author considers that the use of structures such as **IF** $S = S_1$ ... **THEN** ... **END** (case (a) and (c)) is a defensive approach because the checking of the condition is done in the operation body. Then, the use of a pre-conditioned structure: **PRE** ... **THEN** ... **END** is privileged.

[2] Scenarios attached to only one entity or class.

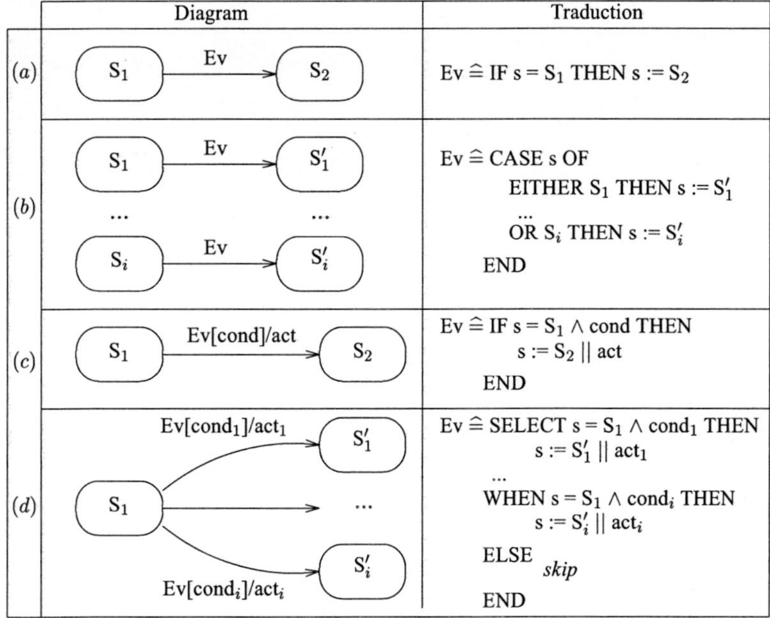

Figure 5. Translation of transitions into B proposed by [31].

4. The Multi-view Development Approach

This section is based on works of J. Souquières an D.-D. Ossami [27] which are based on a multi-modeling approach using simultaneously B and UML. The proposed development process leads to a two-view specification of a same system. This is achieved by preserving consistency and traceability between the formal and the semi-formal view.

The basic idea of this approach is to define "*construction operators*" to evolve simultaneously B and UML specifications. Fig. 6, shows this development process by giving specification states before (*i.e.* S_{old} and S'_{old}) and after (*i.e.* S_{new} and S'_{new}) the application of operations of $\mathcal{O}_{\text{UML}}$ and $\mathcal{O}_{\text{B}}$. This parallel evolution is founded by the hypothesis that B and UML specifications preserve the φ function which traduce a UML model into a B specification.

Consequently, if $S'_{\text{old}} = \varphi(S_{\text{old}})$ then a simultaneous application of $\mathcal{O}_{\text{UML}}$ and $\mathcal{O}_{\text{B}}$ leads to states S_{new} and S'_{new} such that $S'_{\text{new}} = \varphi(S_{\text{new}})$.

The interest of the parallel application of $\mathcal{O}_{\text{UML}}$ and of $\mathcal{O}_{\text{B}}$ is to consider a finer granularity than approaches which derive B from UML. This makes possible to be focused, at the same time, on two sights of each specification increment.

The construction of a UML or a B specification follows two main activities: add components and add data. For illustration, we consider that for UML these notions are respectively classes and attributes. We also assume that, for B specifications, a component is a B machine and a data is a B variable. In the following we consider the *newComponent* and the *newData* operators:

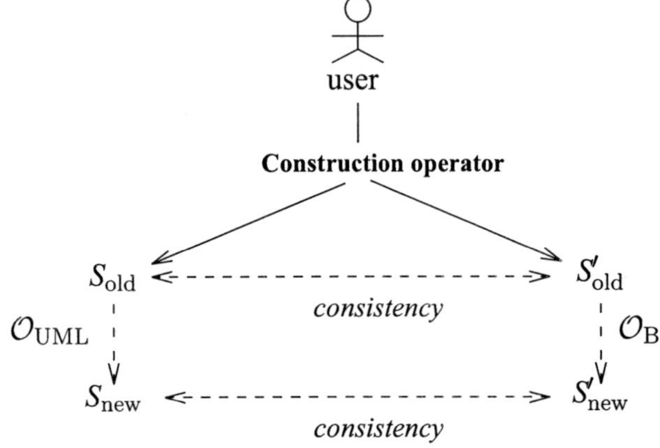

Figure 6. Specification evolution following [27].

Opertator	$\mathcal{O}_{B}$	$\mathcal{O}_{UML}$
newComponent	*newMachine* *addName* *addCompositionLink* *newDataType* *newVariable*	*newClass* *addName*

Operator	$\mathcal{O}_{B}$	$\mathcal{O}_{UML}$
newData	*newVariable* *addName* *addInvariant* $\vert$*addProperty* *addInitialisation*	*newAttribute* *addName* *addType* *addInitialValue* *addMultiplicity* *addProperty*

The translation rules of UML to B proposed by various approaches, in particular those on which this technique is based, can be applied only when the starting point is a UML model (*i.e.* translation UML $\rightarrow$ B $\rightarrow$ UML). Considering this one-way derivation, the technique of simultaneous evolution of the two specifications must still compatible with this translation, and consequently restrictions on B constructs were considered.

This limitation affects considerably a B reasoning because a direct evolution of the formal specification must satisfy particular schemas to be able to guarantee the existence of a similar evolution of UML specifications. These particular schemas are intuitively specified by the derivation rules from UML to B. We think that such a restriction is not easy to put in practice when evolving directly the B model. Indeed, the formal specifications produced by the derivation rules from UML to B are sometimes far from what the developer could have written directly in B. This distance comes owing to the fact that a B developer does not adopt, in general, an object oriented approach and thus, it does not reason in terms of classes and attributes, but rather in terms of abstract machines and B data in a formal approach guided by proofs.

5. From B to UML

Works which studied the derivation of UML diagrams from B specifications want to overcome the formal methods shortcomings. Several references discussed these limits [3, 10] and insisted on the difficulty of understanding of formal methods notations. In software engineering, the readability of specifications is important for the validation and the certification phases. However, these phases, qualified by "*external validation*" by M.-C. Gaudel [10], are not easy when dealing with formal methods because they are generally carried out by persons who are not trained in mathematical notations. The translation of B specifications into UML models allows to assist this external validation by a palet of UML diagrams which are intended to be more readable than formal specifications.

5.1. The Uniform Approach

This approach, proposed by J.-C Voisinet [35], is guided by a set of rules which lead to a partial translation of B specifications into UML class and state/transition diagrams. This systematic translation implies that for each covered B construct only one translation exists. The extraction of UML views from B specifications is then intended to allow to the person who evaluates the B specification to quickly obtain the graphical view. A one to one mapping is established between a sub-set of B and UML constructs. Then, the produced diagrams are not necessarily the best ones for a documentation purpose.

The derivation of UML class diagrams following this approach gives a synthetic graphical view which may be far from the data structure of the B model. In the following, we give some of the proposed rules :

Rule 1. An abstract B machine M is translated into a class S.

Rule 2. Operations become methods of class S.

Rule 3. Integer and boolean variables become attributes of class S.

Rule 4. An abstract set A is traduced by a class E_A, and an association which links E_A and S. Multiplicity associated to S is equal to 1.

Règle 5. An enumerated set D is also translated into a class E_D and an association between E_D and S. An attribute $values$ is added into E_D. Its type is is an ≪*enumeration*≫ class D_VALUES which indicates elements of D.

Rule 8. A relation R between two sets A and B is represented by :

- A class E_A_B,
- An association between E_A_B and S,
- An aggregation link between E_A_B and E_A,
- An aggregation link between E_A_B and E_B,

MACHINE
M
SETS
$A\,;B\,;$
$D = \{elem1, elem2, elem3\}$
VARIABLES
$a,\ d,\ R,\ C$
INVARIANT
$a \in A \wedge C \subseteq A \wedge$
$d \in D \wedge R \in A \leftrightarrow B$
OPERATIONS
Op1 $\widehat{=} \ldots$
Op2 $\widehat{=} \ldots$
END

Figure 7. A simple B machine.

In order to illustrate these rules we consider the B machine M of figure 7 where the data structure is simply defined by two abstract sets (A and B), an enumerated set (D) and four variables: elements of sets a and d, a subset C and a relation R. The behaviour part is defined by two operations: Op1 and Op2.

The application of the previous rules produces the following class diagram which is formed by 5 classes linked by numerous associations.

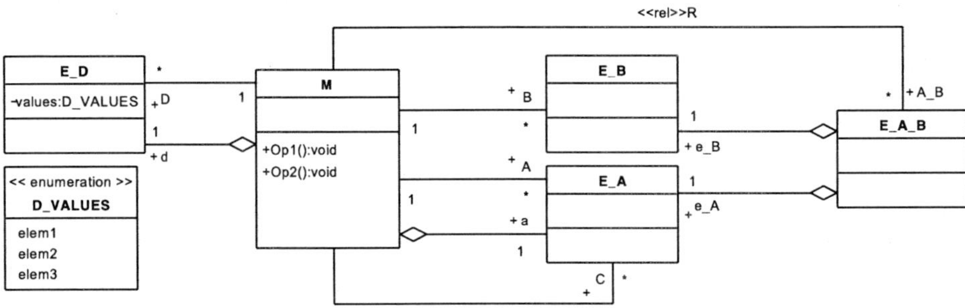

Figure 8. Application of rules of [35] on machine M.

The systematic translation of B machines, sets, relations and functions into classes doesn't seem as the most efficient way to produce a comprehensible UML view. In fact, in this technique the number of classes and associations rapidly explodes when specifications scale up. In the one hand, the translation of a set produces two modeling elements (*i.e.* one class and one association), in the other hand, the translation of a functional relation leads to four modeling elements (*i.e.* one class, one association and two aggregations).

5.2. The Iterative and Incremental Approach

The main motivation of this approach [8] is to allow a great flexibility for the derivation of UML diagrams. Heuristics are applied interactively and following several iterations. Each iteration can be seen as a development increment focused on the user appreciation. Some of these heuristics [8] are:

Rule 1. If a set appears in the domain of functional relations, it can be transformed into a class.

Rule 2. If a set appears in the range of relations without appearing as a domain of other relations, then it can be translated into an attribute.

Rule 3. The inclusion relation between two sets S and E can represent :

- a specilization relation between a sub-class S and a super-class E,
- a possible state S of an instance of class E,
- the set of effective instances S of class E.

Rule 4. A relation $R \in A \leftrightarrow B$ between abstract sets A and B which are translated into classes A and B can be traduced by an association R between these classes or by an attribute R of type B in the class A.

Rule 5. Operations represent class methods and/or transitions in a state diagram.

We can note from these heuristics, which are intended to produce modeling elements of a class diagram, that their intention is to illustrate B data and their relations. In fact, the structural views produced by this technique reflect explicitly data structure of the B model. For example, the invariant $R \in A \leftrightarrow B$ can be translated into two classes A and B linked by an association R. The resulting view is then more intuitive than that which is produced by the uniform approach.

However, many transformations are possible for each B construct. For example, the inclusion relation can be translated following three point of views (Rule 3). The analyst should choose one transformation from this list of rules. The specifications are then completely re-written interactively, element by element. The advantage of this process is that it leads to readable diagrams, but it may be difficult to achieve for great specifications. This disadvantage can be explained by: (*i*) The proposed rules treat partially B constructs and still informal; (*ii*) There is no semantic traceability explicitly defined because transformations are expressed empirically; and (*iii*) A methodological guide is required to assist the analyst to choose the best rules.

5.3. The Semi-automatic Approach

In the previous proposals, two opposite paradigms are studied: either to ensure a strong level of automation leading to complex diagrams, or to produce readable diagrams with a strong level of interaction. In our work [14, 15], we search a compromise between these two paradigms. Indeed, in our solution we try to reduce user interaction while producing readable diagrams.

In order to produce UML class diagrams from B specifications, we propose a transformation process guided by a set of structural and semantic mappings from B to UML in a model driven engineering approach. We define an UML meta-model, giving an abstract B syntax, in order to obtain a homogeneous conceptual framework for these mappings. First, we are interested by the possibility to represent in an explicit way, various transformations considered as relevant for a documentation purpose. Then, in order to select the best transformation, we identify a set of pertinency criteria which allow to significantly reduce the user interaction. These criteria are formalized basing on the following factors:

1. Distribution of the operations on the various classes,
2. The dependencies between operations and B data,
3. Existing links between B data themselves.

Furthermore, we propose a concept formation algorithm which produces, in a semi-automatic way, the static views satisfying these pertinency criteria. The formal framework which found our approach gives a precise and a rigorous analysis of structural aspects of the B specifications.

For the derivation of behavioral UML views, we exploit two complementary techniques: animation and proof. Our proposal, is initially based on an effective exploration of the B model behavior to produce accessibility graphs. Then, we apply a graph abstraction technique to build comprehensible and less complex state/transition diagrams.

6. Conclusion

UML and B are two specification techniques recognized in software engineering; their coupling is justified by the wish of be able to use them together in a software development process integrating structuring and precision. In this chapter, we presented a survey of works which studied the coupling of these two formalisms. These works are motivated by the importance to combine the readability of a graphical method such as UML and the rigour of a formal method such as B.

UML2B. Derivation of B specifications from a UML model aims, on the one hand, to use UML as a starting point of the development process, and in the other hand, to use B tools to analyze and check the formal specifications which result from this derivation. These specifications can also be exploited to check constraints expressed initially in OCL [19] or to produce source code (*e.g.* SQL/JAVA) after a succession of proven refinements [23] ...

B2UML. The research works of derivation of UML models from B specifications adopt the opposite approach: the starting point is B and not a semi-formal specification. Indeed, these works aim at the production of graphical views starting from existing specifications entirely developed following the B method. The major objective is to make B specifications accessible to peoples who are not necessarily familiarized with the mathematical notations.

References

[1] Patrick Behm, Paul Benoit, Alain Faivre, and Jean-Marc Meynadier. METEOR: A successful application of B in a large project. In *FM'99: World Congress on Formal Methods*, volume 1709 of *LNCS*, pages 369–387. Springer-Verlag, 1999.

[2] R. Boulton, A. Gordon, M. Gordon, J. Harrison, J. Herbert, and J.-V. Tassel. Experience with embedding hardware description languages in HOL. In *Proceedings of the IFIP International Conference on Theorem Provers in Circuit Design*, volume A-10, pages 129–156, Netherlands, 1993.

[3] Jonathan P. Bowen and Michael G. Hinchey. Seven More Myths of Formal Methods. *IEEE Software*, 12(4):34–41, July 1995.

[4] Ludovic Casset. Development of an Embedded Verifier for Java Card Byte Code Using Formal Methods. In *FME'02, Formal Methods Europe*, volume 2391 of *LNCS*, pages 290–309. Springer-Verlag, 2002.

[5] Didier Essamé. La méthode B et l'ingénierie système. *TSI, (Technique et Science Informatiques)*, 23(7):929–938, 2004. Hermès.

[6] P. Facon and Régine Laleau. Des spécifications informelles aux spécifications formelles : compilation ou interprétation ? In *Actes du 13ème congrès INFORSID*, 1995.

[7] Harald Fecher, Jens Schönborn, Marcel Kyas, and Willem-Paul Roever. 29 New Unclarities in the Semantics of UML 2.0 State Machines. In *Formal Methods and Software Engineering: 7th International Conference on Formal Engineering Methods, ICFEM 2005*, volume 3785 of *LNCS*, pages 52–65. Springer-Verlag, 2005.

[8] Houda Fekih, Leila Jemni, and Stephan Merz. Transformation of B Specifications into UML Class Diagrams and State Machines. In *21st Annual ACM Symposium on Applied Computing*, pages 1840–1844. ACM, Avril 2006.

[9] Martin D. Fraser, Kuldeep Kumar, and Vijay K. Vaishnavi. Informal and formal requirements specification laguages : Bridging the gap. *IEEE Transactions on Software Engineering*, 17(5):454–465, 1991.

[10] Marie-Claude Gaudel. Advantages and limits of formal approaches for ultra-high dependability. In *IWSSD'91: Proceedings of the 6th international workshop on Software specification and design*, pages 237–241, Los Alamitos, CA, USA, 1991. IEEE Computer Society Press.

[11] Stefan Hallerstede. Parallel hardware design in B. In *ZB 2003: Third International Conference of B and Z Users*, volume 2651 of *LNCS*, pages 101–102. Springer-Verlag, 2003.

[12] David Harel. STATECHARTS: a visual formalism for complex systems. *Science of Computer Programming*, 8(3), 1987.

[13] Lotfi Hazem, Nicole Levy, and Rafael Marcano-Kamenoff. UML2B : un outil pour la génération de modèles formels. In Jacques Julliand, editor, *AFADL'2004 - Session Outils*, 2004.

[14] A. Idani and Y. Ledru. Dynamic Graphical UML Views from Formal B Specifications. *International Journal of Information and Software Technology* , 48(3):154–169, Mars 2006. Elsevier.

[15] A. Idani, Y. Ledru, and D. Bert. Derivation of UML Class Diagrams as Static Views of Formal B Developments. In *Formal Methods and Software Engineering, 7th International Conference on Formal Engineering Methods, ICFEM 2005* , volume 3785 of *LNCS*, pages 37–51, Manchester, UK, November 2005. Springer-Verlag.

[16] Régine Laleau and Amel Mammar. An Overview of a Method and Its Support Tool for Generating B Specifications from UML Notations. In *15th IEEE International Conference on Automated Software Engineering*, pages 269–272, 2000. IEEE Computer Society Press.

[17] Régine Laleau. Conception et développement formels d'applications bases de données. Hdr, Université d'Evry, 2002.

[18] Kevin Lano, David Clark, and Kelly Androutsopoulos. UML to B: Formal Verification of Object-Oriented Models. In *Integrated Formal Methods*, volume 2999 of *LNCS*, pages 187–206. Springer, 2004.

[19] Hung Ledang. *Traduction systématique de spécifications UML en B*. PhD thesis, Université de Nancy 2, 2002.

[20] Hung Ledang, Jeanine Souquières, and Sébastien Charles. Argo/UML+B: un outil de transformation systématique de spécification UML en B. In *AFADL'2003*, pages 3–18, January 2003.

[21] Amal Mammar and Régine Laleau. UML2SQL: Un environment intégré pour le développement d'implémentations relationnelles à partir de diagrammes UML. In Jacques Julliand, editor, *AFADL'2004 - Session Outils*, 2004.

[22] Amel Mammar. *Un environnement formel pour le développement d'applications bases de données*. PhD thesis, CNAM-Paris, Novembre 2002.

[23] Amel Mammar and Régine Laleau. From a B formal specification to an executable code: application to the relational database domain. *Journal of Information and Software Technology*, 48(4):253–279, Avril 2005. Elsevier.

[24] Rafael Marcano. *Spécification formelle à objets en UML/OCL et B : une approche transformationnelle*. PhD thesis, Université de Versailles Saint-Quentin-en-Yvelines, 2002.

[25] Eric Meyer. *Développements formels par objets : utilisation conjointe de B et d'UML* . PhD thesis, Université de Nancy 2, Mars 2001.

[26] Hong Phuong Nguyen. *Dérivation de spécifications formelles B à partir de spécifications semi-formelles*. PhD thesis, CNAM-Paris, Décembre 1998.

[27] Dieu Donné Okalas Ossami, Jean-Pierre Jacquot, and Jeanine Souquières. Consistency in UML and B Multi-view Specifications. In *5th International Conference on Integrated Formal Methods*, volume 3771 of *LNCS*, pages 386–405. Springer, 2005.

[28] Dieu Donné Okalas Ossami, Jeanine Souquières, and Jean-Pierre Jacquot. Opérations de construction de spécifications multi-vues UML et B. In Jacques Julliand, editor, *Approches Formelles dans l'Assistance au Développement de Logiciels (AFADL'2004)*, pages 115–130, Juin 2004.

[29] Guilhem Pouzancre. How to Diagnose a Modern Car with a Formal B Model? In *ZB 2003: Formal Specification and Development in Z and B*, volume 2651 of *LNCS*, pages 98–100. Springer-Verlag, 2003.

[30] M. Satpathy, R. Harrison, C. Snook, and M. Butler. A Comparative Study of Formal and Informal Specifications through an Industrial Case Study. In *Proceedings of FSCBS'01: IEEE/IFIP Joint Workshop on Formal Specification of Computer Based Systems*, pages 133–137, 2001.

[31] Emil Sekerinski. Graphical Design of Reactive Systems. In *B '98: Proceedings of the Second International B Conference on Recent Advances in the Development and Use of the B Method*, pages 182–197, London, UK, 1998. Springer-Verlag.

[32] Antony J. H. Simons and Ian Graham. 30 Things that go wrong In Object modelling with UML 1.3. In H. Kilov, B.Rumpe, and I. Simmonds, editors, *Behavioral Specifications of Businesses and Systems*, chapter 17, pages 237–257. Kluwer Academic, 1999.

[33] Colin Snook and Michael Butler. U2B-A tool for translating UML-B models into B. In J. Mermet, editor, *UML-B Specification for Proven Embedded Systems Design*, 2004.

[34] Colin Snook and Michael Butler. UML-B: Formal modeling and design aided by UML. *ACM Transactions on Software Engineering and Methodology (TOSEM)*, 15(1):92–122, 2006.

[35] Jean-Christophe Voisinet. *Contribution au processus de développement d'applications spécifiées à l'aide de la méthode B par validation utilisant des vues UML et traduction vers les langages à objets*. PhD thesis, Université de Franche-Comté, Septembre 2004.

[36] Martin Wildmoser and Tobias Nipkow. Certifying Machine Code Safety: Shallow versus Deep Embedding. In K. Slind, A. Bunker, and G. Gopalakrishnan, editors, *Theorem Proving in Higher Order Logics (TPHOLs 2004)*, volume 3223, pages 305–320, 2004.

In: Computer Software Engineering Research
Editor: Ari D. Klein, pp. 179-194
ISBN: 1-60021-774-5

Chapter 7

BUILDING PROGRAM COMPREHENSION TOOLS FOR VARIOUS OO LANGUAGES USING DOMAIN ENGINEERING

Lu Zhang, He Li, Dan Hao,
Tao Qin and Jiasu Sun*
Key laboratory of High Confidence Software Technologies, Ministry of Education
Software Institute, School of Electronics Engineering and Computer Science,
Peking University, Beijing, 100871, P. R. China

Abstract

Building various program comprehension tools for various object-oriented (OO) languages has been viewed as a necessity to help maintainers to understand legacy OO systems. Due to the difficulty of building such a tool, several generator-based approaches have been proposed. In this paper, we view building program comprehension tools for OO languages as a domain engineering problem and propose a domain engineering based approach. The basis of our approach is an XML-based intermediate representation for OO source code. Thus, source code in various OO languages can be easily transformed into this common representation and the target program comprehension tool can be built on the intermediate representation with little consideration of the difference in original languages. It should also be emphasized that our approach is a high-level one, and it does not exclude the co-using of previous generator-based language manipulation methods.

1. Introduction

With the accumulation of legacy source code, the importance of analyzing and/or comprehending source code has been widely realized. As a result, more and more program comprehension tools have emerged or are emerging. Usually, building such a tool is a tedious and time-consuming task. Therefore, besides the classic Yacc [13] and Lex [16], several

* E-mail addresses: { zhanglu, lihe, haod, qintao, sjs}@sei.pku.edu.cn

approaches to facilitating the building of program comprehension tools have been reported in the literature using either lexical analysis (see e.g. [22] and [7]) or syntactical analysis (see e.g. [20] and [8]).

In general, it is quite difficult to find a common and easy approach to the above problem. There are two sources of the difficulties. As quite many purposes have been identified for program comprehension (e.g. call graphs, design models, cross-reference lists etc.), such an approach should not be specific to one or two particular purposes. Another difficulty comes from the existence of many programming languages and their dialects. Up to now, what researchers can achieve so far is some general generators, whose input is a set of rules carefully designed for a given language or dialect and a given program comprehension purpose, and whose output is the target program comprehension tool. All the above listed approaches are generator-based approaches.

Domain engineering is a methodology for achieving systematic reuse through analyzing the commonalities and variabilities among systems within a given domain. By clearly separating commonalities from variabilities, developers can avoid repeating the efforts of dealing with commonalities and focus on tackling variabilities, when building different systems in the domain. Typical domain engineering methods include DARE [10], FAST [27], FODA [14] etc. From the perspective of domain engineering, the above generator-based approaches try to capture the lexical and/or syntactical commonalities and variabilities among programming languages. However, as these approaches fail to further explore the commonalities conveyed in the form of common concepts shared by most modern object-oriented (OO) programming languages (e.g. Smalltalk, Eiffel, C++, Java, C#), there is still much repeated work when using these approaches to build various program comprehension tools for various OO languages.

Based on the above reason, we propose a new approach to building OO program comprehension tools aiming at further exploring the commonalities among different OO languages and/or dialects. The central idea of our approach is a common intermediate representation based on XML (see [31] for the XML specification), into which various kinds of OO source code can be easily transformed. From this intermediate representation, program comprehension tools for different purposes can be easily built with little consideration of the original languages. Thus, it is not necessary to repeat the work of extracting OO structure and concepts when building different program tools. To simultaneously use existing techniques for the transformation of source code and the building of the target program comprehension tool, our approach emphasizes on a framework rather than a specific technique.

The organization of the remainder of this chapter is as follows. In section 2, we analyze the domain of building OO program comprehension tools and summarize the commonalities and variabilities in it. Section 3 provides an overview of our approach. In section 4, we present the XML-based representation for OO source code. In section 5, we demonstrate that source code in various OO languages can be easily transformed into the intermediate representation. In section 6, we demonstrate how various program comprehension tools can be built based on the representation. Section 7 discusses the properties of our approach. In section 8, we further discuss research related to our work. Finally, we conclude this paper in section 9.

2. The Domain of Building OO Program Comprehension Tools

The basis of our approach is to view the problem of building various OO program comprehension tools for various languages as a domain engineering problem. In this section, we analyze the commonalities and variabilities in this domain.

2.1. Commonalities

The commonalities among OO program comprehension tools lie in the fact that all the OO languages share the same set of OO concepts. As program comprehension tools usually aim at assisting users to understand high-level structures based on these common concepts, it is desirable to treat these common OO concepts in a uniform way. The common concepts that are directly represented in source code include:

- **Classes**. Most OO systems are mainly composed of classes. In Smalltalk, Java etc., there are no global variables or functions. In C++, using global variables and functions is not viewed as a good style and typical C++ source code does not contain many global variables or functions.
- **Attributes**. Variables belonging to a particular class are also called attributes. In any OO languages, attributes are an essential part of a class. Most OO languages support visibility control of attributes, and an attribute can be either a class attribute or an instance attribute.
- **Methods**. Functions belonging to a particular class are also called methods. Like attributes, methods are another essential part of a class, and follow the same rule of visibility control as attributes. A method can also be either a class one or an instance one.
- **Inheritance**. Inheritance is a mechanism that allows manifesting the generalization relationships between classes. The main difference in the support of inheritance among OO languages is whether and how multi-inheritance is supported.

Besides the above, other relationships among classes (such as associations) are usually not directly represented in the source code. We do not list them here because the acquisition of them requires thorough analysis of the source code.

2.2. Variabilities

The variabilities in this domain mainly come from two sources: different languages and different purposes. An interesting issue in this domain is that the interweaving of the two kinds can complicate the problem.

Language-End Variabilities

The language-end variabilities come from the existence of many OO programming languages, and many dialects of each language. It is typical in this domain to build different tools for different languages or dialects. That is to say, a different set of rules is required to handle a different language in a generator-based approach. For some tolerant generators, handling a different dialect may not require the change in rules. However, the lexical and/or syntactical differences between two languages are usually too large to be tolerated by the same set of rules.

Tool-End Variabilities

The tool-end variabilities come from continuously emerging requirements for new purposes of program comprehension. Typically, a different purpose needs different information from the source code and the extracted information needs to be further processed to achieve the purpose. Therefore, a different set of rules is usually required for each purpose in a generator-based approach. An alternative approach is to extract all the basic information into a database and build each tool for each purpose on the database (see e.g. [11] and [2]). The weakness of this approach lies in the difficulty of building many complicated full information extractors for all the languages and their dialects. Usually, a full information extractor is less tolerant and more specific to one language or dialect.

Interweaving Effect

An interesting point in this domain is the interweaving effect of the two kinds of variabilities. Usually, for each different language and/or dialect, we need different pieces of source code in building the program comprehension tool; while for each different purpose, we need other pieces of source code. In a generator-based approach, source code pieces for both kinds of variabilities are all represented as the input rules for the generator. As a result, whenever a new kind of change (either at the language-end or at the tool-end) comes, we need to rewrite the rules for the generator. That is to say, source code pieces for one kind of variabilities can hardly be reused when new requirements for the other kind arise.

3. An Overview of the Proposed Approach

The basic idea of our approach is to use a common intermediate representation for source code in different OO languages. Thus, we try to dissolve most language-end variabilities at the time of transforming source code in different languages into the common representation. From the common representation, we can focus on tackling tool-end variabilities without much consideration of language-end differences. The overview of our approach is depicted in Fig. 1.

As depicted in Fig. 1, the center of our approach is a common XML-based representation of OO source code, called OOML. For each different language, we build a lightweight converter to transform source code in that language into OOML. With OOML, we can build a program comprehension tool for each different purpose based on parsing and analyzing the OOML representation. As OOML is based on XML, we can use standard XML parsers and APIs to facilitate this task.

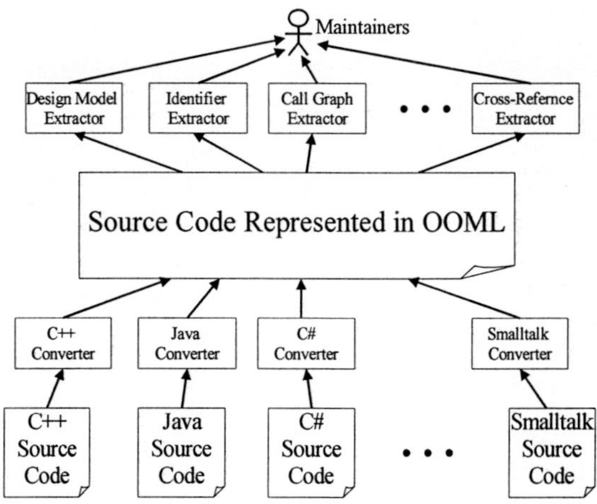

Figure 1. An Overview of the Proposed Approach.

4. An XML-Based Representation for OO Source Code

The XML-based representation is depicted in Fig. 2. For the ease of presentation, we make some simplification.

```
<?xml version="1.1"?>
<Model name="" language="">
    <Class name="" stereotype="">
      <Parent name=""/>
      ...
      <Attribute name="" visibility="">
        <Type name=""/>
        <Multiplicity property=""/>
        <Modifier name=""/>
        ...
      </Attribute>
      ...
      <Method name="" visibility="" isAbstract="">
        <ReturnType name="" multiplicity=""/>
        <Parameter name="" type="" multiplicity=""/>
        ...
        <Modifier name=""/>
        ...
        <MethodBody>source code
        </MethodBody>
      </Method>
      ...
    </Class>
    ...
</Model>
```

Figure 2. An XML-Based Representation for OO Source Code.

As depicted in Fig. 2, OOML is aiming at addressing the commonalities among OO languages; and for the ease of transforming source code in various languages into it, OOML is designed to be as close to programming languages as possible.

In OOML, source code (the model) is represented as a set of classes. Each class is composed of three parts: a list of references to parent classes, a list of attributes and a list of methods. The stereotype property of a class captures the fact that the class may actually be a similar construct in the source code, such as "struct" in C++ or "interface" in Java.

For each class, OOML lists the names of its parent classes. Thus, this representation suits both languages that support multi-inheritance and languages that do not. As interfaces in Java can be viewed as a special kind of classes, there may be several parent classes for one class in OOML converted from Java.

For an attribute, the visibility property can be "public", "private", "protected", or "default". As attributes can be defined as arrays or pointers, the multiplicity property indicates whether the attribute is a plain variable or an array or a pointer. There may be zero or more modifiers for an attribute, such as "static", "volatile" etc.

For a method, the visibility property is the same as an attribute. A method can be either abstract or non-abstract. A method has a return type and the return value can be a plain value or an array or a pointer. A method can have zero or more parameters, each of which has a name, a type and a multiplicity property. Like an attribute, there may be zero or more modifiers for a method.

5. Transforming OO Source Code into OOML

5.1. Basic Strategies for the Transformation

In our approach, the first step of building OO program comprehension tools is to build converters to transform systems in various kinds of source code into OOML. Basically, we have three strategies.

- **No parsing for method bodies**. We can see from Fig. 2 that the code for each method body is just a copy from the original source code. Thus we do not need to parse statements in the source code of method bodies when doing the transformation. As most complicated constructs (such as expressions, branch statements, and loop statements etc.) in an OO language appear inside a method body, copying the method body without parsing can greatly simplify the transformation.
- **Ignoring irrelevant statements**. As what we are mostly concerned with during the transformation is class definition and implementation, we can ignore statements not related to our concern, such as pre-processing statements in C++, "import" and "package" statements in java, and "using" directives in C# etc.
- **No symbol table**. As the transformation is mainly a change of the overall structure, we do not need to maintain a symbol table in the transformation. This will make the transformation much easier.

As most dialects of one language (such as C++, which has quite many dialects) differ mainly in places related to the above three strategies (such as the support of exception handling in C++), the transformation can be tolerant of most dialects. Therefore, we need only to build a converter for one language, not for each dialect.

5.2. Transformation for Sample Languages

In this sub-section, we demonstrate how the source code in Java, C++ and C# can be easily transformed into OOML. We believe that source code in other OO languages can also be transformed into OOML in a similar way. Here we do not claim our implementation for the transformation is the best, and we think the transformation may be easier using techniques proposed in [22], [7], [20] or [8].

From Java Code to OOML

Source code in Java has a similar structure to OOML, and therefore transforming Java code into OOML is an easier task. As we are mainly concerned with class definitions, we ignore the "package" and "import" statements.

In our approach, we treat both classes and interfaces in Java as classes. As the interface definition in Java is similar to class definition, here for simplicity we only describe how to transform a class definition into OOML.

The BNF of the definition of a class in Java is as follows.

[public] [abstract|final] class className [extends superclassName] [implements interfaceName {, interfaceName}]{{attributeDefinition|methodDefinition}}

In the above definition, those inside "[" and "]" will appear zero or one times, and those inside "{" and "}" will appear zero or more times. "{" and "}" represent actual "{" and "}" in source code. "|" is used to connect alternative choices. Italic words represent non-terminals while plain words represent terminals.

On seeing the token "class", we know that it is a class definition. Then we extract the following word as the name of the class. The word following "extends" is the name of one parent class, and the words following "implements" are names of other parent classes. On seeing the token "{", we know we are ready to parse attribute definitions and method definitions.

The BNF of the definition of an attribute is as follows.

[public|protected|private] [static] [final] [transient] [volatile] *type attributeName* [=*value*];

The BNF of the definition of a method is as follows.

[public|protected|private] [static] [final] [abstract] [native] [synchronized] *returnType methodName* ([*parameterList*])[throws *exceptionList*]{*methodBody*}

The main difference between the above two definitions is: In the attribute definition we meet the token "=" or the token ";" after the identifier as the name while in the method definition we meet the token "(" after the identifier as the name. After we distinguish the two definitions, we can extract detailed information of these two definitions.

For example, a piece of sample Java code and its corresponding OOML representation are as follows.

```
class Sample {
   static String str=”Hello World!”;
   static void main(String args[])
   {
      System.out.print(str);
   }
}
```

```
<Class name=”Sample” stereotype=”class”>
  <Attribute name=”str” visibility="default">
    <Type name=”String”/>
    <Multiplicity name=”plain”/>
    <Modifier name=”static”/>
  </Attribute>
  <Method name=”main” visibility="default"
        isAbstract=”no”>
    <ReturnType name=”void” multiplicity=”plain”/>
    <Parameter name=”args” type=”String”
        multiplicity=”array”/>
    <Modifier name=”static”/>
    <MethodBody>
      System.out.print(str);
    </MethodBody>
  </Method>
</Class>
```

From C++ Code to OOML

C++ is a language much more complex than Java. Due to the space limitation, we can only present the main considerations for transforming C++ code.

Compared with Java, there are three main differences in the transformation. Firstly, a class definition in C++ is usually separated into two parts: the declaration part and the implementation part. The declaration part is usually in a header file, and the implementation part is usually in a CPP file. We have to combine these two parts to form the OOML representation. Secondly, there are many pre-processing statements in C++. Our strategy is to ignore these statements. Thirdly, the use of macros in C++ may also cause trouble. Using macros inside the body of a method will cause no trouble, as we only copy that piece of code into the OOML representation. However, the use of macros between class definitions and/or between attribute definitions and method definitions is much more troublesome. Our strategy is to try to ignore them, but strange use of macros can mislead us, although this should not be the usual case.

The BNF of the definition of a class declaration in C++ (in a header file) is as follows.

class *className* [: public | private *superclassName* {, public | private *superclassName*}] {{
[public | private | protected:] {*attributeDefinition* | *methodDelaration*}}}

This definition is similar to the class definition in Java. The main difference is that the visibility of each attribute or method is not on each attribute or method. To acquire the visibility of each attribute or method, we use a variable to store the current visibility. When seeing the token "public" or "private" or "protected", we set the current visibility to "public" or "private" or "protected", and use this value as the visibility of the following attributes and methods. Please note that the visibility related with the type of derivation is simply ignored during the transformation. Constructors, destructors and operators in C++ can be treated as variants of methods.

To transform C++ code into OOML, we still need to extract method bodies from CPP files and combine them with corresponding method declarations. The BNF of the definition of a method in a CPP file is as follows.

returnType className::methodName ([parameterList]) {methodBody}

From this definition, we can see that the central token is "::". The word before this token is the class name and before the class name is the return type. After this token, we can extract the method name and the parameters, which will be used to match against the method names and corresponding parameters extracted from the class declaration. After finding the matched method, we insert the source code of the method body into the OOML representation.

From C# Code to OOML

C# is a mixed language of Java and C++ with extra extensions. Therefore, compared with C++, C# is easier to transform, but we have to deal with those extra extensions.

As source code in C# has a similar structure to Java code, it can be transformed in a similar way of transforming Java code. Furthermore, as there is no use of macros in C#, the transformation will not be disturbed by those strange macros.

The BNF of the definition of a class in C# is as follows.

[new] [public|private|protected|internal] [sealed|abstract] class *className* [: *superclassName*
{, *superclassName*}] {*classMemberDelerations*}

Obviously, we can extract the class name and the names of its parent classes in a way similar to the above way of dealing with Java code.

The attribute definitions and method definitions are similar to those in C++. Unlike C++, the method bodies are combined with method headers in C#. Therefore, we do not need to match the method bodies against their headers. However, there are some extra class member definitions, such as property definitions, indexer definitions and event definitions. Property definitions can be treated as variants of attribute definitions, while indexer definitions and event definitions can be treated as variants of method definitions.

6. Building OO Program Comprehension Tools with OOML

6.1. Basic Strategies for the Building

Basically we have two main strategies.

- **Using XML processors.** We can use existing XML processors to facilitate the tool building. There are quite a few XML processors that can be used for our purpose. The main differences among these processors are two-fold. Firstly, they provide different APIs, and thus differ in the ease of use. Standard APIs include DOM [28], XPath [29], XSLT [30], SAX [26] and STX [4] etc. Secondly, two processors implementing the same set of APIs may use different strategies to process XML documents. Therefore, for building a specific program comprehension tool, using different XML processors may result in differences in the ease of tool building and/or in the performance of the built tool. However, as we do not need to build all the tools using the same processor, we can always choose the most suitable processor to build each tool. In the following, we use expressions in XPath (see [29] for details of the XPath specification) to describe the building of the sample tools.
- **Tolerating language differences.** As code in OOML from different OO languages can still have syntactical differences, we should try to tolerate these differences when building a specific tool. We do not claim that we can always find a tolerant method for all the tools. However, we can demonstrate that it is not a difficult task to find tolerant solutions in many circumstances. If we cannot find a tolerant solution, we have to build different tools for the same purpose for different languages.

6.2. Building Sample Tools

In this sub-section, we demonstrate how three program comprehension tools can be easily built from OOML. We also demonstrate that the difference between the front-end languages can be almost transparent to this kind of tool building. Once again, we do not claim that our implementation is the best.

A Design Model Extractor

A design model is the overall structure of the target system for comprehension featuring the definitions of classes and their relationships. As in OOML each class is tagged with "*Class*", the query "*//Class*" can retrieve a list of class definitions. For a class named "C", the query "*//Class [name='C'] /Parent*" can retrieve all of its parent class names; the query "*//Class [name='C']/Attribute*" can retrieve all of its attributes; and the query "*//Class[name='C']/Method*" can retrieve all of its methods. With these queries, we can easily build a partial design model with the inheritance relationships but without the aggregation relationships and the association relationships between classes.

To build the aggregation relationships for one class, we need to browse the attributes of the class. Any class whose name serves as the type of one or more attributes will have an aggregation relationship with this class. For the association relationships, we need to browse the methods of the class. Any class whose name serves as the type of a parameter of any method or appears in the body of any method will have an association relationship with this class. Obviously, this strategy is applicable for any of the three languages discussed in this chapter.

Although there are cases where the above strategy cannot discover all the association relationships between classes, in most cases the above strategy can fulfill the task of design model extraction satisfactorily.

An Identifier Extractor

Recently, the use of identifiers to build up traceabilities between source code and documentation has become a research focus in program comprehension (see e.g. [9], [18] and [32] etc.). An identifier extractor is a necessity for such an approach. The extraction of identifiers can be performed at two levels: the method level and the class level.

To extract identifiers for method "M" in class "C", we can use the query "*//Class[name='C']/ Method [name ='M']/MethodBody*" to get the body of this method. Then we can parse out the identifiers in the body. These identifiers and the method name and identifiers from its parameters are the set of extracted identifiers for this method.

To extract identifiers at the class level, we need to collect the identifiers for each of the methods in the class and identifiers used for defining each of the attributes in the class. For class "C", query "*//Class[name='C'] /Attribute*" can enumerate all of its attributes.

Once again, this identifier extractor is suitable for all the discussed three languages.

A Call Graph Extractor

The extraction of the call graph has long been identified as a necessity in program comprehension. To distinguish calls to overloaded methods is a very complex task, which involves global type checking; here we only describe a simplified case of call graph extraction with no overloaded methods. Please note that overloaded methods are always a challenge to any lightweight approach to extracting the call graph from OO source code.

The basis of call graph extraction is to extract calls from each method body. Similar to the above extractors, we can use XPath queries to enumerate the method bodies. For a method body, we can further parse it to acquire the calls inside it.

As tokens related to method calls are only ".", "->", "::", "(", ")", "," and user-defined identifiers, we can regard all the other tokens as a single irrelevant token. Thus the BNF of a function call is as follows.

```
[.|->|::] methodName ([tokens] {, [tokens]})
```

On seeing a user-defined identifier between the possible token ".", "->" or "::" and the token "(", we know that the identifier is a method name. The part represented in the non-terminal "*tokens*" will be further parsed to extract possible method names. If no method name is overloaded, we can easily match the names against the methods declared in all the classes. Furthermore, two methods sharing the same name but having different number of parameters can also be distinguished, as we can analyze the part between "(" and ")" to achieve the parameter number for each method call.

In this call graph extractor, we can see that "->" and "::" do not appear in Java code. This is actually a simple strategy to tolerate the differences among the three languages. Although there are also a few cases that some method calls may not be recovered, this simple strategy can recover most calls for all the three languages.

7. Discussion

In this section, we summarize the main properties of the proposed approach as follows.

Firstly, our approach provides a mechanism of systematic reuse in the domain of building various program comprehension tools for various OO languages. A distinct feature of our approach is that it can dissolve the interweaving of the language-end variabilities and the tool-end variabilities in many circumstances. As demonstrated in this chapter, if there are three language-end variabilities and three tool-end variabilities, previous approaches will result in building nine individual tools to cover the nine combinations, while only three converters and three tools are needed in our approach.

Secondly, our approach is a high-level approach, in which many other techniques can also be applied during both the phase of generating the intermediate representation and the phase of building target program comprehension tools. During the source code transformation phase, the basic idea is similar to that of island grammars [20] [21]: Method bodies are passed over into OOML and irrelevant statements are ignored. During the phase of tool building, we can employ different approaches for different purposes. For example, we use a simple string matching approach to extract the design model and a lightweight syntactical analysis approach to extract the call graph.

Thirdly, like many other previous approaches our approach is lightweight, tolerant and flexible. This property can be viewed as a natural result, because we can apply lightweight, tolerant and flexible approaches in the two phases in our approach. Both the source code transformation and the tool building are lightweight, notwithstanding the further gains from reuse. Source code in different dialects and/or source code that cannot be compiled can also be manipulated during both phases. Interestingly, we can employ different techniques to deal with different languages and/or purposes when transforming the source code and/or building the target tools.

8. Related Work

8.1. Lightweight Approaches to Building Program Comprehension Tools

Traditionally, compiler-based approaches have also been used for building the front-end of a program comprehension tool. In such an approach, a compiler-like extractor is used to acquire all the detailed information from source code, and the information is stored in a database. Various program comprehension tools can be built via querying the database (see e.g. [11] and [2]). However, due to the different purposes of program compiling and program comprehension [15], two drawbacks of compiler-based approaches to building program comprehension tools have been identified. Firstly, these approaches are usually heavyweight approaches. Secondly, such an approach is usually not tolerant of partial source code that is not compilable and also very specific to a particular dialect of a particular language.

Over the past several years, program comprehension tool builders are turning to lightweight approaches. In general, there are two kinds of lightweight approaches: lexical approaches and syntactical approaches.

The basic idea of lexical approaches is to view the source code in a given language as a regular expression under a given purpose of program comprehension. As analyzing regular expressions is usually much easier than analyzing source code at the syntactical level, lexical approaches are usually lighter (therefore faster to build) than syntactical approaches [20]. Typical examples of lexical approaches include hierarchical lexical analysis (HLA) [22] [23] and iterative lexical analysis (ILA) [7]. There are mainly two drawbacks of lexical approaches. Firstly, rules in such an approach cannot be easily derived from the grammar of the given language, and therefore writing rules can only be based on careful examination of the given language and the given purpose. Secondly, using such an approach may result in too much imprecision when the grammar can hardly be simplified as lexical rules. In [7], it is claimed that ILA can achieve better approximation than HLA. Please note that imprecision usually also means tolerance and thus there is a tradeoff between too much imprecision and too little tolerance.

Syntactical approaches include the island grammars (IG) approach [20] [21] and the agile parsing (AP) approach [8] [6]. The idea of the IG approach is to only pass those tokens relevant to the given purpose to the actual parser. The relevant tokens are usually called *islands* and the irrelevant tokens *water*. Thus, the program comprehension task can be simplified by not parsing the *water*. Actually, we are using this idea in building converters for transforming source code in various languages into OOML. The idea of the AP approach is to distinguish the common grammar and the variable grammars when facing source code in various dialects. Therefore, the rules for dealing with the common grammar can be easily reused for generating tools for any dialects.

Another related approach is the breadth-first parsing [24], which identifies high-level constructs in the first pass and analyzes the sub-grammar of each construct in the second pass. Our approach can also be viewed as a two-pass approach. However, the aim of the breadth-first parsing is to achieve tolerance while our aim is to achieve reuse.

8.2. XML-Based Source Code Representations

With the emergence of XML as a standard for representing and exchanging structured information over the Internet, program comprehension tool builders have begun to use XML as a means to represent information conveyed by program source code. These representations include GXL [12], CppML [19], JavaML [1] and srcML [17] [5] etc. These approaches can be viewed as using XML-based representations to replace the database used in database-based approaches such as [11] and [2].

The main advantage of these approaches is that standard XML parsers and APIs can be used to acquire needed information. However, there are mainly two drawbacks for these approaches. Firstly, using XML to fully tag program source code may not be a practical approach, as numerous tags will be inserted into the source code [25]. Secondly, fully tagging depends on a full parser, which is usually not tolerant of dialects and/or partial source code.

Thus, these approaches may also suffer from the same drawbacks that compiler-based approaches suffer from.

8.3. Common OO Representation

In recent years, the Unified Modeling Language (UML) [3] has been adopted as the standard specification language for OO systems. As a result, UML can be a good common representation of OO systems.

In this paper, we do not use UML as the intermediate representation for source code, because UML is mainly aiming at modeling rather than source code representation. Therefore, deeper analysis is needed to transform source code into UML than into OOML. In fact, OOML can be viewed as a massively simplified version of UML in the form of XML.

9. Conclusions

In this paper, we have demonstrated how the problem of building various program comprehension tools for various OO languages can be viewed as a domain engineering problem and thus we can apply domain engineering for the building of program comprehension tools. To address the commonalities conveyed by common OO concepts, we designed a common XML-based intermediate representation of OO source code. Based on this representation, we try to tackle the language-end variabilities and the tool-end variabilities separately and thus could dissolve the interweaving effect of the two kinds of variabilities. Future work includes a thorough study of the strength and weakness of OOML, better implementation of source code converters, and a performance study of using different XML processors to build target tools.

Acknowledgements

This research is sponsored by the National 973 Key Basic Research and Development Program No. 2005CB321805 and the National Science Foundation of China No. 90412011 and No. 60403015.

References

[1] G.J. Badros, "JavaML: A Markup Language for Java Source Code," Proc. 9th International World Wide Web Conference (WWW9), Amsterdam, The Netherlands, May 13-15 (2000) 159-177

[2] W.R. Bischofberger, "Sniff – A Pragmatic Approach to a C++ Programming Environment," *Proc. The USENIX C++ Conference*, Portland, Oregon, USA, August (1992) 67-87

[3] G. Booch, J. Rumbaugh, and I. Jacobson, *The Unified Modeling Language User Guide*. Addison Wesley Longman (1999)

[4] P. Cimprich, Streaming Transformations for XML (STX) Version 1.0 Working Draft. http://stx.sourceforge.net/documents/spec-stx-20021101.html (2002)

[5] M.L. Collard, H.H. Kagdi, and J.I. Maletic, "An XML-Based Lightweight C++ Fact Extractor," *Proc. 11th International Workshop on Program Comprehension (IWPC'03),* Portland, Oregon, USA, May 10-11 (2003) 134-143

[6] J.R. Cordy, "Generalized Selective XML Markup of Source Code Using Agile Parsing," *Proc. 11th International Workshop on Program Comprehension (IWPC'03),* Portland, Oregon, USA, May 10-11 (2003) 144-153

[7] Cox and C. Clarke, "Syntactic Approximation Using Iterative Lexical Analysis," *Proc. 11th International Workshop on Program Comprehension (IWPC'03),* Portland, Oregon, USA, May 10-11 (2003) 154-163

[8] T.R. Dean, J.R. Cordy, A.J. Malton, and K.A. Schneider, "Grammar Programming in TXL," *Proc. IEEE 2nd International Workshop on Source Code Analysis and Manipulation*, Montreal, Canada, October (2002) 93-102

[9] T. Eisenbarth, R. Koschke, and D. Simon, "Locating Features in Source Code," *IEEE Transactions on Software Engineering,* vol. 29, no. 3 (2003) pp 210-224

[10] W. Frakes, R. Prieto-Diaz, and E. Fox, "DARE: Domain Analysis and Reuse Environment," *Annals of Software Engineering*, vol. 5 (1998) 125-141

[11] J.E. Grass and Y. Chen, "The C++ Information Abstractor," *Proc. The USENIX C++ Conference,* San Francisco, CA, USA, April (1990) 265-277

[12] R.C. Holt, A. Winter, and A. Schurr, "GXL: Toward a Standard Exchange Format," *Proc. 7th Working Conference on Reverse Engineering (WCRE'00),* Brisbane, Queensland, Australia, November, 23-25 (2000) 162-171

[13] S.C. Johnson, Yacc – Yet Another Compiler Compiler. *Technical Report Computing Science Technical Report* 32, AT&T Bell Laboratories, Murray Hill, New Jersey (1975)

[14] K. Kang, S. Cohen, J. Hess, W. Novak, and A. Peterson, Feature-Oriented Domain Analysis (FODA) Feasibility Study (CMU/SEI-90-TR-021), Software Engineering Institute, CMU (1990)

[15] P. Klint, "How Understanding and Restructuring Differ from Compiling – A Rewriting Perspective," *Proc. 11th International Workshop on Program Comprehension (IWPC'03),* Portland, Oregon, USA, May 10-11 (2003) 2-11

[16] M.E. Lesk, Lex – A Lexical Analyzer Generator. *Technical Report Computing Science Technical Report* 39, AT&T Bell Laboratories, Murray Hill, New Jersey (1975)

[17] J.I. Maletic, M.L. Collard, and A. Marcus, "Source Code Files as Structured Documents," *Proc. 10th International Workshop on Program Comprehension (IWPC'02),* Paris, France, June 27-29 (2002) 289-292

[18] Marcus and J.I. Maletic, "Recovering Documentation-to-Source-Code Traceability Links using Latent Semantic Indexing," *Proc. International Conference on Software Engineering,* May (2003) pp. 125 –135

[19] E. Mammas and C. Kontogiannis, "Towards Portable Source Code Representations using XML," *Proc. 7th Working Conference on Reverse Engineering (WCRE'00),* Brisbane, Queensland, Australia, November, 23-25 (2000) 172-182

[20] L. Moonen, "Generating Robust Parsers using Island Grammars," *Proc. 8th Working Conference on Reverse Engineering (WCRE'01),* Stuttgart, Germany, October (2001) 13-22

[21] L. Moonen, "Lightweight Impact Analysis using Island Grammars," *Proc. 10th International Workshop on Program Comprehension (IWPC'02),* Paris, France, June 27-29 (2002) 219-228

[22] G.C. Murphy and D. Notkin, "Lightweight Source Model Extraction," *Proc. Symposium on the Foundations of Software Engineering,* October (1995) 116-127

[23] G.C. Murphy and D. Notkin, "Lightweight Lexical Source Model Extraction," *ACM Transactions on Software Engineering and Methodology,* vol. 5, no. 3, July (1996) 262–292

[24] J. Ophel, Breadth-First Parsing. *Department of Computing and Electrical Engineering Research Memoandum* 97/12, Heriot Watt University, Edinburgh, Scotland (1997)

[25] J.F. Power and B.A. Malloy, "Program Annotation in XML: A Parse-tree Based Approach," *Proc. 9th Working Conference on Reverse Engineering (WCRE'02),* Richmond, Virginia, USA, October (2002) 190-198

[26] SAX, Simple API for XML (SAX). http://www.saxproject.org/ (2001)

[27] Weiss and R. Lai, *Software Product Line Engineering.* Addison-Wesley, Reading, MA (1999)

[28] World Wide Web Consortium, *Document Object Model (DOM) Level 1 Specification.* http://www.w3.org/TR/1998/REC-DOM-Level-1-19981001/ (1998)

[29] World Wide Web Consortium, XML Path Language (XPath) Version 1.0 W3C Recommendation. http://www.w3.org/TR/1999/REC-xpath-19991116/ (1999)

[30] World Wide Web Consortium, XSL Transformations (XSLT) Version 1.0. http://www.w3.org/TR/xslt (1999)

[31] World Wide Web Consortium, Extensible Markup Language (XML) 1.1. http://www.w3c.org/TR/2003/PR-xml11-20031105/ (2003)

[32] W. Zhao, L. Zhang, Y. Liu, J. Luo, and J. Sun, "Understanding How the Requirements Are Implemented in Source Code," *Proc. of 10th Asia-Pacific Software Engineering Conference (APSEC2003),* Thailand, 10-12 December (2003) pp. 68-77

In: Computer Software Engineering Research
Editor: Ari D. Klein, pp. 195-209

ISBN: 1-60021-774-5

Chapter 8

OAUP: CONSTRUCTION OF ONTOLOGY-BASED ADAPTIVE USER PROFILES

Lixin Han[1,2,3]

[1] College of Computers and Information Engineering, Hohai University, Nanjing, 210024, China

[2] Department of Mathematics, Nanjing University, Nanjing, 210093, China

[3] State Key Laboratory of Novel Software Technology, Nanjing University, Nanjing, 210093, China

Abstract

User profiles play an important role on information retrieval. In this paper, we propose a method, OAUP, of the construction of ontology-based adaptive user profiles. The OAUP method employs collaborative filtering combined with data mining and soft computing to build ontology-based user profiles. One key feature of OAUP is that collaborative filtering, association rules, simulated annealing and fuzzy genetic algorithms are combined to build user profiles. Another key feature of OAUP is that it employs the hybrid algorithm of exploiting the desirable properties of both complete-link clustering algorithms and inference mechanism to build user ontologies. The method can make user profiles strong expressive, more self-adaptive and less manually interfered.

Keywords: Information retrieval, User profiles, Ontology, Collaborative filtering, Soft computing

1. Introduction

Nowadays the amount of information on the Internet is increasing dramatically. The ability of facilitating users to achieve useful information is more and more important for information retrieval system. A user profiles is required to present the information that the user truly need.

Generally, there are two major methods for collecting user profiles [1]. Preprocessing is a method done with a questionnaire. This method is time consuming for users. For the other method, automatic collection is based on the interaction between the user and the system. User profiles are acquired by analyzing the web pages that the user visits. For example a user profile is created by analyzing the content of surfed pages and even by analyzing the length of the document and the time that was spent on the document associated with that content. The cost of automatic collection is not higher than the cost of preprocessing. However, when systems use the acquired information only for their own system, the difference of the accuracy of adaptation may occur. For example, when the user frequently uses a system, the system can achieve an adaptation very well. However, when the user rarely uses a system, the system cannot achieve an adaptation very well.

To solve this problem, we propose a method, OAUP (Construction of Ontology-based Adaptive User Profiles), of the construction of ontology-based adaptive user profiles. The OAUP method is an automatic collection method. The OAUP method is different from the existing other automatic collection methods in that the OAUP method employs collaborative filtering combined with soft computing and data mining to build ontology-based user profiles. One key feature of OAUP is that the method can make user profiles more self-adaptive. A collaborative filtering method is proposed to ensure the completeness and correctness of the text corpus. An algorithm for mining association rules is proposed to extract a set of terms from text corpus. An algorithm of fuzzy genetic combined with simulated annealing is proposed to handle the imprecision of the users' preferences and the inclusion of the users' preferences in the representation of the terms into the genes of the chromosomes in order to keep the knowledge about the users' needs in the population, and to explore the searching space when such needs change. Another key feature of OAUP is that the method can make user profiles strong expressive. An algorithm of complete-link clustering combined with inference mechanism is used to construct hierarchically structured user profiles. The user profiles can maintain sophisticated representations of personal interest profiles. These representations can be utilized for effective information retrieval.

2. Related Work

There are the related works in building user profiles. Desjardins and Godin [2] present an Internet information filtering agent with a search engine using a hybrid evolutionary algorithm to optimize the user profile. The algorithm aims to find such a value added solution by combining a relevance feedback process with a genetic algorithm. Shahabi et al. [3] introduce the GA-based learning mechanisms that utilize the users' navigation behaviors to improve the profiles. Their work extend a hybrid recommendation system, called Yoda [4], which employs a hybrid approach to combining content-based and collaborative filtering in order to achieve higher accuracy for large-scale Web-based applications. Ziegler et al. [5] propose the method designed to balance and diversify personalized recommendation lists according to the user's full range of interests. The method takes into consideration both the accuracy of suggestions made and the user's extent of interest in specific topics. In addition, they propose the intra-list similarity metric to show its effciency in diversifying. In contrast to the above work, the algorithm of fuzzy genetic combined with simulated annealing in the OAUP method is used to handle the imprecision of the users' preferences and to explore the searching space when such needs change. Moreover, the OAUP method can make user profiles strong expressive by building user ontologies.

There are the related works that apply fuzzy genetic algorithms to user profiles. Martín-Bautista [6] et al. present an approach to such an agent, which consists of a soft-intelligent agent that can work offline to filter and rank the retrieved information by using a genetic algorithm with fuzzy set genes to learn the user's preferences. In this paper, genetic algorithms keep the knowledge about the user's preferences, adapt the changes in these preferences and get the feedback from the user; and fuzzy set theory handles the imprecision of the user's preferences and the user's evaluation of the retrieved documents. Later, Martín-Bautista [7] et al. present the improvement of the effectiveness of information retrieval by using Genetic Algorithms and Fuzzy Logic. A new classification for the Information Retrieval models in the framework of the Genetic Algorithms is given. Such classification depends on the aim of the fitness function. They have explained a new weighting scheme based on a fuzzy representation of the occurrences of the terms in the documents, and their representation in the genes of the chromosomes in a GA. In contrast to Martín-Bautista [6], [7], the OAUP method can make user profiles strong expressive by building user ontologies. Moreover, the algorithm of fuzzy genetic combined with simulated annealing is propose to improve congregating speed and accuracy in building user profiles. In addition, the OAUP method uses collaborative filtering techniques to ensure the completeness and correctness of the text corpus.

There are the related works in the construction of the user ontology. Kanjo et al. [1] propose A3, which is a framework for user adaptation. In this framework, the automatic construction of the user ontology and the sharing of the user ontology are enabled in achieving user adaptation. The user ontology is defined as a classified tree of web resources, and is written by RDF(S) and OWL proposed for Semantic Web. They assume that the user ontology represents the user's knowledge, and they use the user ontology as a user profile to achieve a user adaptation on A3. Razmerita et al. [8] address the aspects of ontology-based user modeling and they present a generic architecture for implicit and explicit ontology based-user modeling. They identify the aspects of user modeling relevant to KMSs and integrate them in a generic framework based on ontologies. Middleton et al. [9] present a general ontology-based recommendation system approach. Their two experimental systems, Quickstep and Foxtrot, are built. Quickstep improves user profiles' accuracy via inference and Quickstep is integrated with an external ontology to bootstrap a recommender system for easing the cold-start problem. Foxtrot enhances Quickstep by visualizing user profiles in order to acquire direct user profiles' feedback. Nebel IT. et al. [10] propose a method for the creation of user-profiles through the construction of a central database resource of user ontologies, from which ready-made taxonomies of different types of users can be extracted as a unit. The advantages of the method are its easy adaptability, high speed of operation, automatic completion of inferences to yield new information, and automatic extendibility. In contrast to the above work, the OAUP method combines collaborative filtering, association rules, simulated annealing and fuzzy genetic to make user profiles more self-adaptive and less manually interfered.

3. The Construction of Adaptive Ontology-based User Profiles

The OAUP method consists mainly of the CFTC algorithm for acquiring text corpus, the ST algorithm for extracting a set of terms, the SAFG algorithm for building user profiles and the CLCI algorithm for building ontology-based user profiles. In OAUP, the CFTC algorithm is used to acquire text corpus. The ST algorithm is used to extract a set of terms from text corpus. Based on these terms, the hybrid algorithm SAFG that exploits the desirable properties of both the LOS algorithm for improving local optimal solution and fuzzy genetic algorithms is used to build user profiles. Based on these user profiles, the hybrid algorithm CLCI that exploits the desirable properties of both complete-link clustering algorithms and inference mechanism is used to build user ontologies.

3.1. The Construction of User Profiles

First, we propose the CFTC (Construction of CF-based Text Corpus) algorithm to acquire text corpus. We then propose the ST (Extract a Set of Terms) algorithm to extract a set of terms from text corpus. Based on the ST algorithm, we finally propose the SAFG (Combines Simulated Annealing with Fuzzy Genetic Algorithms) algorithm to build user profiles.

3.1.1. The CFTC Algorithm

Collaborative filtering (CF) methods [11] work by assessing the similarities among users, then recommending to a given user documents that like-minded users accessed previously. Generally, there are two main categories methods in collaborative filtering, that is, user-based and item-based algorithms [12].

In contrast to [13], [14], [15], [16] the CFTC algorithm first employs the widely used Principal Component analysis (PCA) [17], [18] to produce a low dimensional representation, then the CFTC algorithm employs Adjusted Cosine Similarity [13] to compute the proximity between customers and hence we use SOM [19], [20] to form the neighborhood. The CFTC algorithm finally employs the Wavelet networks [21] to rank the relevant text corpus.

In the CFTC algorithm, we assume a set of n users $\{1,\ldots,n\}$, a set of m items $\{1,\ldots,m\}$, and a set of v discrete rating values $\{1,\ldots,v\}$. It is represented as an $m\times n$ customer-product matrix, R, such that r_{ij} is ratings value to the ith customer that has purchased the jth product. We term this $m\times n$ representation of the input data set as original representation.

The CFTC algorithm is described as the following steps:

Input: a set of users $\{x\}$, customer-product matrix R
Output: text corpus
{ PCA is used to produce a low dimensional representation;
adjusted Cosine Similarity is used to compute the proximity between customers;
given initial the weight W_i (i=1,2,….,N), given *maxno* is the iterative maximum number; // initialization;
t=1;
while t<*maxno*
{ $m(x(t))=\arg\min_i \|W_i - x(t)\|$;

$$W_i(t+1)=\begin{cases} W_i(t)+\alpha(t)h_{m(x(t))}(t)[x(t)-W_i(t)] & i\in h_{m(x(t))}(t) \\ W_i(t) & \text{Otherwise} \end{cases};$$

t=t+1;
the neighborhood is formed by a map grid;
principal component analysis (PCA) is used to produce a low dimensional representation;
the wavelet networks is used to rank the relevant text corpus;}}

In this algorithm, t is called the index of the regression step and the regression is performed for each presentation of a sample of x, denoted $x(t)$. $\alpha(t)$ is called a learning rate function, $m(x(t))$ is called the model that matches best with $x(t)$, and $h_{m(x(t))}(t)$ is called the neighborhood function.

The CFTC algorithm is described in detail as follows:

A) learning rate

$$\alpha(t) = [\alpha(0) - \alpha(maxno)] * (1 - k/maxno) + \alpha(maxno) \quad (1)$$

where $0<\alpha(t)<1$, learning rate factor $\alpha(t)$ decreases monotonically with the regression steps. $\alpha(0)=0.48$, $\alpha(maxno)=0.009$.

B) The neighborhood function

$$h_{m(x(t))}(t) = \exp(-\frac{\left\| r_i - r_{c(x)} \right\|^2}{\sqrt{2}\delta(t)}) \quad (2)$$

$$\frac{1}{\delta(t)} = \frac{1}{\delta(0)} + \frac{t}{maxno}[\frac{1}{\delta(maxno)} - \frac{1}{\delta(0)}] \quad (3)$$

where $\delta(t)$ is corresponds to the width of the neighborhood function $h_{m(x(t))}(t)$, which is decreasing monotonically with the regression steps. $\delta(0)=\sqrt{3}\,(Q-1)$ (Q is the side length of a square) and $\delta(maxno)=0.119$.

C) In the Wavelet neural network, the relevant Web pages obtained from all neighbors are more similar to each other than from no neighbors. The algorithm is a hypothesis on that two Web pages are more similar in content if there are more common keywords in their Web pages. The neural network is built using keywords from the Web pages. Each keyword maps into a 0 or 1, so the length of the input vector equals the number of the keywords chosen. The neural network can assign all the Web pages to a relevancy value that is a fraction between 1 and 0. These relevant values may be used to rank these relevant Web pages.

The origin of wavelet networks can be traced back to the work by Daugman (1988) in which Gabor wavelets were used for image classification. Wavelet networks have become popular after the work by Zhang et al. (1992) [22], wavelet neural networks (WNN) combine the time-frequency localization properties of wavelets and the learning abilities of general neural network (NN). Wavelet neural networks may be regarded as a special feedforward neural network. The main characteristic of WNN is that some kinds of wavelet functions are used as the nonlinear transformation function in the hidden layer, instead of the usual sigmoid function. WNN has shown its advantages over the traditional methods such as MLFN, RBF for complex nonlinear system modeling. For clarity of presentation, the basic concepts about wavelet transforms are briefly recalled.

Given a frame $\psi_{m,n}$ in the Hilbert space H, for any $f \in H$, f can be decomposed in terms of the frame elements as follows:

$$F(x) = \sum_{m \in Z^q, n \in Z^q} < f, S^{-1}\psi_{m,n} > \psi_{m,n}(X) \quad (4)$$

where is the frame operator $H \rightarrow H$ and $\psi_{m,n}$ is defined by

$$\psi_{m,n}(X)=\psi_{M_1,n_1}{}^{1}(X_1)\psi_{M_2,n_2}{}^{2}(X_2)\cdots\psi_{M_q,n_q}{}^{2}(X_q) \tag{5}$$

And $m=[M_1,M_2,\text{---} M_q]$, $n=[n_1,n_2,\text{---} n_q]$, $\psi^{i}{}_{M_i,n_i}(X_i)$ is generated by dilating and translating the mother wavelet function in the following form:

$$\psi_{M_i,n_i}(X_i)=2^{M_i/2}*\psi(2^{M_i}x_i-n_i) \qquad M_i, n_i\in Z \tag{6}$$

the index M_i and n_i are dilation and translation, respectively.

In this paper, we can consider the following approximate wavelet-based representation form [22] for the function $f(x)$:

$$f(x)\approx\sum_{m,n}^{N}\omega_{m,n}\psi_{m,n}(x) \tag{7}$$

where $\omega_{m,n}=\langle f,s^{-1}\psi_{m,n}\rangle$ and N is the total number of wavelet function selected. $\psi_{m,n}$ is used as nonlinear transformation function of the hidden units and $\omega_{m,n}$ denotes the connection weights from hidden layer to output layer, formula (7) is regarded as the functional expression of a three-layered WNN modeling function f. In the WNN, 2^M denotes the connection weights from input layer to hidden layer, where n is the bias of each hidden units. If we determine the wavelets represented by index m and n (m and n are taken as integer values), the learning procedure for WNN is based on a fixed set of wavelets.

The wavelets with coarse resolution can get the global behavior easily, while the wavelets with fine resolution can get the local behavior of the function accurately. Therefore wavelet networks have fast convergence, easy training, and high accuracy.

3.1.2. The ST Algorithm

Text corpus in the ST algorithm is acquired by using the above CFTC algorithm for making high-quality recommendations even when sufficient data is unavailable. The ST algorithm is used to extract a set of terms from text corpus.

The ST algorithm is described as follows:

Input: text corpus
Output: a set of terms
```
{ word frequence is counted and ordered by single word;
  the words with higher frequent such as preposition, article, or conjunction are deleted;
  set1=nil; // set1 is used to store a set of terms
  set={the rest of n words with higher frequent } ; //n is the designated maximum
  count=1;
  While count≤ k // k is the maximum number of words in the phrase
  { frequent=nil;
   element=first(set);
```

While *set*<>nil
{*frequent*={the phrase is consist of element and *count* words in the above context }+*frequent*;
frequent={ the phrase is consist of element and the *count* words in the later context }+*frequent*;
element =next(*set*);}
n =*n*-*m*; //*m* is adjusted according to the size of the phrase
set ={calculate the *n* phrases with highest frequent };
s = *n*;
s =*s*- *m*; // *s* is the total amount of the phrases with highest frequent
*set*2={ calculate the *s* phrases with highest frequent };
*set*1=*set*1 ∪ *set*2;
count=*count*+1;}}

The ST algorithm starts from the words with higher frequent, the association phrase is found according to the context until a set of terms is formed. Therefore, the algorithm has less human intervention. The ST algorithm is different from the APRIORI algorithm [23] in that minimum support is adjusted according to the size of the phrase when every loop occurs. Thus, it has better self-adapted.

3.1.3. SAFG Algorithm

First, the LOS algorithm is proposed to improve local optimal solution. Based on the LOS algorithm, the SAFG algorithm is proposed to build user profiles.

3.1.3.1. LOS Algorithm

Simulated Annealing (SA) is a generalization of a Monte Carlo method for examining the equations of state and frozen states of n-body systems [24]. The concept is based on the manner in which liquids freeze or metals recrystalize in the process of annealing. By analogy the generalization of this Monte Carlo approach to combinatorial problems is straight forward [25], [26]. The major difficulty in implementation of the algorithm is that there is no obvious analogy for the temperature T with respect to a free parameter in the combinatorial problem. Furthermore, avoidance of entrainment in local minima is dependent on the "annealing schedule", the choice of initial temperature, how much iterations are performed at each temperature, and how much the temperature is decremented at each step as cooling proceeds [27]. The LOS (Improving Local Optimal Solution) algorithm which introduces simulated annealing is proposed to improve local optimal solution. The LOS algorithm can ensure to break away current local optimal solution and to reduce the computing workload.

The LOS algorithm is based on the following solution form:

1. Solution space is {feature vector};
2. Objective function is $f(\eta_{ij})=\max_{j=1\ldots H}\sum_{i=1}^{k}\eta_{ij}$;
3. New solution is produced by randomly choose another feature vector from neighboring region $N(x)$;
4. Objective function difference is Δf=f(new feature vector)-f(local optimal solution);
5. Accept criterion is P=1 for $\Delta f>0$ or $P=\exp(-\Delta f/t)$ for $\Delta f\leq 0$.

The LOS algorithm is described as follows:

Input: a set of terms, initial solution x_0, function f, initial temperature t_0, initial step q_0, monotone increment function $I(x)$
Output: local optimal solution

```
{ given initial solution x*, function f, initial temperature t0, initial step q0, monotone increment function I(x);
  q=q0; // initialize step q
  t=t0; // initialize temperature t, t=50
  i=1; // initializtion
  at=1; // initializtion
while | Ri – C |>ε //ε is a given enough small positive number, C is an threshold, where C=0.77
{ Ri-1=at/as; //at is the acceptable times of new solution, as is iterative steps number, Ri-1 is acceptable rate
at=at + 1;
as=0; // initializtion
while J<> U //U is the upper limit of step length
{ as=as+1;
 while x∉N(x) // N(x) is neighboring region
 {step length is q and the BFGS optimizer in the quasi-Newton method [28] is used to compute local optimal solution; }
 xi is produced by randomly choose another feature vector from neighboring region N(x) and objective function difference Δf=f(xi)- f(x) is computed;
if Δf≤ 0 or exp(- Δf/t)>random(0, 1)
then { x=xi;
        if f<f*
        then { x=x*;
        f=f*; }
        if at is equal to the given acceptable times
        then break; }
q=I(Ri)*q; // adjustment function I(x) is monofonic increasing function, where I(x)=(x-0.5)^4 +1
}
if f<f*
then { x=x*;
        f=f*;}
Ri=at/as;
if i>2
then // compute self-adjusting temperature
         { if Ri-1<C and Ri<C
           then t=t+TC; // TC is a given constant
          if Ri-1≥ C and Ri≥ C
          then t=t-TC;
          if Ri-1≤ C and Ri≥ C
          then t=t-TC/2;
          if Ri-1>C and Ri<C
          then t=t+TC/2;}
 i=i+1;}}
```

In contrast to the widely used simulated annealing algorithm [25], [29], there are three features in the LOS algorithm. Firstly, the LOS algorithm can self-adaptedly adjust temperature. Therefore it is regarded as time after time optional process. On the one hand, the Boltzmann factor $\exp(-\Delta f/t)$ increases with t. This is useful to break away current local optimal solution and to increase step length in order to look for a better new solution. On the other hand, when acceptable rate meets the given condition, the program can end so as to reduce the computing workload. Secondly, local optimization techniques instead of choosing randomly a new solution are employed in order to compute a local optimal solution. Thirdly, the local optimal solution is recorded during annealing process, in order to protect the current optimal solution from being thrown away. Therefore the LOS algorithm is an intelligent algorithm.

3.1.3.2. SAFG Algorithm

Genetic algorithms (GAs) were introduced by Holland [30]. Genetic algorithms borrow their process from the Darwin natural process of survival. Genetic algorithms are population-based algorithms where variation is brought in by mutation and crossover. By emulating biological selection and reproduction, GAs can efficiently search through the solution space of complex problems. Therefore, Genetic algorithms afford an opportunity to solve various complex problems, even without constructing its formal model.

Fuzzy set theory (FST) is an extension of the classic set theory developed by Zadeh [31] as a way to deal with vague concepts. Hard set theory considers an object as a member of a given set or not, that is, indicator variable is 1 and 0. In a fuzzy set, the indicator variable named membership can take intermediate values in interval [0,1].

To improve ability to local optimization for fuzzy genetic algorithms and adjust the representation of the needs when confronted with the users' feedback, we propose an algorithm called SAFG. The SAFG algorithm is used to handle the imprecision of the users' preferences and the inclusion of the users' preferences in the representation of the terms into the genes of the chromosomes in order to keep the knowledge about the users' needs in the population, and to explore the searching space when such needs change. The SAFG algorithm can make user profiles more self-adaptive.

The SAFG algorithm is different from the existing works [6],[7],[2] in that the SAFG algorithm use essentially a combination of simulated annealing with fuzzy genetic algorithms instead of fuzzy genetic algorithms alone to build user profiles, in order to find a combination that would yield better results than each of its composing processes alone. Therefore the SAFG algorithm can achieve a faster congregating speed and accuracy in building user profiles.

In the SAFG algorithm, each chromosome is a hypothesis on how to evaluate a document according to the information needs. All the chromosomes in the population are competing to predict the users' satisfaction from the documents. Every chromosome in the population of the genetic algorithm contains a set of genes. Each gene in a chromosome is defined by a term and a fuzzy number η of occurrences of the term in documents belonging to the class of documents that satisfy the users' information need. This fuzzy number is characterized by the membership function $T(x)$.

Each gene of a chromosome is specified by a pair $G(t, \eta)$, where t is a term, and η is a fuzzy number characterized by the membership function $T(x)$. The membership function is described as follows: $T(x)=e^{-(\frac{x-\mu}{\sigma})^2}$, assuming that the relative term occurrence frequency is normal distributed $N(\mu,\sigma^2)$, where the parameters $\mu \in [0,1]$ and $\sigma>0$. The estimation of the expected value

μ is given by the weighed average of the relative occurrence frequency of a term t_j. The parameter σ is the standard deviation of the expected value μ.

The chromosome score is calculated as the sum of the gene evaluation of a document. The chromosome score is defined as follows: chromosome score= $\sum_{i=1}^{k} \eta_{ij}$, where η_{ij} is the relative occurrence frequency of the term t_i in the document D_j.

The fitness of the chromosome is the ability of a chromosome to classify a document. The fitness function is defined as follows: $Fitness(x) = \max_{j=1...H} \sum_{i=1}^{k} \eta_{ij}$, where H is the number of documents, and k is the number of genes in a chromosome, i.e. the chromosome length.

The SAFG algorithm is described as follows:

Input: probability of crossover $P_c(t)$, probability of mutation $P_m(t)$, size of the population N
Output: user profiles
{t=0;
initialize $P(t)$;
the LOS algorithm is used to improve local optimal solution;
evaluate $P(t)$;
while t >*size* and $P(t)$<>$P(t+1)$ // *size* is a predetermined, $P(t)$=$P(t+1)$ denote that the average quality of the population does not improve number of generations
{$P'(t)$= crossover ($P(t)$);
$P''(t)$= mutation($P'(t)$);
the LOS algorithm is used to improve local optimal solution;
evaluate ($P''(t)$);
Fitness=α **Fitness*+β ; //*Fitness* is an self-adjusting fitness value,α is a shift factor chosen uniformly in the interval [0, 2], and β is a scaling factor chosen uniformly in the interval [-1, 1]
$P(t+1)$= select($P''(t) \cup P(t)$);
t=t+1;}}

In this algorithm, $P(t)$ denotes a population of N individuals at generation t. An offspring population $P'(t)$ is generated by means of crossover operator from the population $P(t)$. $P''(t)$ is generated by means of mutation operator from the population $P'(t)$. The offspring individuals are evaluated by calculating the fitness objective function values *Fitness* (x) for each of the solutions x represented by individuals in $P''(t)$. Selection operator based on the fitness values is worked to get better solutions.

The SAFG algorithm is described in detail as follows:

A) Initialization

The initialization of the population occurs as follows: For every new gene created in a chromosome, a random term t is selected from the pool of all the indexing terms acquired from the ST algorithm.

B) Crossover Operator

Arithmetic crossover is an operator for real encoded genomes in which an offspring genome is generated by the weighted mean of each gene in the two parent genomes. The effect of crossover operator is defined as follows: $x' = w*x_1 + (1-w)*x_2$, where x_1 and x_2 are the genomes of the parents. The weight w is generated according to the uniform distribution $U(0,1)$.

With an increase in the number of iterations, the self-adjusting P_c decrease. P_c is described as follows: $P_c(t)=K/(\beta*t)$, where t is the number of iterations, $\beta \in (0,1)$, and K is a scaling factor for $P_c(t) \in (0,1)$.

C) Mutation Operator

The mutation operator performed by adding a normally distributed random vector $\vec{z} \in IR^n$ with $z_i \sim N_i\ (0,\delta_i^2)$. $\vec{x} \in IR^n$. The effect of mutation operator is defined as follows: $\delta_i' = \delta_i * (1+0.27*N(0,1))$, $x_i' = x_i + \delta_i' * N_i\ (0,1)$.

With an increase in the number of iterations, the self-adjusting P_m decrease. P_m is described as follows: $P_m(t) = \beta/t$, where t is the number of iterations and $\beta \in (0,1)$.

D) Selection Operator

Selection operator is an essential process in Genetic algorithms. Selection operator removes individuals with a low fitness and drives the population towards better solutions. An important aspect of selection is the selection pressure, which governs the individual's survival rate. It is important to balance the selection pressure. Too strong pressure leads to premature convergence. On the other hand, too low pressure leads to very slow convergence.

We choose the widely used tournament selection [32] as selection operator. Tournament selection can consider fine-tuning the selective pressure by increasing or decreasing the tournament size. In addition, tournament selection is easy to implement and tournament selection has computationally efficient well.

Tournament selection is described as follows:

```
{j = 0;
 while (j<|P (t)|)
 { pick two random individuals I1 and I2 in P(t);
 compare the fitness of I1 and I2;
 insert a copy of the fitter individual in P(t + 1) at position j;
 j=j+1;}}
```

3.2. Constructing User Ontologies

User ontologies may express sophisticated representations of personal interest profiles. Once user ontologies are used to represent user profiles, every user ontology can communicate with other ontologies which share similar concepts and the ontology-based user profiles can be visualized easily. Traditional binary profiles are often represented as term vector spaces, neural network patterns etc. which are difficult to understand by users [9].

We propose the CLCI (Combines Complete-link Clustering with inference) algorithm for automatically constructing user ontologies. The CLCI algorithm can exploit the desirable properties of both complete-link clustering algorithms and inference mechanism to construct user ontologies.

Formula (8) denotes the similarity between two entities A and B.

$$S(A, B)= |A \cap B| / |A \cup B| \quad (8)$$

where a^x is an interest of user profile x, b^y is an interest of user profile y, $|\,|$ is the cardinality of a set, and $A = \{u_{a1}, \cdots, u_{an}\}$ and $B = \{u_{b1}, \cdots, u_{bn}\}$, where $u_{a1}, \cdots, u_{an}$ are the terms of a^x, and $u_{b1}, \cdots, u_{bn}$ are the terms of b^y. The larger $S(A, B)$ is, the larger the similarity between A and B is.

The CLCI algorithm is described as follows:

Input: user profiles
Output: user ontologies
{ i=0;
using formula (8), calculate the proximity matrix D_i containing the distance between a^x and b^y. Treat each interest as a cluster, that is $D_{pq}=d_{pq}$; // D_{pq} is the distance between each pair of clusters, d_{pq} is the distance between each pair of terms
while all terms are not in one cluster
{ $i=i+1$;
find the most similar pair of D_{pq} in the proximity matrix and merge these two clusters C_p and C_q into one cluster C_r, that is $C_r=\{C_p, C_q\}$; // C_r, C_p, C_q is cluster
using formula (8) and the formula $D_{rk}=\max\{D_{pk}, D_{qk}\}$, calculate the proximity matrix D_i to perform merge operation;
class hierarchy can be constructed;
user ontologies are represented as a class hierarchy;
generate some rules from the class hierarchy;
store these rules into the knowledge base;
the widely used Jena2's inference mechanism [33], [34] is used to infer semantic associations from the existing rules in the knowledge base in order to discover more meaningful association instances; }}

In contrast to the widely used complete-link clustering algorithm [35], the CLCI algorithm provides the inference mechanism to find more useful association instances that are not directly observed in the users' behaviour.

4. Conclusion

Nowadays the amount of information on the Internet is increasing dramatically. The ability of facilitating users to achieve useful information is more and more important for information retrieval system. With emergence of Semantic Web, user ontology offers some opportunities for improving on information retrieval system. Ontology-based user profiles typically maintain sophisticated representations of personal interest profiles. These representations can be utilized for effective information retrieval. In this paper, a method called OAUP is proposed for the construction of ontology-based adaptive user profiles. The OAUP method employs collaborative filtering techniques combined with data mining techniques and soft computing techniques to build user profiles. In the OAUP method, the CFTC algorithm is proposed to acquire text corpus. The ST algorithm is then proposed to extract a set of terms from text corpus. Based on the ST algorithm, the hybrid algorithm SAFG of exploiting the desirable properties of both simulated annealing and fuzzy genetic algorithms is proposed to build user profiles. The hybrid algorithm CLCI of exploiting the desirable properties of both complete-link clustering algorithms and inference mechanism is proposed to build user ontologies. The method can make user profiles strong expressive, more self-adaptive and less manually interfered.

Acknowledgements

This work is supported by the National Natural Science Foundation of China under grant 60673186 and 60571048, the State Key Laboratory Foundation of Novel Software Technology at Nanjing University under grant A200604.

References

[1] Daisuke Kanjo, Yukiko Kawai, & Katsumi Tanaka. A3: Framework for User Adaptation using XSLT. In *the Proceedings of the Thirteenth International World Wide Web Conference.* New York, USA, May 17-22, 2004.

[2] Guy Desjardins, & Robert Godin. Combining Relevance Feedback and Genetic Algorithms in an Internet Information Filtering Engine. In *6th Proceedings of the RIAO Content-Based Multimedia Information Access,* Paris, 12-14, April, 2000. Vol. 2, pages 1676-1685.

[3] Cyrus Shahabi, & Yi-Shin Chen. An Adaptive Recommendation System without Explicit Acquisition of User Relevance Feedback. *Distributed and Parallel Databases Journal,* Vol. 14, No 3, Pages 173-192, Kluwer Academic Publishers, September, 2003.

[4] C. Shahabi, F. Banaei-Kashani, Y.-S. Chen, & D. McLeod. Yoda: An accurate and scalable web-based recommendation system. In *Proceedings of Sixth International Conference on Cooperative Information Systems (CoopIS 2001),* 2001.

[5] Cai-Nicolas Ziegler, Sean M. McNee, Joseph A. Konstan, & Georg Lausen. Improving recommendation lists through topic diversification. In the *Proceedings of the Fourteenth International World Wide Web Conference.* Chiba, Japan, May 10-14, 2005.

[6] Maria J. Martín-Bautista, María Amparo Vila Miranda, & Henrik Legind Larsen. A Fuzzy Genetic Algorithm Approach to an Adaptive Information Retrieval Agent. *JASIS* 50(9): 760-771 (1999).

[7] Martin-Bautista, Maria J; Vila, Maria-Amparo; Sanchez, Daniel; & Larsen, Henrik L. Fuzzy genes: Improving the effectiveness of information retrieval. *Proceedings of the IEEE Conference on Evolutionary Computation.* California, CA; USA; 16 July-19 July 2000. pp. 471-478. 2000.

[8] Liana Razmerita, Albert Angehrn, & Alexander Maedche. Ontology-based User Modeling for Knowledge Management Systems. *Proceedings of the 9th International Conference on User Modeling.* University of Pittsburgh, Johnstown, USA, June 22-26, 2003.

[9] Middleton, S.E. Shadbolt, N.R., & De Roure, D.C. Ontological User Profiling in Recommender Systems. *ACM Transactions on Information Systems (TOIS),* Volume 22, Issue 1, January 2004, page 54 - 88, ACM Press, New York, NY, USA.

[10] Nébel, I., Smith, & B., Paschke, R.. A User Profiling Component with the aid of User Ontologies. *Proceedings of Workshop Learning – Teaching – Knowledge – Adaptivity*. Karlsruhe. 2003.

[11] P. Resnick et al., GroupLens: An Open Architecture for Collaborative Filtering of Netnews. *Proc. ACM 1994 Conf. Computer Supported Cooperative Work,* ACM Press, 1994, pp. 175–186.

[12] Breese, J. S., Heckerman, D., & Kadie, C.. Empirical Analysis of Predictive Algorithms for Collaborative Filtering. In *Proceedings of the 14th Conference on Uncertainty in Artificial Intelligence,* pp. 43-52. 1998.

[13] B. M. Sarwar, G. Karypis, J. A. Konstan, & J. T. Riedl. Item-based collaborative filtering recommendation algorithms. In *Proceedings of the Tenth International World Wide Web Conference,* pages 285–295, 2001.

[14] Huang, Z., Chen, H., & Zeng, D.. Applying associative retrieval techniques to alleviate the sparsity problem in collaborative filtering. *ACM Trans. Inf. Syst.*, 22 (1), 116–142. 2004.

[15] Al Rashid, George Karypis, & John Riedl. *Influence in Ratings-Based Recommender Systems: An Algorithm-Independent Approach.* SDM 2005.

[16] Sarwar, B., Karypis, G., Konstan, J., & Reidl, J.. Analysis of recommendation algorithms for e-commerce. In *Proceedings of the ACM Conference on Electronic Commerce. ACM,* New York, 158–167.

[17] E. Oja. *Subspace Methods of Pattern Recognition.* Research Studies Press, Letchworth, UK, 1983.

[18] AM Martnez, & AC Kak. PCA versus LDA. *IEEE Transactions on Pattern Analysis and Machine Intelligence,* 23(2) (2001), pp. 228-233.

[19] T. Kohonen. *Self-organizing maps*. Springer-Verlag, Berlin, 1995.

[20] T. Kohonen, S. Kaski, K. Lagus, J. Salojarvi, J. Honkela, V. Paatero, & A. Saarela. Self Organization of a Massive Document Collection. *IEEE Transactions on Neural Networks, Special Issue on Neural Networks for Data Mining and Knowledge Discovery,* 11(3):574--585, 2000.

[21] DWC Ho, PA Zhang, & J Xu. Fuzzy Wavelet Networks for Function Learning. *IEEE Transactions on Fuzzy Systems* 9(1) (2001) 200-211.

[22] Q. Zhang, & A. Benveniste. Wavelet networks. *IEEE Trans. on Neural Networks* 3 (6) (November 1992).

[23] Rakesh Agrawal, & Ramakrishnan Srikant. Fast Algorithms for Mining Association Rules in Large Databases. *VLDB* 1994: 487-499.

[24] Metropolis, N., A. Rosenbluth, M. Rosenbluth, A. Teller, & E. Teller. Equation of State Calculations by Fast Computing Machines. *Journal of Chemical Physics*, 21:1087-1091, 1953.

[25] S. Kirpatrick, C.D. Gellat, Jr., & M.P. Vecchi. Optimization by simulated annealing. *Science*, 4598: 671-680, 1983.

[26] Cerny, V.. Thermodynamical Approach to the Traveling Salesman Problem: An Efficient Simulation Algorithm. *Journal of optimization theory and applications*, 45(1): 41-51, 1985.

[27] Perry Gray, William Hart, Laura Painton, Cindy Phillips, Mike Trahan, & John Wagner. A Survey of Global Optimization Methods. http://www.cs.sandia.gov/opt/survey/main.html.

[28] Broyden, C.G.. A new double-rank minimization algorithm. *Notices of the American Mathematical Society*, 16:670, 1969.

[29] D. S. Jonhson, C. A. Aragon, L. A. Mcgeoch, & C. Schevon. Optimization by simulated annealing: an experimental evaluation -- Part II (graph coloring and number partition). *Operations research*, 39(3): 378-406. 1991.

[30] Holland J H. *Adaptation in Natural and Artificial Systems*. Mit Press, 1975.

[31] Zadeh, L.A.. Fuzzy sets. *Information and Control*, 8, 338-353, 1965.

[32] David, E.G., Korb, B., & Deb, K.. Messy genetic algorithms: motivation, analysis, and first results, *Complex Systems*, 3(5):493--530, 1989.

[33] Kevin Wilkinson, Craig Sayers, Harumi A. Kuno, & Dave Reynolds. Efficient RDF Storage and Retrieval in Jena2. *SWDB* 2003: 131-150.

[34] J. Carroll, I. Dickinson, C. Dollin, D. Reynolds, A. Seaborne, & K. Wilkinson. *The Jena Semantic Web Platform: Architecture and Design*. HP Laboratories Technical Report HPL-2003-146.

[35] Jain, A.K., Murty M.N., & Flynn P.J.. Data Clustering: A Review. *ACM Computing Surveys*, 31(3): 264-323, 1999.

INDEX

A

B

C

D

J

L

M

R

S

T

U

V

W

X

Y